D0149442

Sri Gyanamata

July 4, 1869 – November 17, 1951

"Never did I see in her face, in her eyes, anger or anguish or pain; only the sweetness of God."

—Paramahansa Yogananda

GOD ALONE

The Life and Letters of a Saint

Sri Gyanamata

A Disciple of Paramahansa Yogananda

Self-Realization Fellowship
FOUNDED 1920
Paramahansa Yogananda

A publication of
SELF-REALIZATION FELLOWSHIP
Founded in 1920 by Paramahansa Yogananda

ABOUT THIS BOOK: In 1932 Sri Gyanamata entered the monastic ashram founded by Paramahansa Yogananda on Mount Washington in Los Angeles. Her duties as a monastic in the Self-Realization Fellowship Order included answering letters to the society from members around the world; she was also a revered spiritual counselor for the other nuns in the Self-Realization Fellowship ashrams, whom she often guided and encouraged through personal notes. At Paramahansa Yogananda's request, excerpts from her letters were printed as a regular feature in *Self-Realization* (the society's magazine, founded by him in 1925); many of her short prose pieces also appeared in the magazine over the years. To preserve her wealth of inspiration and insight, and make it available to all, in 1984 SRF monastics compiled her writings into this volume—including Paramahansaji's eulogy at her memorial service; a biographical sketch of her life; letters written to her by Sri Yogananda and fellow disciples; and photographs from SRF archives.

Authorized by the International Publications Council of
SELF-REALIZATION FELLOWSHIP
3880 San Rafael Avenue • Los Angeles, CA 90065-3219

Self-Realization Fellowship was founded by Paramahansa Yogananda as the instrument for the worldwide dissemination of his teachings. The Self-Realization Fellowship name and emblem (shown above) appear on all SRF books, recordings, and other publications, assuring the reader that a work originates with the society established by Paramahansa Yogananda and faithfully conveys his teachings.

~First Edition, 1984. This printing, 2009~

Library of Congress Catalog Card Number: 84-52361

ISBN-13: 978-0-87612-200-6
ISBN-10: 0-87612-200-4

Printed in the United States of America on recycled paper

10545-J1021

CONTENTS

List of Illustrations . . . . *v*

Preface, by Sri Daya Mata . . . . *vii*

PART I: THE LIFE OF SRI GYANAMATA

1. The Life of Sri Gyanamata 3
   - Childhood and Early Years 3
   - Searching for Love 5
   - Into the Realm of Spiritual Thought 7
   - Gyanamata's Interest in India's Wisdom 9
   - Gyanamata Meets Her Guru, Paramahansa Yogananda . 10
   - Instant Recognition Between Guru and Disciple 12
   - Physical Suffering and Divine Healings 14
   - "This Is Your Home" 16
   - Gyanamata Enters the Self-Realization Monastic Order . 17
   - Reverence and Humility Before a Christlike Master . . . 19
   - Teaching Others Through Her Example 20
   - Exuding Peace, Compassion, Well-Being 22
   - The Letters of Sri Gyanamata 24
   - Her Years at the Encinitas Hermitage 26
   - Communing With God Through Meditation 29
   - "Endure That Which I Shall Send You" 30
   - Through Her Suffering, She Helped Others 32
   - Divine Inner Strength 33
   - Her Final Words: "Too Much Joy!" 34
   - She Left the Body in the Highest State of Samadhi 35
   - Spiritual Footprints for All to Follow 37
2. "The Dewdrop Has Slipped Into the Shining Sea," by Paramahansa Yogananda 38
3. "I Shall Never Be the Same Again" 53

PART II: THE LETTERS OF SRI GYANAMATA

4. Right Attitude 65
5. The Guru-Disciple Relationship 93
6. "All I Know Is That I Must Please You" 116
7. Renunciation 127
8. Wisdom From Gyanamata 135
9. "More and Better" 150
10. Loyalty and Receptivity to Truth 155
11. Devotion 164
12. "Suffering Can Be a Pathway to Greatness" 174
13. Divine Healings and Spiritual Experiences 193
14. Gratitude to God and Guru. 206
15. Rajarsi Janakananda. 229

PART III: LETTERS TO SRI GYANAMATA

16. From Sister-Disciples 237
17. Letters From Paramahansa Yogananda 244

PART IV: SRI GYANAMATA'S PERSONAL DIARY AND MEDITATIONS

18. Personal Diary. 269
19. Meditations 285

ILLUSTRATIONS

Facing page

Sri Gyanamata *(frontispiece)*

Gyanamata as an infant. 8

Gyanamata at age nineteen 8

Paramahansa Yogananda, guru of Sri Gyanamata 9

Gyanamata with her son and husband 24

Paramahansa Yogananda with a group of disciples and students, 1937. 25

Gyanamata as a young woman 56

Paramahansa Yogananda with class in Seattle, 1924 57

Gyanamata with her son and daughter-in-law. 88

Gyanamata with her mother in Seattle 88

Paramahansa Yogananda and Gyanamata feeding fish in Encinitas, 1939 89

Gyanamata at SRF International Headquarters, 1935 120

Self-Realization Fellowship International Headquarters . . . 121

Paramahansa Yogananda and Gyanamata, 1941 152

Self-Realization Fellowship Hermitage, Encinitas 153

Gyanamata meditating at "spiritual wishing well," SRF International Headquarters, 1935 184

Inscriptions in base of wishing well 185

Altar niche in Gyanamata's room 185

Sri Rajarsi Janakananda and Sri Daya Mata, spiritual successors to Paramahansa Yogananda 248

Paramahansa Yogananda in Temple of Leaves. 249

Gyanamata with book, Encinitas 280

Gyanamata on Encinitas Hermitage grounds. 281

Gyanamata by meditation caves, Encinitas, 1937 281

The Spiritual Legacy of Paramahansa Yogananda

Paramahansa Yogananda (1893-1952) is widely recognized as one of the preeminent spiritual figures of our time, and the influence of his life and work continues to grow. Many of the religious and philosophical concepts and methods he introduced decades ago are now finding expression in education, psychology, business, medicine, and other spheres of endeavor—contributing in far-reaching ways to a more integrated, humane, and spiritual vision of human life.

The fact that Paramahansa Yogananda's teachings are being interpreted and creatively applied in many different fields, as well as by exponents of diverse philosophical and metaphysical movements, points not only to the great practical utility of what he taught. It also makes clear the need for some means of ensuring that the spiritual legacy he left not be diluted, fragmented, or distorted with the passing of time.

With the increasing variety of sources of information about Paramahansa Yogananda, readers sometimes inquire how they can be certain that a publication accurately presents his life and teachings. In response to these inquiries, we would like to explain that Sri Yogananda founded Self-Realization Fellowship to disseminate his teachings and to preserve their purity and integrity for future generations. He personally chose and trained those close disciples who head the Self-Realization Fellowship Publications Council, and gave them specific guidelines for the preparation and publishing of his lectures, writings, and *Self-Realization Lessons.* The members of the SRF Publications Council honor these guidelines as a sacred trust, in order that the universal message of this beloved world teacher may live on in its original power and authenticity.

The Self-Realization Fellowship name and the SRF emblem (shown above) were originated by Sri Yogananda to identify the organization he founded to carry on his worldwide spiritual and humanitarian work. These appear on all Self-Realization Fellowship books, audio and video recordings, films, and other publications, assuring the reader that a work originates with the organization founded by Paramahansa Yogananda and faithfully conveys his teachings as he himself intended they be given.

Self-Realization Fellowship

PREFACE

BY SRI DAYA MATA

President and spiritual head of Self-Realization Fellowship/ Yogoda Satsanga Society of India

This presentation of the life and letters of Sri Gyanamata,* exalted disciple of Paramahansa Yogananda, fulfills our long-felt desire to share with others the inspiration of her example and wisdom. A soul of rare divine insight, she mastered the science of supreme spirituality by reducing the complex principles of "do's and don'ts" to the simple formula, "God Alone." Centered in that nucleus, she had a clear perspective of the right direction in which to turn her thoughts and actions at each decisive moment. Through this centeredness of heart and mind she found the perfect love of God.

My strongest personal memories of "Sister"—as we called her—are of her quiet humility, her incisive wisdom in matters both spiritual and practical, her stoic imperturbability, her motherly concern for everyone who came into contact with her. Illumining all these qualities was her complete dedication to God alone: seeking only Him, doing His will always, serving Him unconditionally. She was delicate, almost fragile, in physical health and appearance, but she emanated the limitless spiritual strength of those who reflect the soul's oneness with God.

Gyanamata, though a many-faceted spiritual diamond, will perhaps be most remembered for her perfection of

* "Gyanamata" means "Mother of Wisdom." "Sri" is a title denoting respect; in reference to a saintly personage, it means "holy." *(See also page 18.)*

attitude in all circumstances; and, as an extension of that wisdom, her understanding of the role of the Guru. Because of the clarity of her own spiritual perception, she saw in Paramahansaji the manifested love and wisdom of God. She emptied the chalice of her life of all else that it might be filled with the blessings of God that flowed through the channel of her Guru. So pure and unbroken was her attunement that Paramahansaji said he guided her spiritual life mainly through her intuition.

Gyanamata was not a young woman when she entered the ashram, but she accepted neither age nor physical infirmity as obstacles to spiritual endeavor. Thus Paramahansaji could say of her at the end of life that she was free, a liberated soul, reunited with God; and that further incarnations would not be imposed on her.

Gyanamata's influence had a profound effect on those of us who knew her personally. It is our prayer that as you share with us the unique insights into her saintliness to be found in these pages, you too shall receive inspiration and guidance from the "spiritual handbook" of her life.

Los Angeles, California
November 1984

PART I

The Life of Sri Gyanamata

CHAPTER 1

The Life of Sri Gyanamata

During a talk given in Los Angeles in 1940, Paramahansa Yogananda—the great master from India who founded Self-Realization Fellowship—said of his disciple Sri Gyanamata: "Of all the women I have met in America, I think the one who has found highest favor with God is Sister Gyanamata." Eleven years later, at her funeral service in Encinitas, California, he declared: "A great saint has gone away....But she has left spiritual footprints...for all souls that are in despair, that they might trace her footsteps...to my Father's home. Those spiritual footprints will always be here."

A "great saint," one of the foremost disciples of a God-illumined master, yet one whose exalted life was lived in relative obscurity—who was this humble soul who found such favor with God?

Childhood and Early Years

Born Edith Anne Ruth D'Evelyn on July 4, 1869, Gyanamata was the daughter of John and Isabella D'Evelyn of Woodbridge, Canada, and the eldest of their three children. Her predominant memories of those earliest years were of the church her family attended in that small Ontario town: "I can still see the little white English church amidst the pine trees. When I was about four years old I used to stand on the kneeling bench in the church in order to bring my head above the top of the pew, and I sang the hymns with all my heart. When I was about six, I listened to a sermon in St. George's Cathedral in nearby Toronto. The clergyman said that God would not allow us to depend upon anything but Himself. I thought about the application to myself, and understood it perfectly."

Her father, a young medical doctor, had died when she was but four; and after living for a few years with relatives in Toronto, her mother remarried and the family moved to Madelia, Minnesota, where Gyanamata grew up. Hers was not at all an easy, carefree childhood. For one thing, the family was poor. Gyanamata said that although her mother's family—the well-to-do founders of Woodbridge—were in a position to help them with their financial difficulties, they did so begrudgingly and then only sparingly, "because," she said, "they could not condone the 'unconventional' ways of my mother." Her mother had, for example, married at a very young age and, they felt, "beneath her station"; she refused to wear a widow's cap (the custom of the day) when her husband died; and, though a religious person, she would not attend church "merely for show," as they would have liked. "Mother could not stand hypocrisy in life," Gyanamata recalled. "And she would tell me everything—the unkindness of her family, all of her heartaches and sorrows. I witnessed many, many tears at a very young age."

These childhood struggles no doubt had a strengthening effect on Gyanamata's character—she learned early to deal with suffering in life. Like her mother, she also developed an aversion to hypocrisy and the fickleness of worldly living; this nourished an already strong desire to discover the deeper, eternal truths of life. "I am sure that my steady progress toward the Master* began right then," she said.

Finding public school somewhat shallow, she terminated

* A respectful title often used by disciples when referring to Paramahansa Yogananda—one who had attained self-mastery. It serves as an English equivalent for "Guru," the customary Sanskrit term for one's spiritual preceptor.

her formal education after the eighth grade. With Sri Gyanamata, as with many great men and women throughout history, learning was mostly a matter of self-education. Gyanamata had an insatiable appetite for Truth, and was constantly reading and reflecting on the thoughts of the world's deep thinkers—especially religious philosophers and saints. Further, she was determined to *apply* the wisdom she distilled from her reading, so that from her early childhood, each of life's circumstances became for her an opportunity to learn a new lesson. The whole world became her classroom; her "teachers," the experiences she encountered in her growing desire for spiritual unfoldment.

Gyanamata once related an incident that typified her attitude in those early years. She had a friend at school—a pretty, vivacious, impudent girl—who was a favorite with the young male teacher. Gyanamata longed for a word of approval from him, too; she decided to adopt the mannerisms of her little friend in an attempt to gain his favor. But all she received was a severe reprimand for her impertinent behavior. Characteristically, she thought this over carefully, and gleaned a valuable lesson: "I decided that from that day forth, I must act naturally and follow my heart's natural inclinations." She was nine years old at the time.

Searching for Love

Through adolescence and into womanhood, Gyanamata's independent spirit matured. "I never allowed anyone to force anything upon me," she said. "And when I saw anything that I wanted, I always went after it fearlessly." Her heart was seeking love. "But," she recalled, "I was absolutely unimpressed by the opposite sex. As far as I was concerned, they simply did not exist. When asked to go anywhere, the answer was always the same: *No*. One day, my brother relayed the comment of one of my male acquaintances: 'It will be a brave man who marries your sister!' My mother was always telling me that I would be lonely in old age if I did not marry. I replied, 'Well, it makes no difference to me. For one reason only will I marry—that is for love.' Then I met Mr. Bissett."

Clark Prescott Bissett was at that time a young divinity student who had been given the assignment of conducting summer services in the little Episcopal church that Gyanamata attended in Madelia. A kind, sincere, deeply religious gentleman with a striking personality, the Reverend Mr. Bissett won the hearts of all who knew him—especially the heart of Edith D'Evelyn. "I was really in love with love," Gyanamata said. "I wanted true love, and Mr. Bissett was the soul of kindness. I loved him dearly. When I think of his incarnating again, I picture him as a philanthropist, or one who establishes a house for orphans." It was in 1899, when she was thirty years of age, that they married.

Soon after their marriage, her husband changed his mind about his vocation and entered law school in Minneapolis. "This study was very easy for him," Gyanamata recollected. "He had great powers of concentration, so he finished the course and passed the bar examination in one year!" It was while he was in law school that their only child was born—Clark Prescott Bissett, Jr., whom Gyanamata affectionately called "Rex," because, she explained, to her he was "king of the household of Bissett."

In time, the Bissetts moved to Seattle, Washington, where Mr. Bissett practiced law and later became a professor and acting Dean of the Law School at the University of Washington. Because of the sympathy, guidance, and understanding he gave to his students, they affectionately called him "Father-in-Law." "We must have been married for fifteen years before Mr. Bissett found the work for which he was really fitted," Gyanamata later reminisced. "It was when he entered the profession of teaching. His students loved and were inspired by him. They rose to their feet as one man when he came into the classroom, and at the university he spent the happiest and most successful years of his life." In her humility, Gyanamata failed to mention how much of a part she herself played in his achievements—encouraging him and helping him in every way to become the success he was. Her son later recalled how she often worked "behind the scenes" writing speeches for Professor Bissett. He used to tell her, "You know my thoughts better than *I* do!"

Rex studied under his father at the university and later became a lawyer in Seattle. He recalled how his father's learned friends often engaged in philosophical discussion with Gyanamata—being attracted to her deep wisdom and delightful humor. Frequently Mr. Bissett's lawyer friends would good-naturedly admit defeat after a tussle of wits with her. So keen and penetrating was her wisdom that these scholars would advise others not to venture into a debate with her unless their facts were ironclad!

Into the Realm of Spiritual Thought

Gyanamata's main interests, however, were always spiritual; in fact, she once confided to a close companion: "You know, as far back in this life as I can remember, I have never had a thought that did not have the thought of God behind it." She was always hungry to hear more of God and of the way to bring Him closer in her own life. Consequently, she attended in Seattle several lectures on philosophy and religion and read a great deal on this subject, collecting over the years a great library of select spiritual literature that she later donated to Self-Realization Fellowship.* With her, reading was not merely for the purpose of gathering intellectual knowledge. "Religion," she said, "consists solely in realization." Gyanamata read only for spiritual understanding and inspiration—to lift her mind again and again into the realm of spiritual thought. She once wrote of this in a letter to Paramahansa Yogananda:

"It is always a great satisfaction to me not only to feel but to see clearly mentally, and to be able to put what I feel into words. When I gave you my books, you said that you wondered how it was that I could be so intellectual and at the same time so devotional. I knew that I had never read for the purpose of study and scholarship, but I did not know how to state it to you. Now I do....I read because I wanted to be in the company of the saints. I know now also how to say what I've always wanted to live for: it is for spiritual achievement."

There was nothing limited about Gyanamata's intellectual scope. Through her reading, her mind commingled with the thoughts of all the world's great thinkers—regardless of their race, creed, color, or religion; she perceived the Essential Unity behind all the different religious forms. On her library shelves could be found the great scriptures of all

* The Bissett private library—originally one of the largest on the Pacific Coast—also included biographies and letters of great men and women in history, especially Abraham Lincoln. Professor Bissett, a nationally known authority on the life of this great statesman, wrote a work in two volumes on Lincoln as a man of law. At one time, his was recognized as one of the largest collections of Lincolniana in the world. This collection has since been purchased and donated to Washington State University, at Pullman, Washington.

Opposite: *(Left)* Gyanamata as an infant. *(Right)* Gyanamata at age nineteen.

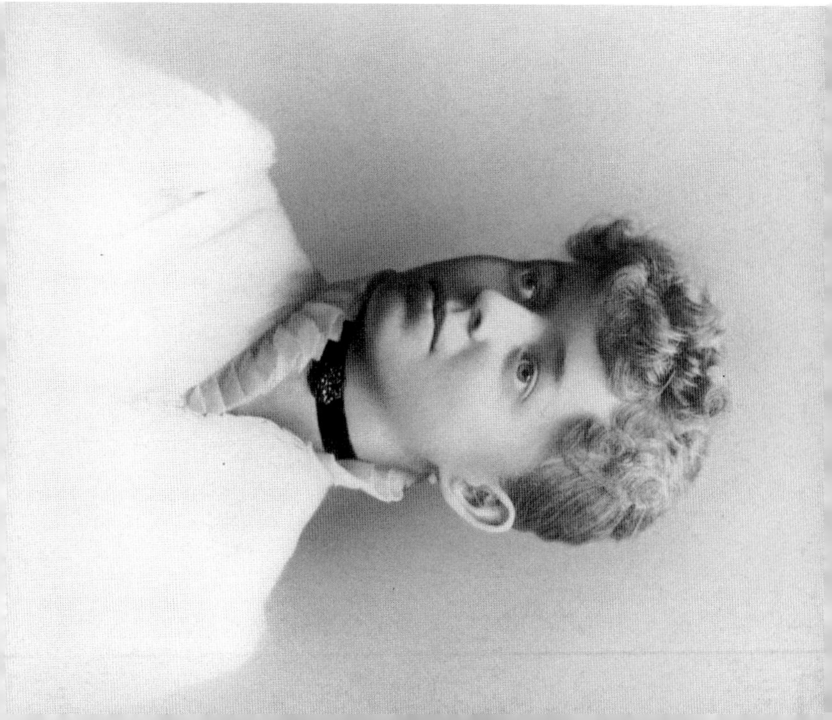

Paramahansa Yogananda

Founder of Self-Realization Fellowship; beloved guru of Sri Gyanamata. Gyanamata once said that this was her favorite photograph of Paramahansaji.

true religions—the Bhagavad Gita, the Bible, the teachings of Lord Buddha; anthologies on the philosophy of religion; books by and about the saints of all religions, the mystics of all climes and times (she seemed to have a special affinity for the teachings of Meister Johannes Eckhart, a fourteenth-century German Christian mystic); poetry from such diverse sources as the great medieval master Kabir, the seventeenth-century English mystic George Herbert, nineteenth-century American bards Longfellow and Whitman, and India's Nobel-prizewinning twentieth-century poet, Rabindranath Tagore.

Gyanamata's Interest in India's Wisdom

While Gyanamata was living in Seattle, Tagore gave a lecture there on India's literature and religion. He was invited to the Bissett household for dinner. There Gyanamata was introduced to him by a mutual friend, who said: "This is Mrs. Bissett. She is a great admirer of yours." "And of your country," added Gyanamata. Later she remarked: "When I said that, his handsome, grave face broke into a smile. If you have ever been in a darkened house when someone suddenly opens the curtains and a flood of light pours into the room—that was the effect of Rabindranath Tagore's smile."

There were several reasons for Gyanamata's interest in Tagore's homeland. The first was a very practical concern: Her son Rex had developed an extreme case of nervousness, and she had been studying yogic methods of curing this disease. Second, she was very much attracted to Indian philosophy. After reading her first book on Hinduism, she declared, "I shall never be the same again." Gyanamata developed a great respect and love for India's spiritual heritage through her extensive reading of the *Upanishads,* the Bhagavad Gita, and other great Indian scriptures, as well as through the writings of and about great Indian saints.

Gyanamata Meets Her Guru, Paramahansa Yogananda

From her study of India's wisdom, Gyanamata soon recognized the necessity of having a true guru* to guide her to the Infinite Goal. A few teachers came into her life during this period, and though she learned some valuable lessons from them, she realized that none of them was a true master—one who knows God. She resolved that until she could find such a guru to instruct and discipline her, she would make life itself her "guru." She would meet every experience with a true disciple's attitude, striving to understand and learn from every circumstance, as she had for years, but now accepting it as though it were a lesson coming from her guru. However, she continued to long for the spiritual training that would enable her to progress more rapidly toward God. When that desire became very intense, it happened that Paramahansa Yogananda came to Seattle.

Paramahansa Yogananda had been sent to the United States four years earlier by his Guru, to teach in the West the ancient spiritual science of Kriya Yoga. He had arrived in 1920 in Boston, where he had been invited to represent India at a Congress of Religious Liberals. Following the congress, Yoganandaji had remained in Boston for three years, teaching the Self-Realization principles of meditation and balanced living. At the end of 1923, he embarked on the first of several cross-continental speaking tours, during which tens of thousands in all of America's major cities attended his lectures and classes teaching the sure and scientific way to know God. In 1924, he came to Seattle, the fourth stop on this lecture tour.

* Spiritual teacher. Verse 17 of the *Guru Gita* describes the guru as "dispeller of darkness" (from *gu*, "darkness," and *ru*, "that which dispels"). The guru helps the disciple to dispel the darkness of ignorance of God and let in the light of God-consciousness.

Gyanamata herself did not plan to attend Paramahansa Yogananda's classes, for she felt that her interest in the teachings of a long-haired Hindu might cause unfavorable comment that could place her husband in a difficult position at the university. However, she very much hoped that her son, who had agreed to attend, could give her the teachings. Rex was among Paramahansaji's first students in Seattle. He was very enthusiastic about what he learned; but when he came home from the first class, he told his mother that he had taken a vow not to reveal to others the techniques of meditation he had been taught. However, he subsequently approached Paramahansaji with the problem, and secured the Guru's permission to pass the teachings on to his mother.*

In the Self-Realization teachings, Gyanamata found everything her heart and intellect had been seeking during her previous years of spiritual study. She later wrote to Paramahansa Yogananda: "All the great masters have told men to seek God. But never before has there been given a complete technique by which men can carry on that search day by day. You came on earth to give that detailed instruction."

The following year, Paramahansa Yogananda returned to Seattle, and was invited by Rex to dinner at the Bissett home. It was on a Sunday, July 12, 1925. This was Gyanamata's first meeting with her Guru†—an occasion for which she had waited years, and which she never forgot. She later wrote in her diary: "I see myself coming down the years, from the days

* The reader may be interested to know that throughout his life Rex continued with his enthusiastic practice of the Self-Realization Fellowship teachings. He and his wife Hughella, also a devoted lifetime member of SRF, often visited Gyanamata after she entered the Self-Realization ashram. In some of her letters, Gyanamata refers to gifts that the three of them sent to Paramahansaji.

† In one of her letters, Gyanamata mentions that she had seen Paramahansaji a year earlier, in 1924, but this was her first meeting with him.

when I was an unhappy little Canadian girl, to that day when I saw standing before me a Hindu swami in the ochre robe of renunciation,* the answer to my prayers and longing. *All* had led up to that moment. I ask myself sometimes: 'Should he come again, with what words would I welcome him?' I know that again there would be the same silence, with no words at all except, 'Bless me, that I may realize God.'"

Instant Recognition Between Guru and Disciple

Gyanamata often told of the instant recognition between guru and disciple at that first treasured moment: They meditated together; then Paramahansaji told her that she had been one of his disciples in a previous incarnation. Recognizing the spiritual receptivity Gyanamata had attained through her efforts in past lives, the Guru was able, at that first meeting, to give her the direct experience of God as the great Amen or *Aum,*† the creative cosmic vibration. Years later she wrote to him: "Do you remember my taking you upstairs to my room when you came to my house in Seattle? Silently you looked at my pictures of holy men; and then, turning your back to the long row of windows, you prayed for me very softly and gave me my first blessing, the one that enabled me to hear the *Aum.* After that, as long as I remained in Seattle, a vase of orange flowers (that were sometimes fresh blossoms and sometimes artificial ones) stayed on the floor to mark the spot where you had stood."

* An ochre robe is the traditional attire for members of India's most ancient monastic order, the Order of Swamis.

† *Aum*—the "Word" or "Holy Ghost" spoken of in the Bible—is the all-pervading vibration of God that upholds creation. It may be experienced when the consciousness is attuned through the practice of meditation techniques, such as those taught in the *Self-Realization Fellowship Lessons. Aum* is heard as the sound of rushing waters, bringing a feeling of great peace: "...and his voice [was] as the sound of many waters" (Revelation 1:15).

A curious and significant incident occurred during that first meeting: Many guests were seated at the dinner table, and on the table was a novel saltshaker. Its leaded base caused it to spring upright whenever it was pushed over. Several of the guests played with it in turn, but no one could make the toy stay on its side.

"Then," Gyanamata recalled, "after several of the guests had tried it, the Master took the saltshaker and examined it thoughtfully for a few minutes. He pushed it down with his finger—it came up. He pushed it down again and again, looking at it intently—each time it came up. Once more he pushed it down, and when he raised his finger, finally it stayed down! Everyone was astonished. But he simply said, 'The mind was determined that it should stay down.'" Later, he recalled, "[At that time] I heard the voice of God: 'For the benefit of Sister,* lay it down.'...I remember well that occasion, for I knew then that God would draw her to this path."

"Swamiji† departed that night," Gyanamata continued, "but the next day there were other guests at the table, and my son told what Swamiji had done. He passed the toy from hand to hand, and it flew upright for everyone, as before.

* At this first meeting, Paramahansa Yogananda immediately recognized the high spiritual stature that Gyanamata had attained in previous incarnations, and he intuitively knew she was destined to follow the path of renunciation in Self-Realization Fellowship. Since "Sister" was the title customarily used in the West for women renunciants, he called her that from their very first meeting. Later, when he gave her the vows of *sannyas* in the Swami Order, her monastic name "Gyanamata" (which included the title *mata,* "mother") formally superseded the title "Sister." *(See page 18.)*

† Paramahansa Yogananda was known as "Swami Yogananda" or "Swamiji" (the suffix "ji" denotes respect) prior to December 1935. At that time his guru bestowed on him the highest monastic title—*paramahansa*—signifying one who has proved his attainment of the supreme, irrevocable union with God. In this book he is referred to by the latter title, except where it would mean changing a direct quote, as in this instance.

When it came to me, I pushed it down as the others had, but it did not fly up again—it remained flat on the table! I was aghast. Everyone exclaimed, 'She's done it, too!' But I knew that 'I' had not—the Master's vibrations were still with me." In later years, Gyanamata often referred to this event, saying that she recognized it as a sign that she would follow in the footsteps of her Guru.

Physical Suffering and Divine Healings

After that first meeting, Gyanamata did not see her Guru again for five years. For Paramahansaji, these were years of almost ceaseless travel, during which he taught the science of yoga in cities large and small throughout the United States. Gyanamata thought of him constantly and wrote to him often. During this period, she suffered from a heart attack and several other serious illnesses. "When things were very bad," she said, "I asked the Master's prayers. He was in New York at the time, and I in Seattle. I figured out how long it would take for my letter to reach him, and just at the time I felt he should get the letter, I felt his healing vibrations as I sat in my meditation chair—they shook the chair....The tremendous roar of *Aum* rolled over and under the house—at first I thought it was a truck passing over the cobblestone street outside...." There was no truck. The Guru's powerful vibrations had healed her.

During those years in Seattle, Gyanamata's external role was one of assiduous but unassuming service to her family. Though herself frail in body and suffering from various physical ailments, she cheerfully performed her household duties and helped her husband with his speeches; at the same time she attended to their adopted daughter, a homeless teenage girl who was bedridden with a serious case of arthritis, and also to her ailing mother, who required constant attention. All this was done cheerfully and without the slightest complaint.

A frequent guest in the Bissett home during these years, Miss Josephine Porter, told of the effect Gyanamata's exemplary conduct had on her: "I was an intimate in her home from 1911 until she went to California in 1930, and I can say that Sister's extraordinary patience was one of her most amazing attributes. For many years, her mother—who lived with her then—demanded constant attention. If Sister was not in sight, she would call for her: 'Edith! Edith! Where are you? Come here this minute!' No matter if she was upstairs or down, no matter what she was doing (except when, on occasion, she herself was suffering from one of the severe migraine headaches that she had endured from early life, until Paramahansa Yogananda healed her), Sister would always answer in a sweet, serene voice, 'Yes, Mama, I'm coming.'"

In 1930, Gyanamata was again experiencing great physical suffering, and the doctors did not have much hope of her surviving. "When I was x-rayed in Seattle," she said, "the doctors found that I had enlargement of the heart, hardening of the arteries, and a stoppage in the left kidney. They said they could not help me."

Though she was not expected to live long, Gyanamata went on cheerfully as if nothing were wrong. Her husband, who had been planning a trip to Europe, decided to drop his plans. Not knowing this, she asked him when he expected to leave. "I can never leave you again," he said. "That's awful!" she replied. "Must we both sit here together waiting for each other to die? Let us live as if we have fifty years more before us." He went on with his plans, and she decided: "I'll go part of the way with you. I have always wanted to go to Mt. Washington."*

* Site of and frequently used name for the Mother Center and International Headquarters of Self-Realization Fellowship in Los Angeles, California.

"This Is Your Home"

So it was decided that she would spend the winter at her Guru's ashram, and return in May to Seattle. As things turned out, Professor Bissett did not go to Europe, but instead bought a house in La Jolla, California—a small town on the Pacific coast, about 100 miles south of Los Angeles—where they went to live. Whenever Paramahansaji was in residence at the Self-Realization Fellowship Headquarters, Gyanamata would visit, in order to be near her Guru. Her health returned, owing, she often said, to Paramahansaji's healing vibrations. She grew to love Mt. Washington, and all the residents came to love her. One day the Guru told her: "Your devotion is felt throughout the house. This is your home. Come here whenever you want to."

Mr. Bissett accompanied his wife on one such visit, and said to Paramahansaji: "Sister feels more at home here than anywhere else." The Master replied, "Yes, she has lived in this vibration for a long time." Gyanamata later related that she "interpreted this remark to mean that, from the first contact between my Guru and myself, I had lived in his vibration."

Indeed, those who knew her claimed that Gyanamata "lived in his vibration" throughout the remaining twenty years of her life, demonstrating a unique attunement with her Guru. She mentally followed him as he carried the Self-Realization teachings from city to city, country to country, all around the world, until she came to feel that inwardly there was no separation between them. She once wrote him: "For sixteen years I have followed you from point to point, until now I do not feel your absence at all—for where you are, there I am also—*always* standing invisibly before you, humbly and patiently awaiting the moment when I will receive a word and a smile from you." Distance was no barrier; no matter how many miles separated them, whenever the

Guru would send a special inner blessing to her, she would feel it, recognize it as coming from him, and would write him a letter of gratitude. Sometimes she would sign her letters to him with the name "Gyanamata of Yogananda," an affirmation of her love and attunement with her Guru.

Gyanamata Enters the Self-Realization Monastic Order

In 1932, Mr. Bissett brought his wife to Mt. Washington and asked Paramahansaji if he would allow her to live there permanently after his passing. Mr. Bissett had had a premonition of his coming death, and he knew she wanted to live at Mt. Washington after he was gone. Indeed, he did die shortly thereafter. Gyanamata was naturally distraught at the loss of her husband, and her emotional trauma was compounded at that time by financial difficulties. After a while, she meekly wrote Paramahansaji, asking for permission to come and live at the ashram. Unfortunately, the letter was delayed in reaching him, so she did not get a reply for a long time. She had prepared herself for the possibility that he simply could not take her—a difficult test indeed—but finally the letter came.

"Dear Divine Soul," wrote Paramahansaji. "I knew long ago that your home would be at Mt. Washington. Have you to ask my permission to come here? I already told you it is your home, which you have made sacred by your divine personality. Your whole soul was to be with us, so the Divine has granted your wish. Your mansion in heaven with God and Guru is always ready there."

With deep gratitude, Gyanamata replied, in the final letter to her Guru prior to her entering the ashram: "Dear Master—You may be weary of listening, but I am never weary of thanking you for the wonderful way you have opened the door to me after Mr. Bissett's death. I wish I could express this in words that would glow on paper as the thought does in my heart. That you *want* me is the crest-jewel of my life."

She was joyously received at Mt. Washington, and Paramahansaji gave her the honor of becoming one of the first Self-Realization Fellowship monastic disciples to take the final vows of renunciation. On July 20, 1932, Paramahansaji conducted a formal Vedic ceremony in which he initiated Sister into the venerable Swami Order, giving her the monastic name and title, "Gyanamata"—Mother of Wisdom. He explained that for her it signifies "Mother of Wisdom through Devotion." Although formally it was now unnecessary to call her "Sister," as her new name included the title "Mata" (Mother), the Guru continued to call her "Sister" as he had done from their first meeting in Seattle, and so was she known by all. "It was my greatest pleasure," said the Guru, "to be the divine instrument to make you a sister to all mankind."

Though a latecomer to the monastic life, being already in her sixties when she came to live at Mt. Washington, Gyanamata had long practiced an inner renunciation—sacrificing selfish motive and attachment to worldly goals to follow her heart's natural love for the Divine Goal of life. "The last chapter in life is the most important," she said; and she made a superhuman effort in her ashram years to live a life of perfection for God and Guru. "God Alone" became her motto, and a sign with these words hung above her bed during all her years in the ashram *(see photo facing page 185)*. Each year, Gyanamata reaffirmed her motto by inscribing the date of the anniversary of her monastic vow on the back of the sign.

In her later years, she wrote to Paramahansaji: "The words that hang above my head, 'God Alone,' are there because I took a vow not to forget my Goal, even for a moment, and never to let anything come between you and me. I never have. You have been the polestar of my life."

Reverence and Humility Before a Christlike Master

Sri Gyanamata had a natural attitude of deep respect, humility, and reverence for her Guru—an attitude that was born of her deep wisdom. Though almost everyone who met Paramahansa Yogananda respected him, very few outside of a handful of close disciples in the ashram were capable of comprehending the greatness of his spiritual stature. Gyanamata was one of the first Westerners who did. She recognized that he was no ordinary spiritual teacher, but a true Christlike master, one whose consciousness is attuned with God. She once told Paramahansaji: "The awareness of the height of your God-conscious state never leaves me for a moment," and she treated him with the reverence and humility that is implicit in such understanding.

"Sister was so humble and considerate," recalled one of her younger sister-disciples, "that anytime Guruji would come into the room, she would approach him, touch his feet,* and depart. I once asked her, 'Sister, why do you leave when Master comes in?' She said, 'I don't want ever to give him the slightest cause to feel that he must give me any notice. I don't ever want him to feel that he must utter one word to me.' Did you ever hear of such humility? Such was her attunement and reverence for the Guru."

During her last years, when she was forced by illness to remain in her room most of the time, Gyanamata enjoyed looking out the window at her Guru as he came and went.

* Bowing down and touching the feet of persons held in high spiritual regard is a traditional form of greeting in India. It is called a *pranam,* literally "complete salutation."

Sometimes she would send a little message to the Master, asking him to look up at her window from the car as he departed. He would smile and gaze toward the window, where he saw the beaming face of his loyal disciple, little Sister, smiling down at him. It was so characteristic of Sister: She who could have asked for anything in the world from her God-illumined Guru asked only for a glance in her direction. Sometimes he would send her a special blessing—a prayer or healing vibration—which she would always consciously receive; other times she would just find herself attuned to his thoughts. In her bedroom one Sunday morning, she turned to one of the other nuns and said that the Master had just revealed, in his Sunday lecture service, that the Divine Mother had said to him: "Dance of life or dance of death, know that these come from Me, and rejoice. What more dost thou want, than that thou hast Me?" Later in the day, when Paramahansaji came to visit her, Gyanamata commented on how much she had liked Divine Mother's words. The Guru smiled and replied, "Oh, so you heard, did you?"

Teaching Others Through Her Example

It is said that the humble soul never knows its own greatness. Certainly this was the case with Sri Gyanamata. She would sometimes say to the young ashram residents, "Oh, if only I had my health, I would show you how to be good disciples." Yet, as her great influence on the other disciples demonstrated, she *was* showing them, all the time. Unlike the scholar, who teaches through study, theory, reason, and mere words, Gyanamata taught through the example of her life—through experience.

She fully grasped the scope and importance of the guru-disciple relationship—the divine law that only through the teachings and blessings of a true guru may a human soul return to God. She understood that just as a person who wants to become a physician must go to an experienced physician to learn the profession, so one striving to commune with God must go to someone who knows Him—a true guru. And once having found him, it is the duty of the disciple to become attuned to the God-conscious state of the guru. By attaining the divine consciousness of which the Master spoke, even though she was not often in his physical presence, Gyanamata demonstrated that *inner* attunement and receptivity to the guru is far more important than outer contact with him—and she was able to transmit that understanding to the other devotees.

Her example had especially great inspiration for the young monastic disciples whom the Guru was training.* One of these was Sri Daya Mata, spiritual successor to Paramahansa Yogananda and president of Self-Realization Fellowship since 1955. "Gyanamata was like a mother to all of us young devotees here," Daya Mata recalled, "and how we adored her! Never have I met anyone like her—a true disciple in every sense of the word. I have seen many, many divine souls in my travels over the years, but I tell you truthfully that Sister was one of the greatest. She spent her whole life here striving to attune her will with the will of God and Guru. Such wisdom, such dedication, such devotion!—and you know, she hardly had any contact with Master. It wasn't necessary for her to be in his physical presence to be attuned to his will. Her words and the example of her life have been and continue to be a source of great inspiration to me."

Tara Mata, late SRF vice-president and editor-in-chief, was another disciple who deeply valued the example of Gyanamata, saying: "I never had such respect for any other

* In honor of the invaluable training Sister gave to the monastic disciples, the nuns' living quarters constructed at the SRF International Headquarters in 1967 were named "Gyanamata Ashram."

woman as I had for her. Paramahansaji often spoke of Sister at length, saying how she always got his thoughts because she was a disciple in tune with her Guru. Indeed, she was a saint incarnate; as with all of them, you wouldn't at first suspect it."

Gyanamata liked to think of herself as God's servant, and externally hers was often—out of choice—a background role. At Mt. Washington, she was given many assignments: cooking, housecleaning, receiving guests, writing letters in response to students' requests for spiritual guidance. When she once mentioned to one of the nuns that she did not consider herself a naturally hard worker, that nun exclaimed, "Well, no one would ever suspect it!" Whatever her task, Gyanamata performed it willingly, silently, efficiently, cheerfully, and with deep concentration.

"She never talked much," recalls Mrinalini Mata, vice-president of Self-Realization Fellowship since 1966, "but when she spoke, ah! such keen wisdom!" That was Gyanamata's way: Though blessed with the deep understanding of a *gyana* yogi,* she did not advertise her wisdom or her greatness. With quiet reserve and dignity, simply, patiently, and humbly, she went about her duties, living her holy life for God alone.

Exuding Peace, Compassion, Well-Being

But her spirituality was never of the "holier than thou" variety, nor was she the least bit aloof or indifferent toward others. On the contrary, she invariably knew how to make others feel at ease and welcome, regardless of whether she was with visiting dignitaries, doctors, lawyers, kitchen employees, market workers, or children.

* One who follows the path of wisdom to union with God. Through the discriminative power of the intellect, the *gyana* (or *jnana*) yogi becomes established in the omniscient wisdom of the soul.

Once Gyanamata was in the kitchen of the Encinitas Hermitage, quietly preparing breakfast for her Guru, when a group of about five young teenage girls—children of some guests at the Encinitas Hermitage—entered the room. They were engaged in an animated, lively discussion about the latest hairstyles. Sister listened quietly as she finished preparing Paramahansaji's meal. After delivering it to the Master, she slipped into her room and emerged with a recent issue of *Ladies Home Journal,* which contained a multiple-page display of the latest hairstyles. She presented this to the girls with a big smile, saying simply: "This might help you." Then she returned to her room. No judging, no criticism, no complaints that such things are too "trivial" to waste time thinking about; Gyanamata's understanding was broad enough to encompass all phases of development.

All who came into the range of her acquaintance were silently attracted and uplifted by the peace, compassion, and sense of well-being that she exuded. When she went to purchase food, the workers at the market would spontaneously approach her with their personal problems, finding strength and practical direction in her suggestions. A physician who sometimes attended Gyanamata said that she became his "confessor." He would bring his troubles to her, and she would help him to put them into perspective and thus gain more control over his life. Sometimes, after treating her, he would just sit quietly in her presence, gazing at her face, which radiated the sweet serenity that is the mystery of the spiritually strong who have suffered and emerged victorious. He developed a high regard for her spiritual state, and often remarked that she helped him far more than he did her.

The spiritual help she radiated often brought material benefits. Not a few visitors would return, after spending some time in Gyanamata's presence, to thank her for physical healings they had received. But she would always say, "It was the Guru's healing—through me." She once told Paramahansaji: "I consider myself a storage battery for your holy vibrations."

Even animals felt the benevolent vibrations of her spiritual magnetism. During the early days at Mt. Washington, the area was still rather remote and there were many wild animals—coyotes, skunks, raccoons—living in the vicinity of the ashram grounds. One young skunk took a special liking to Gyanamata, and used to follow her around the garden. One day, unknown to Sister, it followed her up the stairs into the Administration Building reception hall. Everyone was alerted to be careful, and before the visitor could become alarmed and release its "perfume," Gyanamata led her striped friend back outside and peace was restored.

The Letters of Sri Gyanamata

Since she preferred to remain silent, Gyanamata's favorite means of communication with other devotees was often the letter. When she felt a note would be of service to others, Gyanamata would take the time to compose one of the gems of wisdom collected in this volume. She once explained, in a short note to Sri Daya Mata, then a young disciple at Mt. Washington: "The spoken word vanishes and is forgotten. Because of this I have decided to write you all notes that may be preserved, if you feel that these thoughts are of value or inspiration."

These letters were usually short and to the point, such as this one, sent to Daya Mata:

1. See nothing, look at nothing but your goal, ever shining before you.
2. The things that happen to us do not matter; what we become through them does.

Gyanamata with her son, Rex *(left)*, and her husband, Professor Clark Bissett, at their home in Seattle

3. Each day, accept everything as coming to you from God.
4. At night, give everything back into His hands.

To Paramahansa Yogananda, Gyanamata wrote freely and often. In contrast to the instructional tone that characterized her notes to the younger disciples, these letters to her Guru had a deeply reverential, devotional tone—a reflection of her constant awareness of his great spiritual stature. She always desired complete understanding, harmony, and attunement with his wishes in everything; once, after a hurried conversation with Paramahansaji, she wrote him a short note, saying: "I am not sure that I made myself plain, so I am writing this [to explain]—because I cannot, even for a moment, endure the thought that everything is not perfectly clear between yourself and me." Gyanamata desired perfection, and wanted no flattery from her Guru—only the truth. Often she would ask whether her actions or attitudes were appropriate and correct in a certain situation, and would end her letter with: "Please tell me plainly that I may correct myself, and live perfectly."

On certain appropriate occasions, she would just place a little note of greeting at the Master's door, such as this one on Christmas Day, 1941: "For recognizing me in Seattle as one of your disciples from the past—for receiving me when

---

Opposite: Paramahansa Yogananda with some of the disciples and students who gathered at the SRF International Headquarters to welcome him home after a seventeen-month trip to Europe and India, New Year's Day, 1937. At Paramahansaji's right is Rajarsi Janakananda *(see page 229)*; second from the Guru's left, in dark suit, is Dr. M. W. Lewis *(see page 163 n.)*; seated in front are Sri Gyanamata (looking away from the camera toward her guru) and some of the other Self-Realization nuns, including Sri Daya Mata, Ananda Mata, Durga Mata, and Tara Mata, dressed in silk saris, Christmas gifts brought to them from India by Paramahansaji.

I had no one else to turn to—for holding me to the path, when, bewildered by an agony of pain, I knew not which turn to take—for everything that has come since, up to the present day—for all you are that I know you to be and for all you are that I cannot know—I offer you reverence, gratitude, devotion, and love. But not enough, oh, not enough! It can never be enough."

Paramahansaji was deeply touched by all the loving thoughts and letters he received from Gyanamata; and he would sometimes respond with a note of appreciation to her. Because of his many responsibilities, the Master was unable to write often. "But," he once wrote, "I do write to you ever in my heart and spirit."

In 1935, Paramahansaji returned to India for a last visit with his guru, Swami Sri Yukteswar. Before leaving, he demonstrated his complete trust in Gyanamata by placing her in charge of the Mt. Washington headquarters. "I am so happy," he wrote to her, "to feel I can send devotees safely to one who helps them and inspires them with my ideal. I cannot tell you what a relief it has been since you have been there." The Guru knew that in Sister he had a loyal, faithful disciple who would represent completely the desires of his heart. "Please let everybody know," he wrote to her in 1933, "that in my absence you are the spiritual head of the institution, and everybody should obey your wishes, for I know they are impartial and God-directed."

Her Years at the Encinitas Hermitage

When Paramahansa Yogananda returned from India in 1936, he was happily surprised to learn that Rajarsi Janakananda, then known as Mr. James J. Lynn,* a successful

* In 1951 Paramahansaji bestowed on Mr. Lynn the monastic title of Rajarsi Janakananda. Until that time, the Guru lovingly referred to him as

American businessman and one of Paramahansaji's most advanced disciples, had purchased for his Guru substantial acreage on the cliff-lined coast at Encinitas, California, and had built on it a beautiful hermitage overlooking the Pacific Ocean *(see photo facing page 153)*. Paramahansaji put Gyanamata in charge of his new Encinitas ashram. She assumed the responsibilities of spiritual counselor and hostess, taught Sunday school, and at the same time attended to many other duties.

Daya Mata recalls how, in those early days in Encinitas, friends from all over the world would stay for a time as Paramahansaji's guests at the Hermitage. "On weekends," she related, "we would have as many as twenty-eight guests. We younger ones would move out of our rooms and sleep on the floor in front of the fireplace in the large reception hall. Sister would give up her room too and we couldn't find out where she went to sleep. Finally, I asked her, 'Sister, where do you go when you give up your room like this? Master doesn't expect this of you.' After all, she was an older woman, almost seventy.

"'No, dear, I must do it,' she replied.

"'But where do you go?' I asked.

"'Well, I just put up an army cot in the laundry room.'

"When she said army cot, she meant it—it was the very *hard* kind of army cot. And for years, that is where Gyanamata often slept—on an army cot in the Hermitage laundry room."

Paramahansaji commented on this in a talk some years later: "I never gave Sister a robe, but inside she is a true

---

"Saint Lynn." In 1952, Rajarsi became the spiritual successor of Paramahansa Yogananda and president of Self-Realization Fellowship, a position that he held until his passing on February 20, 1955.

renunciant. She is filled with the love divine. She has conquered within. On one occasion, some guests arrived at the Hermitage at two o'clock in the morning. I called for Sister and asked her: 'Could you give up your room for these guests?' Instantly she answered, 'Oh, yes,' with the greatest willingness. So I said to her, 'Sister, you sleep in my study.' And she remained quiet. I didn't understand then why she was quiet. Three days later, where do you think I found she had been sleeping? She had taken an old army cot and placed it in the laundry room. 'Sister,' I asked her, 'why didn't you sleep in my study?' She replied, 'I didn't want to blaspheme it.' I told her: 'Rather, you would sanctify it.'"

As time went on, Gyanamata's fragile body no longer permitted her to take such an active part in the Self-Realization work, but there was no ego-reaction in having to "step down" and assume lesser responsibilities—she continued always with her willing spirit to perform what little duties and services she could. With typical wit, she told the Master, "You can get anyone to teach, but who will bring up the milk bottles?"

One of Gyanamata's sister-disciples at the Encinitas Hermitage told of this incident:

"God will work through those who are willing instruments. It happened that Master called on the Hermitage intercom to ask if Sister would do some service for him. I answered the phone. I knew that Sister's body was very weak, and thinking that possibly someone else could perform the assignment instead, I started to explain this to Master. Sister overheard me from the room nearby and called out, characteristically, 'Say "yes," and make it snappy!' I hastened to do so, of course. Later, she called me to her and explained: 'Anytime Master asks that I do something, don't hesitate; say "yes" quickly. If it is something difficult, I'll figure out later *how* to do it; but always say "yes," and make it snappy.'"

Communing With God Through Meditation

A humble servant of God, known to only a few, playing an all but obscure, behind-the-scenes role on this earthly plane, Sri Gyanamata was nonetheless very well known to God and the great masters. Every morning at four, when most people were asleep, Gyanamata was studying the scriptures, reading about the lives of saints, and communing with God in deep meditation. "How thankful I am," she wrote to her Guru, "that I established the habit of turning to God in the early morning! It is then that your holy and powerful vibrations, the power of God flowing through you, reach me best—though if they are very strong I feel them at other times in the day."

This is not to say that each and every meditation was an effortless dip into the Infinite; Gyanamata's diary attests to titanic struggles, especially during her early attempts; but perseverance was no stranger to this soul. A diary entry reads: "Have tried to meditate, but found it very difficult. This morning I ordered myself to wake at 3 a.m. and commenced meditation at 4 a.m., without much apparent result till 6 o'clock. Then suddenly it came. I often compare my attempts at meditation to pushing a boat down the beach into the water: One pushes and pushes, till suddenly it is afloat and the current catches it. I can stay a long time in this state—floating on the current."

Knowing Gyanamata's love for Jesus Christ, one of the devotees asked her, in her later years, if Christ had ever appeared to her. At first, Gyanamata hesitated to answer, but finally acknowledged that he had. "It was at Mt. Washington," she said. "I used to have interviews in those days; I tried to answer people's questions, to help them with their problems, so that Master would not have to do it all. One time, when I opened my door to receive the people, I saw Christ in the midst of them, walking toward me, along with the others. They all came up and greeted me, but I could not take my gaze from Christ. I dropped to my knees as he reached me, and he placed his hand on the top of my bowed head—I could feel the pressure of his hand on my head. He was like a great light. When he left, I rose. Of course the people looked at me inquiringly, but I could not tell them what had happened.

"That was the first time. The second time it was different. I had passed from sleep into bliss, and became aware that I was in a cave. A light was coming from within the cave, and I went toward it. There was a wooden table with a small candle, and Christ was sitting on the other side of the table, looking at me. The light that I saw was not coming from the candle, but from the eyes of Christ—from his whole body, but especially from his eyes. I found it difficult to look at him at first; then, as I made the effort, I felt a wonderful sensation go through my whole being, as I gazed into those eyes. He answered many questions for me. Then I felt myself becoming aware of my physical body. It felt so heavy. I remembered how beautiful the color of Christ's robe was, and the bright light emanating from Him—how dull the things in my room seemed in comparison!"

"Endure That Which I Shall Send You"

One day she was thinking of Christ and his suffering. "I was looking at his picture," she said, "and the thought of his suffering overpowered me. It was as if I were deciding to make more suffering for myself, though such an act is very far from me. As soon as I thought this, I heard the voice of God—aloud, with my ears as well as my mind. The voice said, 'Endure that which I shall send you. That will be enough.'"

This was a message Gyanamata came to fully understand. Physically, she suffered greatly, and through her suffering came great strength. "There is no spirituality without heroism," she wrote. "If I could too soon be released from the furnace of suffering, and admitted into the Temple of Bliss, my character would lack the necessary admixture of steel, which is the product of endurance, and also the means of climbing the heights that tower above me." Perhaps more than anything else, Gyanamata's superhuman endurance proved her complete mastery over this world and its trials. After her passing, Paramahansaji stated that God had told him: "Twenty years of suffering never took away her love from Me, and that is what I prize in her life."

In her later years, Gyanamata saw her body literally waste away. Among other things, she had developed a bad case of pernicious anemia, a condition that is marked by a progressive decrease in number and increase in size of the red blood cells, and by pallor, weakness, and gastrointestinal and nervous disturbances; a diseased kidney; arthritis; neuritis and crippled hands—the list could go on and on. She commented once that she felt as if she had been "thrown into a fiery furnace that burned but did not consume." None of this, however, could discourage her invincible spirit. Crippled hands could not stop her from writing her letters of gratitude to her Guru—for a while she typed with one finger; then later, when even that became impossible, someone typed her messages for her.

Amazing though it may seem, it is true that throughout all this suffering, Gyanamata never once gave the slightest complaint. "Suffering is no problem for me," she said, simply. "We cause our own suffering, building it up bit by bit [in our minds]." Over the years, she had, out of necessity, trained her mind not to accept the idea of suffering or pity. "All my life I have unceasingly striven for self-control in every circumstance," she once wrote to a sister-disciple, "and

I have never experienced even one time when tears helped me, nor one where self-control and calmness failed to help me." She therefore continually turned her attention away from the physical body, with all its inharmony and disease, and focused it on Spirit—the Unchanging, Blissful Absolute. Writing to her Guru, she said: "I have no wish to go into the physical side of my condition. What I would like to tell you is how many times a day I turn from the insistent demands of the clamorous body to the things you have said and written to me, to passages in *Whispers from Eternity** and other books I keep beside me on the bed." Elsewhere, she said: "In times of greatest suffering, I tell God, 'I am your servant.' Each time I calm my mind, the thought comes, 'All that matters is: *God is.*'"

Only one who has experienced extreme physical pain can fully appreciate the triumph in Gyanamata's aloof, stoic attitude toward suffering. Most find it difficult even to maintain a *pleasant* attitude under such circumstances; how much greater the accomplishment when one can joyously practice the presence of God when the body is racked with pain!

Through Her Suffering, She Helped Others

The reader may wonder why such a saintly individual had to go through the prolonged suffering that Gyanamata did. Paramahansa Yogananda explained: "Her suffering was because of the sins of many others who became saintly through her life. There was not a sin of her own I could find. I want you to know that. Such is the mystery of God."

That Gyanamata was able and willing to serve others through her own suffering shows the spiritual greatness she had attained. "The metaphysical method of physical transfer of disease is known to highly advanced yogis," Paramahansaji

* A book of prayers by Paramahansa Yogananda.

wrote. "A strong man may assist a weak one by helping the latter to carry a heavy load; a spiritual superman is able to minimize the physical and mental troubles of his disciples by assuming a part of their karmic burdens. Just as a rich man relinquishes some money when he pays off a large debt for his prodigal son, who is thus saved from the dire consequences of his folly, so a master willingly sacrifices a portion of his bodily wealth to lighten the misery of disciples."

Toward the end of her life, Gyanamata's physical condition had deteriorated to the point that she had to stay in bed most of the time. Knowing that even a little exercise would be good for her, the Master encouraged her to get some each day. Her eagerness to follow faithfully her Guru's guidance was such that even on her last day she had someone help her out of bed to walk across the room. Thus her final acts spoke of her loyalty and devotion. Of those latter days, the Guru said of her, "She helps just by being here—even if she cannot lift a finger." So highly did he regard her.

Divine Inner Strength

Many who knew Gyanamata likened her physical appearance to a flower—tiny, frail, beautiful, always exuding the fragrance of Spirit; but inwardly she was as strong as steel. When the delicate flower would become crushed, diseased, or wilted, this divine inner strength became all the more apparent. One of the nuns who was nursing her said: "Sister had very strong will power. It seemed to me that her body was just falling apart; and once, when I honestly did not see how she could make her body walk, I asked her, 'Sister, how do you do it?' She looked at me with a twinkle in those marvelous blue eyes and said, 'I just say to God, "You pick 'em up, Lord, and I'll put 'em down."'" Gyanamata said that her strength came from her complete surrender to God and Guru. At night, just before falling asleep, she would turn her gaze inward to the spiritual eye* and quietly say to God: 'Now, Thee alone I seek. Send what is best.'"

"Some of my moments during those last three weeks with Sister," said another nun, "were almost too sacred to divulge. But I realize that only through personal contact with a saint can we know some things about her....I believe that throughout the twenty-two months that I was with her, Sister was unable even to draw a deep breath without pain, yet she never complained about anything.

"Each night, during the last three weeks of her life, just before she fell asleep, she had me read to her the Master's beautiful poem, '*Samadhi*.'† Just to see if she really wanted it read every night, I would sometimes say, 'Well, I guess that's everything'; but she would say, 'Except "*Samadhi*."' I was glad she wanted to hear it, because her face looked so peaceful as I read the words—just as if *she* were in *samadhi* at those times.

Her Final Words: "Too Much Joy!"

"The night before her passing, when I left her, she asked me to lock her door on the inside. But when I was outside her room, I noticed that it was so quiet inside—I wondered if she were still breathing. I started to go back in, but as I was re-entering the room, I heard Sister exclaim, 'Master! Master!'—sharply, as if he had been with her, but vanished when he heard me at the door.

"The next afternoon, she told another nun that she would not be there the following morning, and she was

* The single eye of intuition and omnipresent perception at the Christ center *(ajna chakra)* between the eyebrows. The spiritual eye is the entryway into the ultimate states of divine consciousness.

† Published in chapter fourteen of *Autobiography of a Yogi,* wherein Paramahansaji conveys a glimpse of the bliss of *samadhi,* the state in which human consciousness becomes one with Cosmic Consciousness.

not. I was present at the time of her passing. She was resting, breathing very short breaths. She finally succeeded in drawing a few very long breaths, and then her breathing stopped, without a struggle. It was finished. Someone said, 'It was like going to sleep,' but I said, 'No, it was like waking up.' Master, who was away at the time of her passing, was with us in a short time."

Another of the Self-Realization Fellowship nuns was present when Gyanamata spoke her last words. "They came a short while before her passing," she said. "Sister's face was radiant. A big smile illumined her face as she exclaimed, 'What joy! What joy! Too much, too much joy!' Within an hour or so she was gone."

She Left the Body in the Highest State of Samadhi

It was on November 17, 1951, that the "Mother of Wisdom" quietly passed on—at the age of eighty-two. A few days before, her Guru had given a dinner in Encinitas for a number of devotees. Later he explained: "The disciples didn't know why I held that dinner. It was in honor of Sister. I knew she was going. It is a custom in India, when great souls leave this earth, to celebrate with a banquet their release in God."

The story of her passing is perhaps best recounted by Sri Daya Mata, who was with Paramahansaji at the time: "I remember well that last day. One of the nuns came to Master and said, 'Sister's condition is very bad.' So Master went in immediately to see her. She was sitting in her chair at that time. Master said something to her, and stayed with her for some time, blessing her. Most of the time they said nothing to each other—we knew that he was communing with her soul.

"Then he said to a few of us, 'Now come, let us go for a drive.' Guruji had told us that Divine Mother would never let him be in the room when one of the devotees passed away; and thus it happened that he never was physically present when any disciple left the body. We drove around Encinitas and the nearby community for about an hour or so. Not one of us spoke; our minds were with Sister. Master sat absolutely motionless; he was meditating deeply. On the way back to the Hermitage, we stopped at the SRF Cafe* to greet the devotees serving there. After a short time, Master told us to hurry, and said to the driver, 'Now let us go back.'

"When we entered the Hermitage, one of the nuns came up to him and said, 'Gyanamata has just left her body.' Master was very quiet and withdrawn. Finally he whispered, 'Yes,' and went reverently into her room. We all remained at a respectful distance outside the door. He spent some time with her there, in silence, blessing her. We heard him whisper, 'Sister, you went before me.' After a while he motioned for us to come into the room. Quietly we entered and approached Sister's body. With solemnity in his voice, he asked us to feel the temperature of her feet. They were very cold. Then he said, 'Now I want you to feel the top of her head.' This was remarkable—it was very hot, as if on fire.

"Master explained to us: 'This shows that she has left the body in the highest state of *samadhi*. Her soul departed through the highest spinal center, the thousand-petaled lotus† in the brain. Now she has achieved that final state of

* The cafe, located at the front of the Encinitas Ashram Center on Highway 101, served a variety of vegetarian dishes—many of them original recipes of Paramahansa Yogananda's. It was closed in 1966, when its facilities and personnel were needed for other services to the growing membership of Self-Realization Fellowship.

† Yoga treatises explain that there are seven occult centers of life and consciousness in man's spine and brain, through which the soul has descended into the body and through which it must reascend by a process of meditation. By seven successive steps, the soul finally escapes through

mukti [liberation]; she is free. She has no need to return to this world. But we will meet again.'

"After that, Master said to us, 'You must know that her passing symbolizes that I will be leaving this world shortly.' Less than four months later he left his body."

After Gyanamata's passing, Paramahansaji was privately asked how her spiritual attainment compared with that of the well-known Christian saints. The Master confided that she ranked with the greatest of them. At her funeral service, he elaborated: "Sister's life has been like that of St. Francis, who suffered even while helping others. So she stands as a great inspiration. In all those years she suffered, she showed that her love for God was greater; and I never saw one mark of suffering in her eyes. That is why she is a great saint—a great soul—and that is why she is with God."

Spiritual Footprints for All to Follow

Sri Gyanamata has now gone to her beloved God, but she has left "spiritual footprints" for all to follow. In her letters she has left a rich legacy of invaluable counsel. And not only do these letters provide priceless practical and spiritual wisdom, they also offer fascinating glimpses into the character and interior life of an illumined saint of modern America, whose soul embraced the universality of Spirit.

But all description must ultimately fall far short of the heights attained by a God-knowing saint. Only by striving to follow her spiritual footprints to God alone can we begin to appreciate the depth of perception, of divine love and joy, that was the essence of her life and the source of the deep wisdom that was incarnate in Gyanamata.

---

the *sahasrara* or "Thousand-Petaled Lotus" in the uppermost part of the cerebrum into Cosmic Consciousness.

CHAPTER 2

"The Dewdrop Has Slipped Into the Shining Sea"

*Tribute to Sri Gyanamata at Memorial Service**

BY PARAMAHANSA YOGANANDA

Encinitas Ashram Center, November 19, 1951

"Dear Lord, You have taken our Sister Gyanamata, greatest among women disciples of Self-Realization, and freed her in Thee. I send all my love and blessings to her soul, which has merged in Thine infinite Being. But I cannot help missing her spirit incarnate in the dear form of Sister, which was such a great inspiration to us all.

"Gyanamata, Queen of Wisdom, we are contented that thou hast thy freedom in God. But with all our hearts' love and devotion we weep for our loss, that we had to part with thee. We shall always miss having thee here amongst us, imparting inspiration that was felt by everyone. And even though thy spirit now rests with God in eternal freedom, thou hast left here a spiritual vibration that all who are in tune will feel. With all the sweetness of our remembrance of thee, we send our love and wishes for thy rejoicing in freedom in God."

Let us all chant, "*Aum. Aum. Aum.* Amen."

To the mighty Lord and Spirit, in whom I feel the spirit of Sister, I give my love.

* First published in condensed form in *Self-Realization* magazine, shortly after Gyanamata's passing. Here we have drawn on the full transcript of the service, except for omission of a brief ceremony. *(Publisher's Note)*

I ask you to close your eyes and hear my words, what I have to say from my soul. I speak from my love, and ask forbearance for all my personal utterances, which are as from one who loves the Spirit as both Heavenly Father and Divine Mother.

This is a very difficult occasion for me. I cannot say that I am happy, because I terribly miss Sister, and will continue to miss her. Why Spirit makes the delusion of parting with loved ones in death so painful is one of the things about which I often fight with the Divine Father, the Divine Mother.

Someone said to me last night, when there were tears in my eyes, that I should be happy that Sister is free in the joy of Spirit. I said, "I know all that, how happy Sister is, how this glorious chapter of her life is closed, how the pain is gone from her body, and that she is released from the terrific test of my Father in which she helped others through the suffering of her own body. My spirit is with hers in God. But these are tears of love, that on this side I shall miss her."

I said to God, "Lord, You have given me too much love to give. I feel so much for people. It is You who make me love them so."

That bright and humble light that was Sister was extinguished before me, and has commingled with the Great Light. That is my contentment, and my sadness. And I am glad to be sad, glad that she was with us to inspire so much love from our hearts; because there are few rare souls such as she sent on earth to help others find their way to God.

So this is not a funeral service for Sister, it is an expression of my love for her who lived so perfectly. The same perfection Master [Swami Sri Yukteswar] expected of me, she has lived that.

It was in 1925 that I met Sister as Mrs. Bissett in Seattle.

She invited me to a dinner at her home. Immediately I knew her soul from lives past. While we were at the table, I noticed a little novelty saltshaker, rounded on the bottom and weighted with lead so that it couldn't be made to lie down. I tried to do it—twenty times—and then I heard the voice of God: "For the benefit of Sister, lay it down. Speak and it shall be so." I slapped the saltshaker down, and by the grace of God it lay there. I remember well that occasion, for I knew then that God would draw her to this path. I left Seattle, but wherever I was lecturing, all over the country, Sister's letters were always there for me.

In 1932 her husband, who was a university professor, brought her to Mt. Washington, calling her "Sister." I was very much astonished, and asked, "Why did you bring her?" He said, "Would you keep her now? Sister wants very much to live here at Mt. Washington." I said, "What about you?" He replied, "I am going to leave this body in three months." "Have you any disease, any trouble?" "Not at all," he said, "but you will see me go." He was a great man of God. Few people knew that. He went away, and his words were fulfilled. There was no sign of disease in him at that time, but in three months he was dead.

Some time after, I went one day to see Sister in her room at Mt. Washington. I could hear her heart pumping just like a bellows, even from the door. I was very frightened for her, and I called on God.

But she was calm. Though she was lying down, gasping for breath, she said, "Don't pray for me. Don't trouble yourself. Just bless me." Tears rolled down my cheeks. "Sister," I said, "Heaven is with you, and I beg your life from God." She immediately became well, and was breathing normally. And I knew that having begged her life from God, she could not go from this earth without my prayer to God to release her. His troth with me was: "She will not go until you say so." All of you students who know me, know that I am speaking truth.

I found myself in a peculiar position. I took delight in the fact that Sister could not die without my release, and yet I was extremely grieved that I had asked the Father to spare a life that I later found was to be constantly tested by physical suffering. I would not have asked the Father to spare her life had I known then that she was to be tested so strongly. I know what she endured, for I always have suffered with the suffering of those who are close to me; and I have felt that suffering was a sort of compulsion toward being good. Sister didn't need suffering for that reason. Her suffering was because of the sins of many others who became saintly through her life. There was not a sin of her own I could find. I want you to know that. Such is the mystery of God.

Even though I knew Sister suffered not for her own, but only for the sins of others, still I often fought with the Heavenly Father as to why He, in His almightiness and painaboveness, was not helping to relieve her suffering.

I have had continual controversy with my Heavenly Father as to why pain is a test to bring back to Him human beings who are made in His image. I tell the Father that in pain there is a compulsion; persuasion and love are better ways to get human beings back to heaven. Even though I know the answer, I have always fought with God on these points, for He understands me as a father understands his son.

I remember how hard Sister worked, and never complained. She would go up and down the stairs of the three stories of Mt. Washington till her body would drop out of sheer inability to carry on its work. She helped me to help others by always being a peacemaker, by trying to instill in them the right attitude and behavior. Once some people said to her, "Why do you enslave your will in service to God?"

She replied, "It is rather too late to change now. And I think I have made a very good choice. My will is guided by wisdom, not by whims."

Everybody looked to her as an example. Whoever was sincere and came near her was changed. When Madame Ganna Walska* met her, she said, "She is a great saint." Of all the women disciples, she has been one of the greatest. Never did I see in that face, in those eyes, anger, or anguish, or pain—only the sweetness of God. I said to her once, "Sister, your seat is reserved in heaven when you go," and it is so.

One boy only, during all my twenty years of knowing Sister, criticized her that she had talked sharply. When I asked her about it she said simply, "No," and such sweetness was in her eyes. Of course, he was the one who was wrong. Some come to the ashram, you know, and then try to reform everybody except themselves. And so it was, after all, that this boy went away; and I know he has not found God yet. He is still roaming, and will roam throughout this life.

But I had never seen, never heard Sister criticize anybody; never heard a cross word from her lips. All the disciples whose good fortune it was to know her found a new inspiration, and they all said, "She is indeed a saint."

I saw Sister very little, but spiritually I was always with her. Whenever any special thought was in my mind, I would immediately receive a little letter of response from her, so much was she in tune. All those letters are coming out in *Self-Realization* magazine. How many people have told me, "There is life and spirit in those letters!"

In 1935, when I was going to India, Sister asked me to release her. I said, "No, Sister. When I return, I shall laugh again with you." I came back, and we did laugh together

* A well-known opera singer of the time.

again. Many times since, her life seemed to be going, but it didn't go.

Three years ago her condition was very serious. Right before that, Sister had told me (Mrs. Elizabeth Maley was a witness in the room when it happened) that she heard a terrible voice saying, "Yogananda's prayers won't work. I am taking you now." When Sister told me that, I was frightened. It was true that her life was in danger. After a few days, I was praying in my room [in the Encinitas Hermitage], and the Lord told me to come out. I met her doctor, and I said, "You haven't diagnosed exactly what is happening to Sister. It is very critical; but the remedy is very simple. Send her to Scripps-Howard."* So she was sent to the hospital. They found that she had only enough nutrients in her body for one more day. Another twenty-four hours and she would have been dead. She had been suffering from indigestion and canker sores in her mouth, and without telling anyone had been taking almost no food for weeks. All they did at the hospital was give her food injections. But if I had not met the doctor and sent her there, she would have been gone.

I remembered the covenant with God. With Sister's life—a little spark in that great ocean of His light—He still kept the troth, that never would He take her away without my consent. She was saved, and came back from the hospital well.

So through the years God has kept that promise with me. I am not taking any credit; I am telling you exactly as it happened. How great the Spirit is, that His promise is ever true to the devotee! The God that you say is invisible has been visible to me, and has been true in every way. I tell you these things that you may desire to get to Him faster. As much as you can, work with the thought of Him; work only for Him, don't work for yourself. Half of meditation is

* Now Scripps Memorial Hospital at La Jolla, California.

thinking of God in silence, and the other half is doing work for God. Working for Him is karma that is not binding. And no matter if the body falls apart, have communion with God before you sleep. That is the secret. Don't succumb to sleep until you commune with Him.

This is God's world. He takes you; He keeps you. When the doctor says, "Well, I'll heal you," if God makes up His mind to take you, you will go. So live your life for Him.

Last Wednesday, one of the disciples in Encinitas called Mt. Washington and told us, "Sister is suffering awfully." I was in another room, but I began to feel it right away. My heart throbbed and I became very restless. I knew it was Sister. So I took the call; and when they told me how Sister had bedsores, what they described just went through me. I began to cry; I began to pray. And that night, after midnight, I wrote this note:

Mother Divine,
Break the troth of mine
With Thee 'bout good Sister.
Release if You will, Mother dear!
Her test is greater
Than she can bear.
From this nightmare of suffering
Take her to the wakefulness
Of ever new Bliss.

That was when I gave up the covenant that I had with God. Then I couldn't sleep. I sat up and prayed, "Mother, will You listen to me?" And a great light appeared, and I saw Sister in the arms of the Divine Mother. I cried out, "Sister, do not go. Wait!" And even that desire was fulfilled.

When I reached Encinitas the following evening, she was fully conscious. She asked me for *nirbikalpa samadhi;* but I said, "You don't need that. I saw you in God. When you reach the palace, why do you want to go in the garden any more? Divine Mother has taken care of you." And she was contented.

The next day, although I wanted to with my whole soul, God wouldn't let me see her, because He knew I would again pray that she stay here. She was all right, and one of the disciples was carrying word back and forth—keeping me informed of her condition and taking to her my blessings.

The following day, I wanted to go out of the Hermitage; I *had* to go, because death doesn't often happen when I am there. And I knew there would be a big battle between my Father and me. I went to Sister's room; the others didn't know that it was my last visit. I commended her to God and I asked her, "If you have any desire, I will fulfill it right now. You tell me." Three times she said, "No." "Is it true?" "Yes, Sir," she replied, very firmly.

She was just falling asleep, and I went away. Several went with me in the car. I said, "Just drive around, not too far"; and I even asked to have the radio on. But my soul was only one place—with Sister. On our way back, I said, "Stop at our SRF Cafe." I knew it was still too soon to go to the Hermitage. But when it was time to go, those with me were delaying, eating ice cream. "Hurry," I said, "don't delay me now." When I came to the Hermitage, they told me, "She is gone." I shook my head that I already knew. And then I felt a tremendous vibration in this place, and I knew that she was not gone; that everyone who comes here will feel her sweetness ineffable. That sweetness in her eyes I never saw dimmed.

Indeed, a great saint has gone away from this Hermitage. But she has left spiritual footprints here forever, for all souls that are in despair, that they might trace her footsteps and go from the desolate shore of this earth to my Father's home. Those spiritual footprints will always be here. We shall miss her, but whoever is in tune will feel that presence which she has left. God consoled me that way, and I felt better afterward. Otherwise, I could not have been here with you today.

Though I cannot say I rejoice, because of the terrible loss, yet I am contented, because she is free from going through that terrible karma of others. Sister's life has been like that of St. Francis, who suffered even while helping others. So she stands as a great inspiration. In all those years she suffered, she showed that her love for God was greater; and I never saw one mark of that suffering in her eyes. That is why she is a great saint—a great soul—and that is why she is with God.

You who go through just a little suffering, much less than she has gone through these twenty years, should be glad to use the health of your bodies to seek God. Once you are near Him, you will never lose Him again. This is the miracle of God.

How great is His love, just think! He doesn't talk, lest you start an argument with Him. That is why that great Being remains silent; but He can be made to talk if your love is deep enough. Do your Kriya Yoga deeply and talk to Him as I am talking to you. Love Him more. He is invisible, but you have to make Him talk. And if your meditation becomes "chronic" enough, and your love becomes "chronic" enough, He will be with you always.

It is His reality that gives all the unreal changing things their reality. Remember, you did not create yourself, you did not create this earth, you didn't create anything, not even a grain of wheat that sustains you. God created those things. So why do you say that you are the doer? Remember, in the dream you create a villain and you create a hero. They all get their egoity through your own consciousness. So it is egoity that keeps us separate from God. That's our curse—that we think we are the doer of everything: "I own this, I own that; this is all mine, my home, my money, my strength." No, it is *His.* Know that it is His. And as soon as you know that, you are free from the dream. He can't keep your image deluded any more. It remains in name only.

Sister has not to wait for years after her death to be canonized. She is already a saint, and a great saint.

She heard that I had scolded the disciples, saying, "Why didn't you help her to get some exercise so that she wouldn't get the bedsores?" So in spite of her pain and weakness, she got out of bed, with the devotees helping her, and sat on the chair in her room and tried to exercise. Followed my words to the last. Such an example! She passed her final hours on that chair of discipline,* following to the end the vow she had taken as a Sister.

How many more could have been saved if, like Sister, they had only listened. I could have saved them. I work only to do God's will in helping you all. Those who came, and then fell asleep in ignorance, they could have had today what she has. I seldom talk about the advancement of the disciples around me; God has shown me those who are in Him. But Sister and Saint Lynn I have always put before you as examples. Saint Lynn, who has never made himself known, has done so much for the cause and never asked credit. A wonderful businessman he is, and at the same time a great yogi and saint. He never loses his balance with business or with God.

I have seen yogis in the Himalayas who live in caves and profess great renunciation; but all the time thinking of how to get food, and fighting over firewood. That is why for a long time I didn't give you in the ashram robes to wear. I

* After Paramahansaji saw Gyanamata for the last time, and then left the Hermitage *(see page 35),* Sister was carried by the nuns back to her bed.

said, "Make your heart a hermitage, and your robe the love of God." That is what makes a saint.

Follow the example of Saint Lynn and Sister, and go all the way. That is the door to heaven. The door to the world leads to death. If you are faithful to Self-Realization, if you follow to the end, you will meet God.

When Sister's time came, she went through *Gyana Yoga,* or union with God through wisdom. That was her way. When I looked at her for the last time, her eyes were distant, but still they were gleaming in God. That part was beautiful; but saying goodbye to the form—that part was not nice.

But when I looked at her body in the casket, I felt Sister's soul commingled with the omnipresent ether, and I heard the voice of the Father speaking to me from within: "Twenty years of suffering never took away her love from Me, and that is what I prize in her life." I could not say anything more; I realized that the Heavenly Father has a right to test our love for Him with pain, for even twenty years or more, in order that we may claim in exchange our lost eternal, ever new happiness as His image.

Then again I choked with the thrill of God's presence, and I said to myself: "To regain the eternity of ever new joy through twenty years of being unruffled by pain is the greater achievement, through the grace of the Father." I also realized in her life a new phase, as she had worked out her own karma completely in her last life and in this life, and she was drawn by the grace of the Heavenly Father to eternal freedom in this life without the higher ecstasy. This does not mean that Gyanamata did not have the highest ecstasy (*nirbikalpa samadhi*). She had it in her past life. But—even as it says on the little placard in her room: "God Alone"—in this life God's grace alone lifted her pain-unruffled, successful soul to omnipresent liberation.

When Bhagavan Krishna told Draupadi to practice yoga for salvation, she replied, "Krishna, you have asked of me something impossible, for I can't take my mind away from you to practice yoga." Thus, while Sister did practice yoga in this life, her yoga-accomplished soul went beyond yoga, and became so engrossed with God that I had to remind her she was already with Him, that I saw her in God, when she questioned about *nirbikalpa samadhi.* All devotees should remember that only constant practice of yoga brings the grace of God in the highest way, for Krishna told Arjuna: "O Arjuna, greater than the path of wisdom, or action, or any other, is the path of yoga. Therefore, be thou a yogi, Arjuna!"* Sister, being already an accomplished yogi, was liberated by the grace of God alone.

I am very thankful that the Mighty Being listened to the little utterances of my love and spared Sister's life to be with us so many years. That the Master of the Universe would listen to such an insignificant being as I am! I am only a wave on the ocean of His Being. That was a great test that I put God to. How much love the Infinite Lord has that He would abide by what He promised me. He doesn't have to listen to or account to me or anybody; but He can be won by love. Just see, that night after I wrote to God to let Sister go, I was sorry, for I wanted to see her again. So even her release was delayed for me, until I could come to her. That is the miracle of God's love.

That love you must seek. That love you must make the effort for, until you find it as I have. I am living only for Him. I am interested only in His work. To the last breath I shall work for Him, I shall worry about His work; but not for myself, not for me at all. There is nothing else in this world for me, nothing of use, not even this body, I see. I can tell you

* Paraphrase of Bhagavad Gita VI:46.

now that I was to go before Sister. I have long been living on borrowed time. Last year there was a beautiful opportunity to leave the body. For three days I was away from this world, in such joy! But it didn't happen, because I wanted to stay longer to see what would happen after I was gone. That is why I am seeing all these things, even as God told me they would be. So Sister beat me to it. I am sorry that I asked God to let her go. That is the human element in me. But then she would be here still in suffering; so I know I have done right. I leave it to God.

Now I wipe my tears, and though I shall always miss her on earth for what she meant to others and to me, still I shall be contented to feel her presence with the Heavenly Father-Mother omnipresent in Cosmic Wisdom, *Gyana*. Gyanamata, Mother of Wisdom, has commingled her being with the Cosmic Mother of Wisdom.

Someone asked me if I had seen Sister since she left her body. She has come to me many times, but not in form. She had enough of confinement in a body. Now she wears only the robe of infinitude.

In every flower, every leaf, every gust of wind, in the Hermitage where she lived, in every particle of earth, and the twinkling stars and milky ways, wherever Cosmic Wisdom is, I shall feel the spirit of Sister.

During Gyanamata's funeral service, Paramahansaji asked Rajarsi Janakananda to say a few words; and then to place on her body a red and a white rose, symbolizing divine love and goodwill. The following are Rajarsi's words on that occasion:

Sister came to Guru with a soul crying in the wilderness of spiritual desolation. In him she found the Light, and a spark ignited her soul. She received him that she herself might be lifted into the illumination of God.

Sister was truly selfless. She wanted nothing for herself; would do nothing for self; never thought of self, or of the body. She was always engrossed in the thought of God. Her life was an example to all.

When I first came to Mt. Washington in 1933, I found her humble, quiet, always busy for God and Guru. That has been her entire life. She had received from Master what she sought, a spark of the spirit of God, and she was satisfied. She wanted nothing more.

In later years, whenever I met or meditated with Sister, the light of Spirit completely enveloped us. That light was always around Sister. As Master has told you, she is now in the bliss of God. She has what she wanted, what she sought, what she lived her life to attain—Bliss, union with God.

Gyanamata

By Paramahansa Yogananda

On the lap of Light and roses
Our Sister—queen of wisdom—reposes,
Transcending our tears,
Beyond pain and fears.

In meekness immeasurable,
In sweetness illimitable,
She captured the mist fragrant
Of God-love vibrant.

She is joy eternal, forever free from all tears
After four score and two years.
Yet I grieve for our loss, heart-piercing:
For she was a beacon of wisdom's light transmuting,
Shining a bright path for the lost and ignorance-dazed—
Now extinguished to human gaze.

In nineteen thirty-two, she was to leave this mortal shore;
I begged her life from Mother Divine and did implore
Her promise that Sister Gyanamata mine
Would never go
Until I said so.

'Twas fate's irony
That from suffering flesh to set her free,
The same Mother Divine I had to beg again:
"Release her fragile bubble of life into the Mighty Main."

With fading breath did she supplicate—
"What about Nirbikalpa Samadhi state?"
And I replied,
As she died,
"You are with Mother Divine, Sister mine;
I am holding you there.
The path is not needed—you are already there."

CHAPTER 3

"I Shall Never Be the Same Again"

The First and Last Handwritten Letters From Gyanamata to Paramahansa Yogananda

Written one week after their first meeting in Seattle:

> In my early childhood I was
> not happy. The world seemed
> a place in which no one could desire
> to dwell. I turned, with my earliest
> consciousness, to religion for comfort
> and enlightenment, but fear grew
> instead of abating.
> Later, my own spirit taught me
> intuitively, and I was freed from
> some of the worst dogmas of our church,
> such as the belief in hell. I saw
> plainly that "God", even if He were
> no greater than the finite mind could
> conceive, would not do what an or-

In my early childhood I was not happy. The world seemed a place in which no one could desire to dwell. I turned, with my earliest consciousness, to religion for comfort and enlightenment, but fear grew instead of abating.

Later, my own spirit taught me intuitively, and I was freed from some of the worst dogmas of our church, such as the belief in hell. I saw plainly that "God," even if He were no greater than the finite mind could conceive, would not do what an ordinarily

-2-

-dinarily tender-hearted mortal would
never be guilty of. I also saw that
suffering was a necessary part of
my earthly discipline, and that while
I might have to say with Jesus, "Father,
save me from this hour," it was also
possible for me to add, as He did, "yet
for this cause came I unto this hour," at
which thought strength flowed into me.
About the year 1909, a friend lent
me a book containing my first definite
teaching of Hindu truth. Returning the
book I said, "I shall never be the
same again," and this was absolutely

tender-hearted mortal would never be guilty of. I also saw that suffering was a necessary part of my earthly discipline, and that while I might have to say with Jesus, "Father, save me from this hour," it was also possible for me to add, as He did, "yet for this cause came I unto this hour," at which thought strength flowed into me.

About the year 1909, a friend lent me a book containing my first definite teaching of Hindu truth. Returning the book I said, "I shall never be the same again," and this was absolutely

-3-

true. Striving did not cease, however,
and finally, I reached a point where I
clearly perceived that the next, – the
vitally necessary step for me, – was
expressed in the words of Jacob Boehme,
"Stand still from the thinking and
willing of <u>self</u>, and the eternal hearing,
seeing, and speaking will be revealed
in thee; and as God heareth and seeth
through thee. Thine own hearing, willing,
and seeing hindereth thee, that thou dost
not see nor hear God." I was unable
to take this step beyond self, but with
tears and longing, continued to "make it

true. Striving did not cease, however, and finally I reached a point where I clearly perceived that the next, the vitally necessary step for me, was expressed in the words of Jacob Boehme, "Stand still from the thinking and willing of *self,* and the eternal hearing, seeing, and speaking will be revealed in thee; and as God heareth and seeth through thee. Thine own hearing, willing, and seeing hindereth thee, that thou dost not see nor hear God." I was unable to take this step beyond self, but with tears and longing, continued to "make it

Gyanamata as a young woman

Paramahansa Yogananda *(center)* with some of the Self-Realization students who attended his class in Seattle, October 17, 1924. Rex Bissett, Gyanamata's son, is seated at far right in first row.

-4-

hot" for God. At last, one came to me through whose words, but still more through his vibrations, what I had so longed for was brought about. I heard the Voice saying, "Hello! play-mate, I am here!" And because it was so purely subjective, I was able to recognize it as coming from my own Self.

I now wish to approach that Self, by a systematic effort, by the method taught by you.

Early this morning I was moved to write this, because if you honor and

hot" for God. At last, one came to me through whose words, but still more through his vibrations, what I had so longed for was brought about. I heard the Voice saying, "Hello! playmate, *I am here!*" And because it was so purely subjective, I was able to recognize it as coming from my own Self.

I now wish to approach that Self, by a systematic effort, by the method taught by you.

Early this morning I was moved to write this, because if you

-5-

bless my home by your presence, there may be no opportunity to say it, and I wish to lay before you, Reverend Swami, the tribute of the testimony of a western disciple to the power of the truth taught by the Sages of the East.

I sent my son to you, and in my heart I take the dust from your feet for what you have done and are doing for him.

honor and bless my home by your presence, there may be no opportunity to say it, and I wish to lay before you, Reverend Swami, the tribute of the testimony of a Western disciple to the power of the truth taught by the Sages of the East.

I sent my son to you, and in my heart I take the dust from your feet for what you have done and are doing for him.

Praising the Power, which, working in Silence and Darkness, brought you to our city and home, I bow to you upon your departure.

Had I money to give, it should be given to your work; as it is, all I can offer is the earnest desire of my heart. May all obstacles be cleared from your path, and may you establish your school upon a sure foundation, to be a light to lighten the darkness, a City set upon a hill, which can not be hid.

Come to us again, that we may be

Praising the Power, which, working in Silence and Darkness, brought you to our city and home, I bow to you upon your departure.

Had I money to give, it should be given to your work; as it is, all I can offer is the earnest desire of my heart. May all obstacles be cleared from your path, and may you establish your school upon a sure foundation, to be a light to lighten the darkness, a City set upon a hill, which cannot be hid.

Come to us again, that we may be strengthened by personal

strengthened by personal contact and teaching.–

I am your disciple, and the disciple of all the Guru's of India, who, working in Silence, from across the world or beyond the grave, have spoken Truth to the listening ear of my soul.–

Asking your continual blessing and prayers, to the end that the one personal desire of my heart,—God-consciousness,– be granted to the full, I am, Reverend and dear Swamiji,–

Edith D. Bissett.–

Sunday.– July 19th 1925.–

contact and teaching.

I am your disciple, and the disciple of all the Gurus of India, who, working in Silence, from across the world or beyond the grave, have spoken Truth to the listening ear of my soul.

Asking your continual blessing and prayers, to the end that the one personal desire of my heart—God-consciousness—be granted to the full, I am, Reverend and dear Swamiji,

Edith D. Bissett

Sunday, July 19th, 1925

Quite possibly the last handwritten letter from Sister to Paramahansaji:

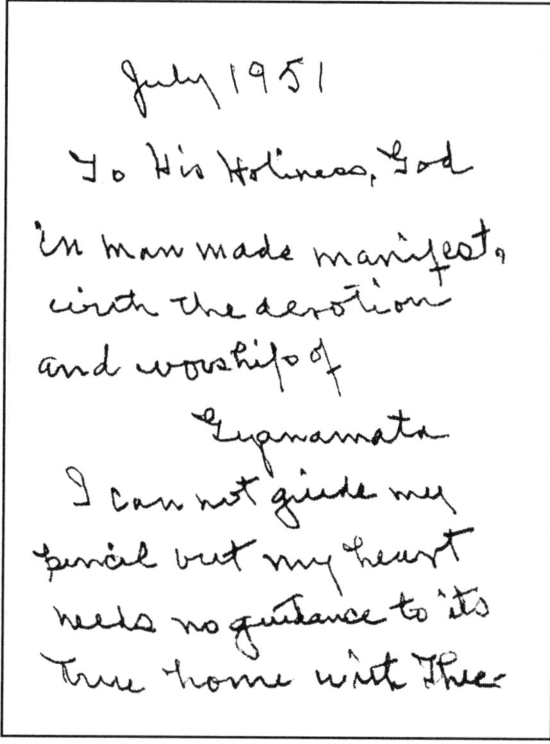

July 1951

To His Holiness, God
in man made manifest,
with the devotion
and worship of

Gyanamata

I can not guide my
pencil but my heart
needs no guidance to its
True home with Thee

July 1951

To His Holiness, God in man made manifest, with the devotion and worship of

Gyanamata

I cannot guide my pencil but my heart needs no guidance to its true home with thee.

PART II

The Letters of Sri Gyanamata

CHAPTER 4

Right Attitude

Paramahansa Yogananda taught that pure, soul-directed thoughts and actions lead to lasting happiness. His teachings show how to cultivate the mental attitude by which one can maintain an inner happiness and peace throughout all the ups and downs of life. This concept of "right attitude"—that there *is* a spiritually correct and proper attitude of mind for every circumstance—Gyanamata understood perfectly. She realized that right attitude is the very foundation of the spiritual path—indeed, of life itself—and so constantly nurtured this quality in her own life.

Gyanamata could not give others the gift of right attitude, but through her understanding advice and sincere concern, she could and did help them to develop that quality within themselves, and thus attain emotional and spiritual maturity.

October 7, 1940

Dear ________,

If I were to give you the gift that I would like best of all to offer you, it would be the right attitude toward God and Guru; toward life; toward your work; toward the others of your group.

But the best gifts cannot be purchased and given. The gifts and graces of the soul must be acquired by patient, daily practice. All will surely be yours in time, for if you do not obtain them in the position to which God has called you, where, in all the world, are they to be found?

The Buddha said: "The profit of the holy life, O monks, lies not in gains and favors and honor, nor in the fulfillment of morals, nor in the fulfillment of concentration, nor in knowledge and vision; but just this, O monks: the sure, unshakable deliverance of the mind. That is the aim of this holy life. That is its heart. That is its goal."

My love, dear, upon your birthday and all the days,
Gyanamata

* * * * *

In the following two letters, written in Encinitas, Gyanamata offers personal counsel to Sri Daya Mata (known at that time by her family name, Faye Wright). The letter dated February 15, 1948, refers to Daya Mata's being put in charge of the Self-Realization Headquarters in Los Angeles. Sister knew that Daya Mata was humbly reluctant to be elevated to the position of leadership that Paramahansa Yogananda had asked her to assume. Gyanamata helped her to gain the right attitude toward these new responsibilities.

July 10, 1946

Dear Faye,

Thinking over the temporary change in the routine of your life—and I think of it continually—I want to write down the points that deeply impress me. Not that you do not know them as well as I do, but I want to add the weight of my experience to yours.

1. *You have nothing that is your own, and you must not cling to phenomena.* This was said to me by my first teacher at a time of great stress and suffering. The effect was as if a bright light had been turned on in my brain. If I had followed this light unfalteringly, I would have escaped many painful experiences.

2. You needed what has happened;* without it, and unless you live it through, you will never know yourself. By your reaction to it you can measure what is personal and what spiritual in your relationship to the Guru. That relationship only exists for what is purely spiritual—for the life and growth of your soul. What is painful now will end in joy, for "ever the greater pain ushers in the greater joy."

3. I consider it of the highest importance that you remind him from time to time of your unchanging reverence, gratitude, devotion, and love. And *in writing,* because written words often produce a more lasting effect than the spoken. Besides, they are permanent; they do not vanish into the air.

4. Since I came to live here I have told you frankly—*too* frankly—the things that took me by surprise and caused me pain. But never have I told you all of the wonderful things that have happened to me—some like big blazing diamonds, some like tiny jewels, set in the pure gold of my relationship to His Holiness. As with me, so with you.

With love in God and Guruji,
your Sister

* * * * *

February 15, 1948

Dear Faye,

I begin this letter doubtfully for several reasons. The body feels less well than usual; but also, I think you know my viewpoint on all points of the devotee's path. So what chance is there of my finding in my little "storeroom" some

* Gyanamata is referring here to the fact that Daya Mata, in her new capacity at the Mother Center in Los Angeles, would now be unable to spend as much time in the physical presence of Paramahansaji, such as when he was in residence at Encinitas.

new piece of wisdom that will inspire you in this difficult task that God has placed upon your shoulders? Why, there is an important point right away—that it is God who has done it. To seek your own will would be to step outside His will. "It is the Divine Will"—that is always a supremely calming thought to me in disturbed moments.

Then follows naturally the question, "What *is* your own will?" I use my oft-repeated illustration. If the Master were to come to you and say, "You are unfitted for this work; it is too much for you; you may return to your home to live with your mother and grandmother"—what would your reaction be? "No!" You want to make good. Then make good! It can only be done by going straight ahead. When you took the vow before the Master in your seventeenth year, you said "yes" to all the moments that followed as a consequence. I have watched the work going on in you, the work of building into your character endurance and courage, without which there is no real spirituality.

I miss you very much, so you see it hits me too. I like people and things to stay put, so to speak, but it is not to be. It cannot be if the work is to be carried forth into all parts of the world.

> Change and decay in all around I see;
> O Thou who changest not, abide with me.*

We will never be Sister and Faye in any other life. So let us do as much as we can for the world while we are here. This, the Master wrote of himself and Mr. Lynn when he was in India. Let us pray that among all the changes and chances of this mortal life our hearts may surely be fixed where true joys are to be found.

Your ever loving Sister

* From the nineteenth-century hymn "Abide With Me."

Dear ________,

An English saint called Mother Julian* wrote the following words: "The soul that willeth to be at rest, when another man's sin cometh to mind, let him flee from it; for the beholding of other men's sins maketh as it were a thick mist before the eyes of the soul, unless we behold them with compassion and holy desire to God; for without this it harmeth and tempesteth and hindereth the soul that beholdeth."

Whenever you are involved in an unpleasant situation with another person, as you are at present, I believe the best method of handling the matter is to decide: "What ought *I* to do, how ought *I* to act?" Then concentrate wholeheartedly on living up to your decision, putting the other person and her actions entirely out of your mind. The first effect of this is that one becomes calm, calm and happy—and you know how important this is in dealing with difficult situations. Whenever I have remembered and lived up to this rule, I have met with surprising success. Whenever I have not followed it but have expected to straighten things out by trying to effect a change in the other person, nothing but friction has resulted, and a lower vibration of my own consciousness. I maintain that holding my own consciousness on a high plane is of the first importance; if I take care of that, everything else will eventually come into line.

I deeply wish that you would be guided by this rule, not only in this particular situation, but in *all* the questions that the years will present before you to be decided and acted upon.

Gyanamata

* Mother Juliana of Norwich, a fourteenth-century English mystic and Benedictine recluse, best known for her spiritual classic, *Revelations of Divine Love.*

December 5, 1940

Dear ________,

This morning I felt the wish to answer immediately the letter I just received from you. It won't be an answer to the detailed statements of your letter, but an answer to the general feeling that arises in me from what you tell me of your life; and it will be an answer to all the letters you have written me in the last four years.

Did you ever stop to divide the things that our friends can do for us from those they cannot do? If we are suffering physically, mentally, and spiritually, they can give us unchanging love, sympathy, pity. They can send for the doctor and the nurse. They can get out the car and take us to the hospital and bring us home again. They can visit us, bring us flowers, buy us gifts thrilling in beauty and usefulness; they can stand by through everything, watching us with the eyes of love. But they cannot find and operate that secret spring that arouses our soul to right action.

The vital, all-important things the soul must do for itself. If we do not want to practice the virtues of calmness, self-control, endurance, fortitude—all that a life of peace calls for—no one can make us do so, or do it for us. Briefly, it is up to us. We have to *practice* peace, deliberately calm ourselves, when everything seems to conspire against our inner quiet.

If our lives are a perpetual search for thrills—thrills such as have come to you from new clothes, beautiful surroundings, cocktails, cigarettes, etc.—it is those things and their results that we will get. If we do not like, if we do not enjoy, *ourselves* and our character, then we must build anew. No one can do it for us. I have not lived for nothing, and I have seen this again and again: In the same environment, with the same surroundings and opportunities, two people will manifest in entirely different ways. The stormy soul will be at warfare in the midst of beauty and comfort, while the soul at peace will be at peace even in poverty. Why?

In the words of Sri Shankaracharya:*

"A father has got his sons and others to free him from his debts, but he has got none but himself to remove his bondage.

"The true nature of things is to be known *personally*, through the eye of clear illumination, and not through a sage: What the moon exactly is, is to be known with one's own eyes; can others make him know it?

"Who but one's own self can get rid of the bondage caused by the fetters of ignorance, desire, action, and the like, aye, even in a hundred crore of cycles?"

The important things are all up to us. The rest are just details that make the body more or less comfortable, and that provide "good times."

With love, dear, always,
Gyanamata

* * * * *

circa 1937

Dear Mrs. ________,

I found the last sentence of your letter very significant. Of your son you say, "He doesn't drink, smoke, or swear, and is considered a fine boy." Then you are to be congratulated, and it seems possible that you are minimizing his good points and exaggerating his faults. A young man sometimes makes no attempt to conceal his weaknesses from his family,

* Great Indian philosopher and reorganizer of the ancient monastic Swami Order. His date is uncertain; many scholars assign him to the eighth or early ninth century.

expecting that they will understand and bear with him, but to the world he presents his more sterling qualities.

You also add that he is "just spoiled." This gives rise to the question, "Who spoiled him?" If you do not altogether approve of or enjoy the harvest of your own sowing, at least face things honestly and place the blame where it belongs. But do not waste time in vain regrets. As a Self-Realization Fellowship mother, you are called upon to be an inspiration to your family, the leader of a little circle that may one day be a meditation group. It is a fact overlooked by many home and social reformers that all improvement must commence with one's self. If one does not manifest qualities that command respect, then nobody will listen to one's words of good advice and counsel.

What have you done for your son? What are you doing for him each day? Remember, I have nothing to go by except your letter, and am basing my advice solely upon that and upon the general principles that ought to govern the relationship of a mother and son. You only mention having given him a big car, and of being willing to support his wife if he marries the right girl—both gifts of doubtful value to a young man. It would be better for him to have to wait for both until he had earned the right to them; or at least until he had given unmistakable proof that he deserved such gifts at your hands, and would know how to use and appreciate them properly.

But do you give him each day a patient, sympathetic attempt to see life from his viewpoint? Do you nag at him about his faults, or are you wisely silent when you cannot truthfully praise? Do you hold up before him a high ideal by trying each day to be in your own life and character all that you wish him to be?

If my questions contain any hints that you can use,

then seize them and act upon them without delay. It may take time, but if you never give up, but patiently, day by day, live before him according to your highest ideals, you will finally command his respect and influence his life. Example is better than precept. Influence is more far reaching than authority.

I will pray that you may be guided to the right action in all things, and that a happy answer and solution be found to all your problems.

Gyanamata

* * * * *

May 26, 1937

Dear ________,

When devotion fails to support us; or when, like you, we think we have none, then *duty* must step into the breach. The more opportunity I have to study the lives of those who are practicing meditation, the more I am convinced that hand-in-hand with it should go the practice of the good old-fashioned virtues. I have been told that meditation itself is enough—but I have no evidence that this is so. And our *paramguru,* Swami Sri Yukteswarji, did not so hold, for to his disciples, the group of boys whom he was training in the best methods of meditation, he said: "Learn to behave."

What does good behavior consist of? In the careful, watchful regulation of our daily conduct to each other *when we do not feel like it;* for of course if one feels like it, such right conduct becomes natural and automatic. Since we are human beings, and not machines, it becomes necessary for us to be vigilant in the exercise of self-control. It can all be put into a few words: We must do what we know to be right, whether we feel like it or not. You have not been doing this. You have simply not been behaving. And I know why: You have been engaged day and night in the thought of yourself. Because of this, a great chance to serve Paramahansaji, a great chance to cement the bond between you and the rest of your group by unselfishly helping them at a time when they needed you, has passed you by.

"We have fought a good fight, brave Crillon, but *you* were not here," said a French king once to a subject who stayed away when he was needed. Let the little self whine if it will. Turn your back on it. Concentrate on your behavior.

You asked me what we could do if we had no devotion. I have told you.

With love in God and Guruji,
Sister

* * * * *

August 12, 1941

My dear ________,

You are so wonderful in many ways, and you have such unplumbed depths of love and devotion—do not spoil all by failure in one point. Daily I watch your life and I know what you want. When you are unhappy your face tells me the story; besides, you have spoken plainly with your tongue.

You want something which, if you are honest (and you have a very honest and sincere nature), you will admit you have not earned, you do not deserve. Try the method of self-control, of silence and patience, of respectful answers. Try to *deserve* what you want, whether you get it or not. Do not tell me that the behavior of A, B, or C is not any better than yours. What is it to you how anyone else acts? It is your own life, your own soul, that concerns you.

I do not think that I have anything that you would like to have. I do not think you envy me any of my duties—but there is no harm in my writing as if you did. I assure you that I have *nothing* that has been given to me without effort on my part—patient, self-controlled, *strenuous* effort, maintained by keeping my eyes fixed upon the goal that I saw before me when I was initiated into *sannyas,* and by asking myself in painful moments, "What did you come for? Was it for favors, or notice of any kind? Or was it for God?"

Are you a weakling? Can your feet not tread the same path that my poor feet are walking upon—the path that leads to the smile of God and Guru, that gives deep peace to the soul?

With everlasting love in God and Guruji,
Sister

* * * * *

November 8, 1938

Dear ________,

I am so interested in the new office plan. If only everyone will cooperate, I believe each will find a new strength—instead of a distraction—in being all together in one room. It will have the same power that group meditation has, though for a different purpose.

The last quarter that my husband lectured at the University of Washington, I went with him every morning. While he was in class I sat in the library, a beautiful building, very much like a cathedral. There were rows and rows of tables, at which the students read, or took notes. Of course there was a strict rule against any kind of noise. I used to feel the force of their silent concentration. It was quite different from being in a room all alone. I would become absorbed in my book, and would become entirely oblivious of everything else; then I would look up and be surprised to find myself surrounded by silent figures. I don't see why it should not be the same with you (the typewriters will be something to overcome of course) if only you will concentrate with all your power.

Gyanamata

* * * * *

February 1, 1936

Dear _______,

All week I have wanted to write you about what happened last Sunday. I cannot feel at peace until I do, because I had the same fault in my youth, and feel a responsibility to warn you of the consequences that result from such an attitude. I suppose no wrong action that I ever performed did as much to cloud my happiness, shut out the light of God, and hold back my spiritual progress as much as the wicked habit of holding on to a desire—*not wrong in itself*—that was impossible to gratify. When I look back and remember how I darkened my days and saddened those who loved me by this hideous, sinful practice, I wonder how God ever had mercy upon me, how I ever won one smile from Him.

The first thing to consider is that these desires are seldom wrong in themselves. This is what gives them their insidious power over us. It is just some circumstance of our life that makes them wrong. But you are mistaken if you think that getting what was withheld from you would lead you nearer to God. This has, now that you have entered upon the path of inner renunciation, become a bondage that must be broken if you are to be free. When I went to the beach last week with my friend, I recognized, as I think I told you, that my bondage, my attachment to the ocean was broken—and I was deeply thankful.

You see, first we have to give up wrong actions. This is not so hard, because we can see the reason. Having accomplished this, we are apt to rest satisfied, thinking that we can now enjoy the things that are rightfully ours. But God says, "No. Come, lay *all* the dear innocent pleasures at My feet. Everything. Hold nothing back." Until we obey that command, we cannot know that God Himself is the gratification, the satisfaction of all desires, and the only real one. He is the Joy, the Bliss that we were seeking on the mountain and beside the sea.

Next I want you to notice the blackest side of this dreadful fault. It is the injustice it causes you to do to others, the pain you give those you love. When your will is crossed and you have a "mood" in consequence, the ones you shut out are the ones you love best. You not only make yourself miserable, but you cast a gloomy shadow over them.

You have a strong will. I suppose that is the cause of your trouble. You cannot give up. But you may turn that will into the instrument of your liberation. You can if you only want to enough. There are times when the strong command of the will is needed, when we ought to give ourselves a good shake and say, "No more of *that* from you!" And if we do this in dead earnest it will work. Try it and see.

If only I can show you how hateful this attitude of the mind is; if only I can give you a suggestion that will aid you in overcoming your enemy, I shall feel that God was patient with me when I was guilty because He intended to use me later on to help you.

Anyway, as long as I live, there will always be Sister to act as a guidepost on the roadway of your life.

With love in God and Guru

* * * * *

In the following two letters, Gyanamata responds to two students who had written to SRF asking for counsel with certain problems.

She gives explicit guidance on the proper attitude one should have toward depression and melancholy, mental suffering, and how to deal with evil spirits. *

November 7, 1935

Dear Mr. ________,

I do truly sympathize with the mental suffering you described, and had in my own childhood an experience of torture, so you see, we are fellow sufferers. It is a mistake, however, to pity ourselves on account of this suffering, because it is through suffering that we learn and grow. I shall always remember the words of someone to me when I was undergoing the greatest suffering of my life. He was not a friend, but a complete stranger, who had the impulse to speak to me one day when I was out for a walk. He said, "It had to be. It was all necessary for you." And I answered, "Yes, I know that what you say is true. I needed it." His reply came quickly, and like a blow from the shoulder: *"Then glorify it!"* That is the point. Since it is suffering that teaches us the truth and turns us toward God, why do we not thank and praise it for the work it does for us?

You speak of your tendency toward melancholy and despondency as being hereditary. This is a mistake. Since you are a student of Hindu philosophy, you must be acquainted with the law of karma. We do not suffer for the wrongdoing

* Paramahansa Yogananda explained that evil spirits, or disembodied "tramp souls," are "roaming in the ether seeking human vehicles for expression and experience in the physical world. These souls are of low type, with strong attachment to this world, which prevents them from natural adjustment to the better life in the astral world. Instead of remaining in the astral world, they hover between the astral and physical planes and are occasionally successful in possessing someone whose mind is weak and dwells on a low level of consciousness. The 'devils' that Jesus cast out [see Matthew 8:16] were tramp souls."

of others—only for our own. You brought this tendency to be melancholy over from a past life, and the reason for it lies in that forgotten life, not in something which you have inherited from your ancestors. The memory of the shock over your grandfather's tragic death may strengthen your tendency toward melancholy, but it would not cause it.

No doubt you have fought against it, and you should continue to fight with ever-increasing strength and vision to the end. Whenever we see that some habit, mental or physical, is dragging us down—as you see this tendency to despond does—at that very instant we ought to begin the fight against it. It is a very great mistake to say or to think that we are bound by the acts of another. We ourselves, through endless incarnations, have built the character we now possess. Since we ourselves did it, we can and must undo our work and build better, more noble mansions for our souls.

Never read nor listen to accounts of suicides, murders, or anything similar. Such things do happen on this plane, but they do not furnish suitable food for our souls. When that "huge, clammy hand from the mire" reaches for you out of the darkness, first firmly deny its power over you—even Jesus had to say, "Get thee behind me, Satan"—and then turn, wide open, toward God in whatever way is easiest for you. Try to feel His presence in the beauties of nature, or in the companionship of some helpful friend or inspiring book, or do anything else that uplifts you. Do not forget that I have had to do all these things myself, *so I know.* And most important of all, meditate as much as possible. Meditation is the method by which we fry the seeds of karma so that they cannot germinate and bear fruit in some future life.

You say that God has been very kind to you. Your letters show me that you do not fully realize how kind He has been. Melancholy is said to be the greatest bar there is to the realization of God; yet in spite of it, you have had the Bliss experience six or eight times. God manifests as Bliss, so He came personally to you to help you in your suffering. Keep those experiences in your mind as much as possible, shutting out all sad thoughts.

You say that at times you feel as if the connection between yourself and God has been severed. This is impossible. Man cannot cut asunder this connection, because "in Him we live, and move, and have our being."* The aim and goal of all spiritual work, discipline, study, and meditation, is to become *conscious* of this fact—to contact this abiding Presence within us. That is the only difference between the saint and the sinner. One is conscious of his lineage; the other is not. Fortunate people—like yourself—those whose karma is sufficiently good, feel the touch of His hand upon their souls. The others will when the time is ripe.

Very sincerely yours,
Gyanamata

* * * * *

Dear Mrs. ________,

How did you contact the evil entities that are tormenting you? Was the lady whom you served as secretary a spiritualist, or are you? Did she hold seances, and do you attend them? If so, the first thing for you to do is discontinue the practice. Next, keep yourself in a positive state of mind. They gained access to your mind and consciousness by reason of your negative attitude. They do not attack one who is positive.

Since it is you who opened the door to them, it must be you who puts them out. Plant your feet firmly and say, "Get

* Acts 17:28.

out! And stay out!" Keep yourself in a positive state of mind constantly, and fill your mind with thoughts of God. Act as you do when you want to make a dark room light. You do not fight with the darkness. You simply *bring in the light,* and the darkness is dispelled. Read spiritual books constantly—the Bible, the lives of holy people, anything that is inspiring and that appeals to you. In this way you will surround yourself with light. Evil spirits are in the darkness; they cannot penetrate the light. But if you become negative and your aura* becomes dark, they come nearer and nearer to you, and at last they gain admittance.

Next, and this is very important, sing or chant—loudly, softly, or mentally—the word *Aum.* It is pronounced "Om." Surround yourself with the atmosphere of *Aum* by keeping it in your mind and on your tongue constantly. The method is to draw the letters of the word out, thus: "O-O-Om, O-Om, O-Om-m-m-m." When you go to bed at night, write, with your finger, the word *Aum* on your pillow.

Gyanamata

* * * * *

In the following three letters, Gyanamata discusses the right attitude that one should have toward one's body—its food, its health, its age. The first of these is a report to Paramahansaji of interviews she had with two of the many students who sought her advice and counsel during her years at the Encinitas Hermitage. She faithfully informed her Guru of the salient points of these interviews, to be certain that he approved of the counsel she was giving.

Paramahansaji:

________ wouldn't eat the pancakes served at breakfast.

* Yoga teaches that the aura, or life energy radiating from the human body, reveals one's physical, emotional, and mental condition through variations in color and intensity.

He also said that one morning there was no milk and no toast (the toaster being broken).

I told him that one's *attitude* toward one's food is more important than the diet itself. That, while I would like to have a perfectly balanced diet, if I could only have *one*—the diet or the attitude—I would take the attitude. I told him that he would have to concede something, and advised him to eat a flapjack or two; that as he was working out of doors, they would not hurt him, especially if he had the right attitude.

I told him to pray silently before eating: "O Lord, this is the food Thou hast given me. Therefore it must be the best for me." I also told him how, when we had careless cooks at Mt. Washington, I had eaten burnt rice, applesauce, and bread and butter for my supper, and counted it all joy because I was near you. He seemed to feel better for the time being, and thanked me.

Mr. ________ says he likes to work for you because you are a perfectionist. You notice every little thing that is not right, and point it out to him, and he is glad to make it right. He says that if something is not perfect, you are not fully satisfied, and that he feels the same way about his work. He only hopes that what he has done will stand the test of time.

Gyanamata

* * * * *

Thursday morning

Divine and Blessed Master,

I well know that what you wish me to manifest is complete surrender to God, a surrender that gives no place for concern for the body. How lovely, how heavenly this ideal is I have no words to express. But I think you do not really mean me to give up *care* for the body, because if I do this, it will be of no use to you.

On one occasion, when I was able to completely ignore the demands of this body, I carelessly exposed myself to a cold. You told me that such an act was not a spiritual act, because if I became ill as a result, I would not only bring needless suffering upon myself, but would also encumber others, who would then have to care for me. "An imprudent action is not a spiritual action," you said. So I feel that all the proper care I can take of this poor and useless body (useless except to the degree it is useful to you and this work) is a truly spiritual action.

With deep devotion,
Gyanamata

* * * * *

My Blessed Master,

I cannot wish to live for a great number of years, like the woman you mentioned who has celebrated her 100th birthday. I can't help wondering, "What else has she to celebrate?" Length of life—what is that worth? Jesus was just thirty-three. His Holiness your Master Sri Yukteswarji was eighty-one when he decided to go. Swami Vivekananda died before he was forty. These names come to me.

But I do not wish to be "a deserter in the face of the enemy." Since you regard this poor life as useful to you and the work, I will do my best to hold to it as long as it helps you. I would like to believe that I will go quickly when the time comes, as I wish never to be a burden to you and the others. I would also like to be able to say, of my little life, "It is finished," as Jesus said of his great one. Nothing left undone that I *could* have done.

I have, then, these ambitions: To be near you, which is the desire that brought me from Seattle. To serve you; to be loyal to you to the last drop of blood in my body; never to fail you through carelessness. To make as perfect a manifestation of your teaching as possible. To go quickly at just the right moment. To leave nothing unfinished.

With deep devotion,
Gyanamata

* * * * *

My Divine Master,

The habit of explaining everything to you is so well established that, though I do not think it is necessary, I am writing to explain what I wrote you about ________'s meditation, but expressed so badly that perhaps you could not understand it.

Please note that I made no inquiry into the truth of ________'s statement about me. I did not come to you and ask if I had been with you in the incarnation about which he spoke. The thought stirred a certain amount of interest, but I knew it was not important. What is important is what I am *now*—what I have become because of all my incarnations. My best, my most important memory is what I am. You teach that it is folly to dwell upon the past or the future. The day that I am earnestly looking forward to, if I may look forward that much, is the day on which I shall know myself to be free from all incarnations, when I shall see them lying dead around me, like withered leaves that have fallen to the ground around a tree.

Whatever, whoever I have been in the past, in this—the most important incarnation of all—I am Gyanamata, the work of your hands. Please pray for me that I may stand firm and unshaken to the end.

With reverence, gratitude, devotion, and love—but not enough, O not enough!

Gyanamata

In the next two letters, Gyanamata discusses the proper attitude one should have toward progress in meditation. The first was written to her Guru only a year after their first meeting.

Seattle, September 28, 1926

The Rev. Swami Yogananda:

Dear Master,

Rex was brought home last Saturday. He is steadily improving. It is expected that in two weeks he will be able to sit up in a chair, and about the first of November commence to walk with crutches. I do not know how much muscle and tendon he has lost. I realize that in telling me about it, everyone presents the most hopeful side. The doctor says that when standing erect, with legs apart, he will not be able to draw the right leg up to the left, because the necessary muscles for that action are gone. Another doctor says that when sitting, he will not be able to cross the right leg over the left. He has suffered from nervous indigestion, and has to be very careful about his diet, but that is better now.

Rex says that he often thinks of you, and that he attributes his freedom from fever and pain to your help. He believes that without you, the history of his case would be very different. He is even now exercising the left leg, and says that he feels sure that his practice of the SRF Energization Exercises will do much to help him regain use of the right. His nurses have commented on his unusual muscular control and strength, due of course to the exercises.*

I will now use your gracious permission to write you about my spiritual practices. Since the 18th of July, my routine—at best, never what I could wish it to be—has been much interrupted. But I know that the real hindrances are in myself. If I can overcome them, the others will be of no importance. So I will say nothing about them.

* Rex eventually recovered completely from this injury.

[Patanjali* said:] "Yoga is the suppression of the transformations of the thinking principle. Freed from them the Self attains to self-expression." Joy followed by pain, calmness by irritation or resentment—these are only transformations of the thinking principle. If the mind does not admit nor recognize them, what, where, are they? Opportunities to practice evenness of mind are given me every day—so if I will it strongly enough, my hindrances may be turned into *sadhanas* [spiritual disciplines, through which the disciple progresses]. This has been much in my mind lately, and the implied confession, made to you, will, I believe, put me on honor to do better.

I am writing just what comes to me, in the sure confidence that if in my eagerness and ignorance I write what is unimportant and unnecessary, you will excuse it. [Sister then describes in detail her personal experiences in seeing the spiritual eye, and feeling and hearing the divine vibrations of *Aum*. She concludes:]

I feel no bliss at all. I just quietly watch what goes on. I do, however, feel some effect or result of my poor imperfect practice. It is that when vibrations, quietness, and light come, I am not tired that day, no matter how early I have wakened....But it is the feeling of peace and well-being that I would put into words if I could.

Of course, I wish that I could progress a little faster, though just now I think that if I could feel bliss in proportion to the strength of the vibrations and the brightness of the light, I would be content to wait indefinitely [without making the effort to change]. But I know how obstinate my mind is, and how bad are the mental habits to which I have so long been in bondage. It is a state of blessedness just to

* Ancient exponent of Yoga, whose *Yoga Sutras* outline the principles of the yogic path.

be able to attempt the practice of meditation. To stand at the same door through which those Shining Ones passed who have spoken to me through the printed page, giving me light, peace, and courage to follow Them—what joy for me! I am ashamed to even express a wish for more, knowing that with Their blessing and yours, I must in the end win full success.

If I may, I would like to tell you of my one experience of Bliss-consciousness. [This took place before she met Paramahansaji.] For a week I had a continuous flow of Bliss-consciousness. I seemed to be in two states of consciousness at the same time. The inward bliss and light glorified my surroundings and every act. I shall never forget a few moments that I spent in a dark attic. No moment of my life, whether spent in church, in prayer, or in some act of love and devotion, compared to this one! During this week everything of a pleasant nature increased my bliss, while anything unpleasant caused me pain almost unendurable. Night found me wearied to the point of tears. Day came, and my first eager question was, "Is *IT* still here?" And I received an immediate, but indescribable answer.

I thought I was always going to remain in this state, high above my former pettiness and selfishness. A friend regarded these experiences as "gifts of the Spirit," not to be worked for, but "conferred." But I longed to be taught that practice which would not leave me at the mercy of chance emotions or experiences; and my earnest wish for a master, which had sprung into being with my first Hindu book, was greatly increased—if that is possible—though it remained unsatisfied until I saw you and realized that he whom I had been watching for had come! "When the pupil is ready, the master appears." Now, on days when success seems far from me, I remember your coming. My Joyful Mystery!

The goal that my face is turned toward, however far distant it may be, is liberation, supreme *mukti.* That this may be my last enforced life, my last life of entanglement in earthly illusions, help me!

My humble thanks always for your favors.

With gratitude and devotion,
Edith D. Bissett

* * * * *

Dear ________,

It is not because of a lack of intelligence that the saints are unconscious of favor or neglect, of whether they have their rights or not, of whether the best or the worst is given them. It is because their minds are in God, and therefore all material things have become the same to them, that they are not concerned about their bodies and earthly joys, and therefore cannot be made unhappy about them. Or, if they do notice that something is withheld from them that they could enjoy, they say: "How could I, who fall so far short of the perfection that I ought to manifest, expect to receive more than I do?"

I think that most of us would like to be able to test the reality of those moments in meditation when God seems to come near. Are they genuine, or do they come as a result of a process of self-hypnosis? Is not this the severest test of all: What do we manifest in our daily life as a result of our meditations? Are the beautiful buds and flowers of humility, love, and unselfishness, and that deep peace of the soul—which, like charity, "seeketh not her own," and which gives promise of a rich spiritual harvest—visible on the tree of our lives? Do they send forth a fragrant vibrational perfume? If not, how can we be sure that we have found the Pearl of Great Price, God, the Divine Mother, in meditation?

Gyanamata

Gyanamata with her son Rex and his wife Hughella on grounds of the Self-Realization Fellowship International Headquarters

Gyanamata and her mother, outside the Bissett home in Seattle

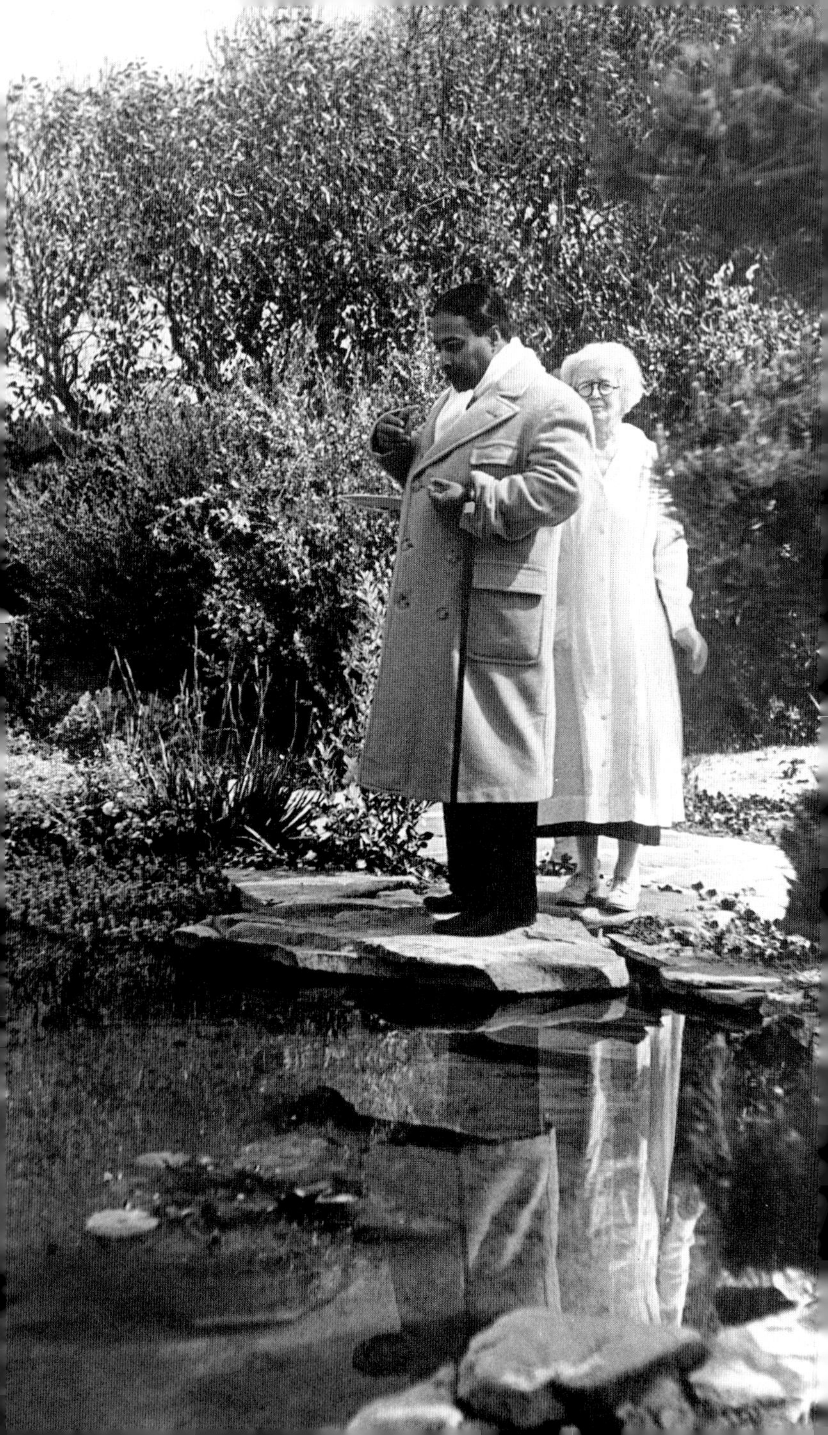

Dear ________,

The saints have a way of expressing in a few words thoughts that others might take hours to express. I quote an example:

> Suso describes a vision he had of Meister Eckhart* after death....The Master [Eckhart] told him that he was in great glory, into which his soul was transformed and made godlike in God. Suso inquired what exercise was best calculated to advance a man who wished to be taken into the abyss of the divine essence. Eckhart's reply was that he must die to himself in entire detachment, receive everything as from God, and keep himself in unruffled patience with all men.

These three instructions, plus meditation, contain the only rule of life that any disciple needs: detachment; realization of God as the Giver; and unruffled patience. As long as we fail in any one of these three, we still have a serious spiritual defect to overcome.

Reading the Bhagavad Gita the other day, this thought came to me very strongly, that calmness is the soil, and the only soil, in which all that we most desire to be will grow.

With love in God and Guruji,
Gyanamata

* * * * *

Dear Mr. ________,

First I want to apologize for the length of time that your letter has remained unanswered. The delay was unavoidable, but it did not arise from lack of interest or appreciation of the confidence in me you have shown.

* Meister Johannes Eckhart and the Blessed Henry Suso were fourteenth-century German Dominican friars and mystics.

Opposite: Paramahansa Yogananda and Sister feeding fish in lotus pond on grounds of Encinitas Hermitage, 1939

You did make a mistake in changing your name. Not that it is wrong in itself to make the change; there might be circumstances in which such a change would be wise and necessary, such as business, or the inheritance of property. But to do so with the hope of improving or changing one's so-called fate, or to hasten one's development in any way, shows lack of understanding.

Since you are a student of Hindu philosophy, you no doubt know that one of the highest teachings is that man, at the apex of his being, is divine, one with God. To contact that Self is the goal, the aim, and end of all yoga practices. To contact this Self in deep meditation is Bliss, and is also the source of all truth. To contact it intuitionally gives inspiration, wisdom, genius. Self-realization means all of these things.

Since the above is true, why should one look to anything lower for inspiration, for help, for guidance? You say that since you changed your name you have had many costly experiences. The change of name did not bring them about. Just at that time, karma became ripe, and you began to reap the results of actions done earlier in this life, or in a past one.

To improve the circumstances of your life, to raise yourself physically, mentally, and spiritually, *change your attitude.* Meet trials with courage, determination, and fortitude. When you need help, meditate deeply and try to contact God, but look to no lower source than to Him and to your guru. Pray and affirm: "I will reason, I will will, I will act, but guide Thou my reason, will, and activity to the right thing that I should do."

Gyanamata

Dear ________,

> Prayer is the heart's sincere desire,
> Uttered or unexpressed,
> The motion of a hidden fire
> That slumbers in the breast.*

Many years ago I read a volume of sermons by an English clergyman. I only remember one short one on prayer, and of that I can recall only two statements. He said that in all the rope used by the British Navy a red thread was woven, adding that through all our prayers must run the red thread of surrender to the will of God. Above all our own wishes must stand the wish that God's will should prevail. His kingdom come, His will be done, on earth as it is in heaven. What a vision of peace this opens up before the eyes of the soul!

During the same period of my life, late one afternoon, I was kneeling in prayer in the chapel—I was thinking of something that was coming into my life that filled me with apprehension. I knew that it was not the will of God that I should be saved from the experience. Even at that moment it was moving toward me. Suddenly God told me the prayer He would listen to, and I said quickly: "Change no circumstance of my life. Change *me*."

There are experiences that the soul never forgets, but which cannot properly be expressed. My prayer was answered instantly. I was changed. Trying to put this into words, all I could compare it to was a window being opened in an overheated room, and a cool, refreshing breeze blowing in. It is not getting our own way that gives joy; it is attunement with the Divine Will.

* First stanza of the poem "What Is Prayer?" by James Montgomery.

The concluding words of the clergyman's sermon expand this further: "Pray until praying causes you to cease to pray." What a boundless vision of peace! The tearful eyes are dried. The praying lips close. The soul is absorbed in the blissful thought that in the will of God lies its highest good. For in the end He will give Himself.

Gyanamata

CHAPTER 5

The Guru-Disciple Relationship

Of all the advice given by Sri Gyanamata to those she counseled, some of the most valuable had to do with the proper attitude that a disciple should have toward the guru. Although the devotion, respect and veneration inherent in the guru-disciple relationship has been a long-standing tradition in India, the concept was foreign to Westerners in the mid-1900s. Gyanamata was one of the first who clearly grasped the spiritual importance, value, and intimacy of this sacred bond.

She realized that far from being personality worship, the obedience and reverence given by the disciple toward the guru is born of the highest wisdom, for a true guru is a vehicle of God for the emancipation of souls. Gyanamata understood that the guru-disciple relationship is rooted in divine law; that only through the teachings and blessings of a true guru—through attunement with his enlightened consciousness—can a soul ascend the path to union with God. Even though Gyanamata was not often in her Guru's physical presence, she attained the divine consciousness about which he taught, demonstrating that inner attunement and receptivity to the guru is far more important than outer association with him.

Gyanamata constantly strove for perfection as a disciple. Through her example and letters, she offered invaluable counsel to other devotees on how to establish and perfect this unique, divine relationship in their own lives.

Dear _______,

The Master has come from the other side of the world to seek and gather his disciples around him. You have welcomed him joyfully. Perhaps you have said, as I did, "He came for me," shutting out all the others in order to make this great moment more intensely personal—that the thought, "I have met my Guru! He has come! Now I must be receptive to him," might burn with a living, deathless flame on the altar of your devotion.

What follows? That, each disciple will discover for himself. None may have another's. The time will come when you will realize that this is so. Therefore, have no jealous or resentful thoughts, which poison both soul and body.

As the soul is before God, so the disciple is before the spiritual teacher—either in the wrong, or, in the case of the disciple before the guru, free to make a suggestion if it is done in a respectful and detached manner.

One thing is outstandingly necessary—the right attitude toward the Guru. The importance of having the right attitude toward the Guru cannot be ignored. Without it, the disciple is like an automobile without a steering wheel, or a boat without a rudder. With it, he need have no fear. He will safely pass through all that may chance.

Gyanamata

* * * * *

April 4, 1951

Dear _______,

One may have many teachers but only one guru. He appears when the hunger for God is so strong that it will take no denial. His object, his purpose in the life of the disciple is not only loving kindness, but also firmness. He does not hesitate to give what we call "pain," if by that pain the disciple will draw closer to God. It is like a painful operation that has as its object the benefit of the patient.

The greatest thing in the life of the disciple is to be able to look in the face of the guru and say, "I will accept anything. Treat me in any way that seems best to you in order that in the end I may be what you are."

Gyanamata

* * * * *

Dear ________,

I want to finish my talk this way because it is not likely that I will have a chance alone with you. Besides, I do not want to discuss personalities, but to lay down some principles that I *know* will help you, for they are true, basic, timeless.

First: The meeting with the guru is *not for pleasure.* It is a hand-to-hand conflict between his God-conscious soul and the newly awakening soul of the disciple.

Second: A master does not care whether you suffer or not, whether your feelings are hurt or not, because he knows that when his work for your soul is accomplished, all suffering will be over for you. One night at dinner, not long ago, our Guru said: "All suffering is from Satan." It was some time before I got the meaning, though it is obvious. A perfect soul is all Bliss. You *cannot* hurt its feelings nor bring tears to its eyes.

Third: Your feelings were hurt? What of it? Resolve that for you will dawn the day of absolute liberation from all petty feelings!

Fourth: Do you remember my telling you that when I first came to the Mother Center, I determined that, whatever happened, I would not be daunted nor ask explanations. I would try to *see eye-to-eye with the Guru.* The result has justified the experiment, and not long ago he praised me because he has never had to explain anything to me.

Fifth: Make a few simple rules for yourself. If the Guru seems to be displeased with you, ask him to show you wherein you were wrong (if you do not already know) that you may improve. If you wish to explain yourself, do so, for he always welcomes explanations—but do so respectfully, with sincerity that cannot be mistaken, and with humility. Now, what does that word "humility" mean? Nothing wormlike or groveling. It means the simple, straightforward admission that you are not perfect, and that you know you get nothing in the way of blame or discipline that you do not deserve. *Never* stay away from him as you have done. If you get only suffering, come just the same. Remember how the saint kept coming when his guru, to test him, would not speak to him.

Sixth:

> When Love beckons to you, follow Him though His ways are hard and steep.
>
> And when His wings enfold you, yield to Him though the sword hidden among His pinions may wound you.
>
> And when He speaks to you, believe on Him, though His words may shatter your dreams as the north wind lays waste the garden.*

Dear one, the above is just the experience you are having!

Please do not throw this letter away, even if you do not like or understand it. Keep it until you do.

Gyanamata

* * * * *

Dear ________,

There is an old saying that I want you to consider: "One

* From *The Prophet,* by Kahlil Gibran.

can hold a penny so close to one's eyes that one cannot see a dollar." You are doing this in maintaining your attitude toward your duties here—housecleaning. You told me that you saw things that ought to be done, and since no one else undertook them, you did, and were scolded because you would not stop until they were finished, regardless of how late it became. If you would put cleaning in its place, and pleasing the guru and obedience above all else (where they belong), you would have escaped this scolding. If you are scolded, it is because the guru does not want you to labor so hard at this kind of work—and also, you are really doing it to please yourself.

If you look closely, I think you will see that the worst of your troubles are caused by your doing what *you* think ought to be done, instead of what the guru wants you to do. What is the sense in calling him the guru-preceptor if we do not really believe in his superior wisdom?

It all boils down to this: We incarnate here on this plane in order to learn certain lessons, gain necessary experiences, do work we are fitted to do. We take up our appointed positions, and we cannot have what belongs to another. We get our own—neither more nor less. It is only by cooperating with our karma that we find the path of peace and blessedness. Please think this over. Think deeply. It is the voice of one who loves and admires you that is speaking.

The words of a poor
Sister

* * * * *

October 2, 1942

My dear ________,

I want to give you the exact words of that saying of the Buddha's which I tried to quote to you the other day, because it is so very important. My mind is filled with it for days at a time. “He whose conquest cannot be conquered again, into whose conquest no one in this world enters, by what track can you lead him, the Awakened, the Omniscient, the Trackless?” The mental picture this brings to me is that of a figure standing on the highest peak of a snowy mountain range. No pang of pain, no sorrow that stabs and burns can touch this soul, for his conquest cannot be conquered again.

I felt some anxiety lest you misunderstood me, fearing that it might have appeared to you that I was making the most of, and enjoying, the opportunity to talk of myself and complain. *No.* There was a particular point that I wanted to illustrate and impress upon you: Four-fifths of the iceberg lies below the waves. We never contact that part of it. We see only the shining peak, the smaller part. So it is with the relationship of the guru to his disciples. His consciousness is so vast that the disciple can only touch on a small phase of it at a time.

The point that I tried to bring before you was that the Guru is the vehicle of God at all times, whether his action is entirely unconscious or deliberately planned for the disciple’s good. Every moment of his life, consciously and unconsciously, he is working for the good of his disciples’ souls. And it is very interesting to watch the result of his unconscious acts. I have never asked him questions, even when there was something that I would like to know about. This is one of the things for which he has praised me. But about two weeks ago I had an experience that I wanted to know about, and thought I would ask him a question for once.

“What was it?” I said. His answer was, “God through me.” God had come to me through him. Just three words—and it covers the whole of the relationship of a master and disciple. God through him, always, and in everything.

You said, while we were talking, that you had no longer

any feeling. I think you will remember this, even if I am not putting it exactly right. We make too much of feeling, even admitting that the right kind of feeling is very enjoyable. What does it matter how you feel? Bear your lot as long as it is the will of God that you should do so. Act rightly, and in due time the right feeling of peace and joy will come.

You asked me if I had ever thought of going away [from the ashram]. No, not for a split second. I knew what I wanted long before I came. I did not come for honor, nor for pleasure, nor for favor. I came for God. Some things surprised and disappointed me, but I moved on, from point to point, until I had the full vision of the guru-disciple relationship. I saw that if the Master had [not disciplined me and instead had] treated me with what is called "kindness" I would never have known myself nor my spiritual needs. "Thou, O Lord, givest to each man his portion, and I, receiving it, acknowledge it to be good."

I do not want to appear to exaggerate the "discipline" side of my experiences with the Guru, but rather the other side, which is all joy and wonderful honor! Once on a card he wrote of my "countless divine cooperations" with him. On another, "May your devotion shine like a special star in the skies, for generations of mankind to be guided to God and ideal Guru-devotion." Ask your heart if it would not thrill with joy if these things were said to you.

Dear ________, your past incarnations had advanced you to the point where you were ready for a place very near to the Master. Are you willing to sink permanently below that level? To sell your divine birthright for a mess of pottage composed of temper and self-will?

The only real pain, the only real joy there is, flows from within. We do not, cannot, enjoy what others are. What does it matter to you and me how great, how wonderful, how

God-conscious our Guru is, if we have no God-realization of our own? Let us press on, accepting either praise or blame, until we have become those "whose conquest cannot be conquered again."

With love in God and Guruji,
Gyanamata

* * * * *

Dear ________,

All your moments with the Guru, whether you are meditating, listening to his teachings, eating, enjoying some pleasure, or exercising on the tennis court, are for *one* purpose: your development, your liberation. *He* does not come into the matter at all, just exactly as I do not come into this letter, which is being written purely for your sake. You tune your mind to him, and keep it tuned perpetually to a worshipful attitude in order that the channels of that mind which are clogged with ignorance, prejudice, and all sorts of wrong notions may be cleared out, and the pure love, devotion and service of your soul may flow unobstructed to God.

You are with him because he is God-conscious and you want to be God-conscious too. This is the reason for every moment of contact you have with him. It's all for *your own sake.* So be with him in the same deeply reverential attitude that you have when you come out of the temple within after meditation, when you put your folded hands to your forehead, and whisper *"pranam."*

Gyanamata

* * * * *

Sunday, January 28, 1940

Dear ________,

I am not writing this to offer you my love and sympathy.

I believe you know you have both every day of your life and under all circumstances. I want to ask you again the question I put to you some time ago: Do you ask Paramahansaji's help that you may overcome this tendency of yours, which causes him so much trouble and you so much suffering? *Do you ask him to pray for you?*

The Christian is always warned against attempting the work of self-mastery in his own strength. He is told to look to God, and draw upon His power. When the attention is withdrawn from the self and its weakness and focused upon the One Source of Strength, the doors and windows of our being are opened toward heaven to receive a blessing that does not fail to come. Our way of doing this is to ask the prayers of the Master.

The thing about the life of Brother Lawrence that has stood out in my memory ever since I read the book *The Practice of the Presence of God,* is the simplicity of his relationship with God. When he failed, when he did wrong, he said, "That is the way I am; that is the way I shall always be *unless You help me.*" This simple prayer, this simple attitude of the mind, shows the truest humility. It says, "I know well that I am nothing, but let Your power flow into me and I shall be saved. I shall be all that You want me to be, all that I long to be." Tears and groans of shame and agony will not do for the soul what the above simple prayer will do.

So, dear ________, whom I long to see established in peace, approach the Master in this way, if you have not already done so, and ask him to direct the power of God that flows through him to you that you may be liberated from this bondage.

With love, as ever, in God and Guruji,
Sister

July 16, 1942

Dear _______,

In one respect I was very fortunate from the first—in the understanding I possessed of the relationship between guru and disciple. I did not mistake it for a friendly one, nor a social one, nor one for work or service, nor for pleasure. It is solely spiritual, so deeply spiritual that it passes away beyond my sight and understanding. Though you can only dimly apprehend this divine relationship at this time, trust yourself to it. The Guru will lead you out of the slums of "self" onto the heights of spiritual realization.

You stand where the road of your life forks. You cannot follow both paths. You must make a choice. There are two things of supreme importance in your life: your Guru and "that something" (I do not know what to call it) that separates you from him every now and then. You cannot follow both. If you would have the one, you must let the other go. Which shall it be? Which do you choose? Will you keep "that something" that has dragged you down, and will surely drag you deeper and deeper if you hold to it, and let him go? Or will you renounce this obstructing principle and hold firmly to him, walking the path of spiritual joy? He cannot help you, great master that he is, unless you give him your willing cooperation.

With warm love from the heart of
Sister

P.S. My relationship with the Master has been, and is, a wonderful relationship—mysterious, soul-satisfying, deepening with the years. If I have caused you to think anything else, I have unintentionally misled you.

* * * * *

June 19, 1940

Dear _______,

> The soul of man is immortal, and its future is the future of a thing whose growth and splendour have no limit. The principle which gives life dwells in us, and without us, is undying and eternally beneficent, is not heard or seen, or smelt, but is perceived by the man who desires perception. Each man is his own absolute lawgiver, the dispenser of glory or gloom to himself; the decreer of his life, his reward, his punishment.

This is an exact statement of the truth. We come to the guru asking him to give us liberation and the joy of realization; and so he can and will, but only if we cooperate with him. If the soul resolutely clings to the things that drag it down to earth, no miracle happens to release it. It may continue on this way as long as it chooses. At last the guru, however patient and long-suffering, has to say, "Take your own course."

Look into your heart, look back over your life, and tell me if you have ever persisted in any action that you absolutely felt no desire to do? No. When we really do not want to do a thing, *we simply don't do it.* When any action is persisted in, it is not simply a matter of habit, though habit counts. If you look closely you will have no trouble in discovering the red thread of desire. You *wanted* to do it, no matter what the consequences.

Whenever I think on this point, there comes to mind an experience I had in La Jolla. On a certain day, in a moment of intense feeling, I saw myself confronted with two courses. I felt within me the power to take either. I said to myself that I was free to choose—and I chose the lower, to my undying regret. It represented what I most wanted to do, in spite of clear vision and understanding. Whatever you do or don't do, dear girl, resolutely and honestly face yourself.

One of the reasons why people do wrong and foolish things is because in a moment of great emotional stress they forget everything and everybody—except themselves and their own wrongs, real or fancied. A little unselfish thought taken for those they really love would save them.

I know you meditate, but do you keep up the practice of spiritual reading? I consider it very important. Our consciousness does not rise into the spiritual ether unaided. And next to meditation, what help is so effectual as reading with concentration the lives and writings of those saints who have left records of their sufferings and successes on the pathway that leads upward to God?

They met the tyrant's brandished steel,
The lion's gory mane;
They bowed their necks the death to feel:
Who follows in their train?

They climbed the steep ascent of heaven
Through peril, toil, and pain:
O God, to us may grace be given
To follow in their train.*

With the love of one who is only a poor
Sister

* * * * *

Divine Master,

Some time ago I read the life of a saint called "The Sage of Sakori." It was very interesting, and because of one important incident, it will always stand out in my memory. This guru sometimes threw stones at his disciples, not playfully, but in anger. Those who, with devotion, picked up the

* From the hymn, "The Son of God Goes Forth to War," by Bishop Reginald Heber (1783–1826).

stones and carried them home, found that they had golden nuggets. Those who left them lying on the ground missed the blessing.

I had read all the lives of saints that I could get, but found nothing similar in them. An outstanding and marvelous truth was taught by the incident. If the guru "throws a stone"—that is, assigns a duty or gives an order that is disagreeable and painful to the disciple—the attitude in which he receives it and performs it determines whether he shall receive the blessing or not. If he "picks it up and carries it home"—that is, receives it humbly and carries it out cheerfully—he will find he has a golden nugget. All depends upon his attitude.

* * * * *

October 8, 1942

My Divine and Blessed Master,

During the last two or three years, my attention has been caught by what you have told us of your Master's methods [of training disciples]—his inexorable methods—and I thought what it would be to be able to stand before one's spiritual teacher and say, "I do not ask for any favor, or even kindness. Give me what you know I need that I may attain perfection, that I may attain to a conquest that cannot be conquered again." If Your Holiness had taken the course with me that I have seen you take with others, I would have accepted it, I am sure; but I would not have come to know what I now know. It would not have provided the fiber of which my character stood in need.

I believe that any ordinarily good teacher can discipline a student by some process of rewards and punishments. What I refer to is much more subtle. God often uses the guru as His vehicle without any conscious cooperation from the guru; and God was flowing through you to me in the way I most needed. That is the answer to my whole life for years: God and His will for me flowing to me through you.

The spiritual training you have given me has been, and is, perfect. The guru cannot be judged, if he is to be judged at all, by the rules that apply to a friendship between equals. I have always known this. So beginning at the very first, if anything happened that disappointed me or caused me pain, instantly my soul asked, "What did you come here for? Was it honor, distinction, favors, or pleasure?" As promptly the answer came: "No. For God. For God alone."

Knowing that you are praying for me all the time, that you are doing much for me in God, I have never expressed any especial need to you. Now my need has become so great that I ask you, when next you pray for me, to give me strength to overcome fear—to surrender myself so completely into the hand of God, that fear may leave me, and peace take its place.

Lord, it is my chief complaint,
That my love is weak and faint.
Yet I love Thee, and adore,
O for grace to love Thee more!*

Gyanamata

* * * * *

August 3, 1938

Blessed Master,

Something you said in the letter you wrote me from Salt Lake City keeps coming to my mind. It did not seem necessary to answer it at the time, but again and again it comes. I will cease to think of it once I have written to you about

* From a Christian hymn; words by William Cowper, 1768.

it—besides, you have told me that, for you, "there is satisfaction in the spoken or written word."

It was what you wrote about seldom talking to me.* I have always understood this. Speaking from your side, there are probably reasons for this that I do not know, but there are others that I well understand. I do not attract it from you. I have never attracted any sort of social intercourse from *anyone* in all my life. Those who loved me, and what friends I had, liked to know that I was in the house, that I was around somewhere. That satisfied them. How much less could I expect to have little friendly talks with *you*?

Speaking from my side, I don't think I have needed that sort of guidance from you. If human twinges have visited me at times, I have always recognized them for what they were—and have repudiated them. I am never really lonely for anyone. Only for God. If my consciousness is raised the tiniest bit, so that the Self—the radiant denizen of my inner being—seems so much as a hair's breadth nearer to me, all sense of isolation leaves me.

And greatest reason of all, the awareness of the height of your God-conscious state never leaves me for a moment. I am sure that I am speaking quite exactly and truthfully when I say that. I am sure that I cannot state this more strongly than I feel it. Can I, then, possibly desire that you "talk" to me?

I came to you old and ill. If, in spite of those limitations, I

* Owing to his extensive traveling to give lectures and classes in the Self-Realization teachings in scores of American cities, and his responsibilities as founder and spiritual head of Self-Realization Fellowship and the SRF monastic order, Paramahansaji had little time to speak or write often to Gyanamata. But the Guru explains, in one of his letters to her *(on page 246)*, how he felt that this outer communication was not necessary, due to their inner attunement.

have been able to serve and please you in a few small matters, if I have at all succeeded in making this what I wanted it to be—the one perfect relationship of my life—how great is my good fortune! The wonder of it all! that I should have come as near as this to you, even if I can never draw any nearer.

With gratitude, devotion, and love,
Gyanamata

* * * * *

April 2, 1940

Dear ________,

The spoken word vanishes and is forgotten. Because of this I have decided to write you all notes, which may be preserved if you feel that the highlights of what I said to you yesterday have value or inspiration.

What I said then and what I am writing now were stirred in me by what you said in the lovely note that accompanied your gift—about my attitude to the Master. This attitude I seem to have brought over from a past incarnation. It was in full force when I came from Seattle to Mt. Washington, and has never failed me in any situation in which I have found myself. I want to mention the ways in which it may be developed in those who do not have it, or want to increase what they already have.

1. Keep ever before your mind his divinity, his God-conscious state. He is God in man made manifest. I am sure you will see at once what this one rule, kept ever in the mind, will do for your soul and your outward behavior. Indeed, all the rest that I have to say is but an amplification of this one idea. The soul is never in the right, can never justify itself, when standing before God. You cannot imagine yourself answering back, or arguing with God; and he, the Master, is the vehicle through whom God flows to you. Therefore,

when you stand before him, you stand before God. I do not simply stop talking when he comes into the room, I *feel* still within. I listen. I am intent.

2. Preserve this attitude of inner and outer silence even when you are in the kitchen helping him cook, or when you serve him in any capacity. It is a state of deep peace.
3. When you are serving him, preserve a meditative silence. Talk quietly, if some subject comes up, but do not chatter, and speak *one at a time.*

This is the true way to minister to the Guru; the way to have the peace of God that passeth understanding; and the way to give aid to that Master who is carrying the burden of this world-movement.

Put the above into active practice, and you shall see for yourself whether I am right or not.

With love in God and Guruji,
Sister

* * * * *

March 7, 1948

My Divine Master,

When I called you this morning, you said something that I did not catch. The few words I did hear seemed to mean that my little offering should have been accompanied by a note. If this did not seem necessary to me, it is because a spring of devotion flows ceaselessly from my heart to you in an unbroken stream, and has now for twenty-four years, beginning at the time I first met you. Nothing has ever disturbed it.

Looking back over those years, I feel perfect satisfaction in one thing: No matter what you refused or withheld from me, I never thought you were in the wrong. I always knew that any pang I might feel came from the shadow thrown on my life by desire—wanting something for myself. That if I were what I ought to be, what I hope to be, there would be no shadow, no sign of the cross. Your treatment of me, your directing of me, has been perfect. As I tell the young disciples, if the years have given me anything of value, it is our relationship; it is because you have been what you are to me. In other words, I am as I am because you are as you are.

Material offerings can be given only now and then; but the stream of reverence, devotion, gratitude, and love that flows to Your Holiness from this poor heart never ceases, day or night.

Gyanamata

* * * * *

January 5, 1943
Your Birthday

My Divine Master,

My knowledge of your measureless and unceasing blessings seems very deep to me, though it falls short of being as deep as I could wish. Yet for a long time I have regarded my relationship to you as being that of a receiver, container, and, in some instances, a transmitter of your blessed vibrations. If you wanted for some reason to hold the streamlined train, and I were on board, it would not move until I got off.*

You speak of not having been demonstrative. I never expected nor sought what might be called a social or friendly relationship to Your Holiness. Even if you had offered it, I would not have been able to maintain it; because, in each of the brief moments in which I am in your presence, I am filled with the thought of your God-conscious state. I am silent, as in a temple.

* A reference to the miracle performed by Lahiri Mahasaya for his disciple Abhoya (recounted in Chapter 31 of *Autobiography of a Yogi*).

The reverence, gratitude, devotion, and love I feel for you come from deep down in the vibrationless region of my soul.

Gyanamata

* * * * *

Dear Children,

Yesterday you put the question, "What is the last word in discipleship; what would be the distinguishing mark of the perfect disciple?"

You know that I am always quiet when in the presence of the Master. This is not a pose, intended to win his approval, nor is it altogether because I know this to be the proper way to behave. It is because I have an inner feeling of stillness. I seem to be listening intently. So his words sink into my mind and heart to be pondered upon, sometimes for years. Because of this I often get the answer to a mental question in his very words.

Yesterday, when my mind asked me that question, it immediately flashed before me a scene that had taken place at Mt. Washington years ago. And I got my answer. It was the day of a certain student's spiritual wedding ceremony. We were gathering in front of the Center, and Paramahansaji was telling us where to stand, etc. He gave Mrs. ________ a red rose to wear. She said, "But I don't *want* a red rose. I want a pink one." He answered, "What *I* give, *you* take."

Here was my answer. The quick, or at least open, mind; the willing hands and feet—these, brought to perfection, would be the last word, the distinguishing mark, the very perfection of discipleship. "Be swift to meet Him, O my heart; be jubilant my feet!" I do not mean that we must like the order, whatever it may be. That will not matter if only there is the ready response.

How far off from the goal we are, O Lord! "Yet we love Thee and adore, Oh, for grace to love Thee more."

And so, dear young sister-disciples, I wish you all the joys of Christmas, knowing the greatest of these to be the surrender of the will to God. Meister Eckhart said: "In absolute obedience there is never any 'I will,' but only an unconditional renunciation of all that belongs to self." He also says that no man ever surrenders himself so perfectly in this life that he is unable to push it a little further.

I know I shall hear your screams of joy when you open your gifts on Christmas morning! As for me...well, I don't know what will happen when I open all those packages that lie on my floor under my Christmas tree! And I can only say a feeble "thank you" to the dear givers.

With love in God and Guruji,
from The Poor Sister,
Gyanamata

* * * * *

February 14, 1949

Dear _______,

If I could, I would like to engrave upon the heart of the disciple two basic truths: First, you can have only your own; and your own will surely come to you. Indeed, you cannot escape it. Second, that the Guru is always the guru, in every act and utterance, even if he is not consciously acting as such.

In our hearts, perhaps subconsciously, we really prefer what our karma gives to us to that which another receives, knowing that it is what we need. For the disciple to permit the thought that he is being unfairly treated to enter his mind is fatal. The will of God flows to the disciple through the Guru at all times. If we accept our discipline in the right spirit, it will strengthen our character as nothing else could.

With love always,
Gyanamata

* * * * *

To Ananda Mata (known at that time by her family name, Virginia Wright), who was later appointed by Paramahansaji to the Self-Realization Fellowship Board of Directors:

Dear Virginia,

I would have loved to see you, but feel it is better that you stay there with the Master. He needs the support of you all, even now that he has passed into a higher state. Thank you for telling me about him; it helps me, with what the others have told me, to follow him along Calvary. First the suffering, then ecstasy and *sabikalpa samadhi,* then *nirbikalpa samadhi,* the highest state of all, where the saint can look both ways at once, and see himself as man and God.* He was in that state before, only not as deeply.

What a high privilege to be with him!
Gyanamata

* In helping to lift the karmic load of disciples, a guru sometimes works out on his own body some of their karma. In his compassionate love, Paramahansaji lightened the burden of many a disciple, and for this reason the great master suffered certain physical disabilities during the last few years of his life. This is the "suffering" that Sister refers to here.

Regarding the two kinds of *samadhi* mentioned by her, the Guru explains: "In the initial states of God-communion (*sabikalpa samadhi*) the devotee's consciousness merges in the Cosmic Spirit; his life force is withdrawn from the body, which appears 'dead,' or motionless and rigid. The yogi is fully aware of his body condition of suspended animation. As he progresses to higher spiritual states (*nirbikalpa samadhi*), however, he communes with God without bodily fixation; and in his ordinary waking consciousness, even in the midst of exacting worldly duties." Both states are characterized by oneness with the ever new bliss of Spirit, but the *nirbikalpa* state is experienced by only the most highly advanced devotees.

Dear ________,

Last night after you left, ________ told me of the Master's refusal of material aid for his body, and some of the things he said. I at once understood his aim. He will not allow the God-consciousness to which he has attained to slip even a few inches lower. For us to suggest or try to persuade him to accept what *materia medica* offers would not only be useless, it would also be unkind. It might, I think, produce in him a sense of isolation and loneliness, to find that the group who are so near him were weak in faith, and turned to the doctors in moments like this, instead of to the power of God that flows through him.

Gyanamata

* * * * *

Sunday

Dear Faye and Virginia,

About the subject of the Master's work being carried on when he leaves the body: The work will undoubtedly be different, but it does not necessarily follow that it will be a difference of which the Master would disapprove. I think we should remember what Jesus said to the Apostles about his passing: "The Holy Ghost will bring to your remembrance whatsoever I have said unto you." So will it be in this case. The Holy Vibration will bring to your remembrance all things that your Master has taught you. Gratitude, devotion, love, and obedience to the founder of this work will be strengthened a hundredfold. Jesus said that the Holy Ghost, the Comforter, would also teach them all things, but would not come until he went away.*

* Gyanamata's prediction came true. Years later, Sri Daya Mata described her experience at the time Paramahansa Yogananda left his body: "As I knelt over my blessed Guru, I could see that his soul was leaving the body;

Please, dear sister-disciples, accept the thanks that comes straight from my heart for all you do for me. When I want anything, when I need any help, it is Faye and Virginia to whom I turn, and who listen to me with astonishing patience. Just here you are sure to say something about what I do for you. Well, I hope so, and I know how it is done: Because of my attitude toward His Holiness, I am able to remind you of things which perhaps your position so close to the Master makes you momentarily forget.

With love in God and Guruji,
Your Sister

---

and then a tremendous force entered my being. I say 'tremendous' because it was an overwhelming blissful force of love, peace, and understanding. I remember thinking, 'What is this?' My consciousness was lifted up in such a way that I could feel no sorrow, I could shed no tears; and it has been so from that day to this, because I know beyond any doubt that he is truly with me."

CHAPTER 6

"All I Know Is That I Must Please You"

Gyanamata could not bear the thought that there might be even the slightest misunderstanding between herself and her Guru. She clearly recognized the importance of honest, open communication in the guru-disciple relationship, and therefore wrote freely to Paramahansaji, telling him her innermost thoughts, not so much for his information—since she has said that the Guru already knew her innermost thoughts—but for the unfoldment of her own understanding. Paramahansaji has mentioned in his autobiography that the sensitive minds of highly advanced souls feel keen pain if any mistake is made in their conduct or their perception of truth.

These letters are very intimate; Gyanamata chastizes herself severely when she perceived a flaw in her character, or if she thought that she might have caused Paramahansaji any grief—so sincere was she in her desire for complete attunement with the Guru's wishes. "All I know," she wrote him, "is that I must please you."

Divine Master,

My mind works so slowly that it is just this moment that I see how dreadful what I said to you must have seemed. I express myself so badly at times; how could you possibly understand me?! I said that my prayer to you was to grant me sufficient length of days, and quietness of days, that I might feel God as Bliss before I leave the body. This sounds as if I wanted things made easier for me, that I wanted to be left alone to meditate! Oh, how could I ever have said such a thing—put words together that do not at all express my meaning!

My meaning was that since you are God in man made manifest, and that by your divine power you have healed me and lengthened my days, you would—by the same divine power, the power of your meditation—sufficiently lengthen them, and by your vibrations breathe quietness into my mind and life, that I might see Him before I die. But it sounded—what I wrote—as if I had no sooner commenced to work for you a little than I became tired and complaining. Oh, dreadful thought! Please permit me to do anything for you or the work that is possible.

And, oh, please give me a sign that you forgive my stupidity—it was nothing worse.

With deepest devotion,
Gyanamata

* * * * *

Wednesday, August 24

Divine Master,

I do not write these long-winded letters for your information—or, only very slightly. Sometimes there is something I wish you to know and, while you can intuitively find out anything that goes on if you wish to, still, for the sake of our own development, we ought to express ourselves occasionally to you. You are my mental and spiritual clearinghouse.

Yesterday I wrote you three times in one day; I wrote repeatedly, as the thoughts came to me, not only because I was sorry if I had given you cause for disappointment in me, but because I feared that if I did not do it quickly, the whole matter would pass out of your mind. My temperament does not allow me to be satisfied with a solution like that. If I have placed myself in the wrong, I *must* admit myself to be in the wrong and ask for forgiveness—especially if it is you whom I have displeased.

Your words to me on Monday night started me thinking; still more, what you said in class, until I could not evade the question: Did my earlier letter to you have a meaning, or possible interpretation, unsensed by me as I wrote it, that had made you think I was complaining, that I was worked too hard for the good of my meditation? I did not know, until you told me yesterday afternoon, that the devotee always feels this way about his meditation; but even if I had, it would not have made any difference. Once the question took possession of my mind, I could not rest until I stood before you and repudiated it.

As I begged you to read my letter immediately, my deep devotion to you, and an overwhelming sense of what I owe you, reduced me to tears. Even now, as I sit here quietly writing, or at any time when I think of you in this way, tears well up in my eyes. I can easily weep at any moment, if I think of that aspect of our relationship. I call it weeping for God—as indeed it is—for all the longing of my soul for Him I pour out to you in these letters, in the devotion of my heart, in the tears that the thought of you brings.

If I come upon you unexpectedly as I go about the [Mt. Washington] Center, I am transfixed inside, and I feel as if some great good had suddenly befallen me—as indeed it has, for you always look at me with blessing in your eyes. "This is not mawkish sentimentality," I tell myself. "It is the proper attitude of my soul toward my Guru—the vehicle of God." Is it surprising then, that feeling this way, I was overwhelmed at the thought of having disappointed you?

I do not mind being old. In many ways I like it. Even when under strain it has been, and will be more and more, the most peaceful and richest period of my life. But I very much dislike—indeed I detest—the outer physical signs of old age. If I ever behave in a weak or "old" manner, my soul feels indignant and outraged, as if I had insulted it unbearably. So, though I knew that my tears yesterday were justifiable, I was ashamed of shedding them before you.

When I asked you to make me a Sister, I did so purely for my own good. I did not consider that I had anything to offer the Center worthy of its acceptance. I thought everything would go on as before, and that probably I would remain in my room in seclusion more than ever. I even felt a little self-conscious about it, since I could not assume the duties that would be expected to go with it. I did it because I wanted to take a vow before God and Guru to banish all except Them from my mind, and give the last of my life to meditation.

What I most wanted to say about this is that I am very much surprised and flattered to find how my position is developing. It is not all title. There are many little things in which I find I can be useful, and the title gives me authority I would not otherwise have. The guests come to me to arrange the details of their life for them, and when I receive strangers and tell them that I am a Sister, I find that they are willing to talk and listen to me as they never did before. My help is asked by the regular workers. All this gives me great satisfaction.

While emotional outbursts are always to be avoided, and for myself I intensely dislike them, always feeling that I have degraded myself even if one seems to happen without my volition, still I am sure that they occasionally do good, if they go deep enough. I had one the other day which I mention only because I know you will be glad to hear that through it I found the cure for something that had been troubling me.

The cure lay in the resolute control of my mind by the operation of my will. I saw that there was no use to ask help from the guru, nor to put my trust in the deepening of meditation—I must help myself first. The mere thinking of this thought took effect immediately. I deliberately "forsook this mental upheaval" as I had vowed before God and you to do, and it took instantaneous effect. I have since had other experiences of my ability to instantly control my mind, *if I chose to do so.*

In concluding this letter, I ask a special favor of you—that you will not spare me on account of my age if I ever merit reproof. While still a little girl, I resolved that I would develop the strength of a man—and I detest and despise all signs of weakness in myself. I want to face all truth, about myself first of all, even—no, most of all—when it is painful. I want to be done forever with all delusions. Away with them! For I cannot be what I want to be until I face what I am. I would rather you said to me, "What is the matter with you? This is unworthy of you," than have you deal tenderly with me on account of an aging body, which I already repudiate as no part of my self. It would hurt me if you did speak this way, I admit it. But I prefer it to any kind of coddling. I would brace up, study my faulty action closely, and see wherein and why it had failed to please you. I have come to you for Self-realization, not self-pleasing.

From a heart that is weary of all save God, I thank you for your astonishing goodness to me.

With devotion that will never wane,
Gyanamata

P.S. I did not have an opportunity to thank you for including

Sri Gyanamata in front of Administration Building at SRF International Headquarters on Mt. Washington, 1935

me in the gathering last night. Your disciples were thrilled when they arrived at the theater and saw the large placard, announcing that Sid Grauman took pleasure in welcoming the distinguished guest, Swami Yogananda, and we stood long before it.* I was the first of my party to spy it, and point it out to the others. Then each one, as he saw it, beckoned to the others and pointed to it.

Your talk was beautiful. Your face was full of joy, and your words expressed a certain simplicity that I often note, wonder at, and especially admire in you. Only a dull and insensate person could have looked at your face and listened to your voice and words without feeling that love which made you incarnate, and which inspires you to toil daily for the sake of others. All, *all* for us!

* * * * *

My most blessed Master,

This morning I am filled with shame at the remembrance of my silent reception of your beautiful Christmas gift, and nothing will restore my self-respect except to tell you the secret reason—something I never expected to express to you nor to anyone else. I am doing it purely to please and to relieve myself. You, who are a discerner of the hearts of men, may have known it all along. Still, it probably escaped your attention because it is something so different

* Mr. Grauman had invited Paramahansaji to come to his famous Grauman's Chinese Theater in Hollywood to give a brief talk on the art of living.

Opposite: Self-Realization Fellowship International Headquarters, 1982. The octagonal structure at lower left is the Wishing Well Mandir, a shrine protecting Paramahansaji's spiritual wishing well. On the base of the well are the imprints of his hand- and footprints and the handprints of Gyanamata *(see also photos facing pages 184 and 185).*

from what you would expect from me. I am counting on the patience with which you always accept and read the thoughts and emotions that I from time to time pour out upon paper to you.

I have always desired, craved, and longed for a gift of a certain type from you. I had in mind no definite article, only that it must meet two essential requirements: It must have no intrinsic value, and you must feel the impulse to give it, without its being suggested to you. When I was initiated into sisterhood, I hoped that you would give me upon that occasion some small object, one that would be to me a token of the relationship between us. Since you did not do so, I had made one of those little Yogoda emblems* that I now wear on the end of a string of *tulsi* beads. But this was only the beginning of that desire, which has grown with time....

Then came the desire that you *make* something for me with your own hands, as you made the emblem over the Encinitas Temple door. A piece of wire twisted into a bangle for *me* by *you* would have been a treasure that could not have been purchased from me with the diadem of a king!

I know that I have accomplished something important for myself by telling you the truth about this. I shall never have this wish again. Perhaps I may find that I am now entirely out of the power of "Desire, my great enemy."†

And I am now free to thank you humbly for your beautiful gift, and to begin to enjoy possessing and wearing it.

With deep devotion,
Gyanamata

* The Self-Realization Fellowship/Yogoda Satsanga Society emblem, shown on the title page of this book.

† A reference to one of the chants in Paramahansa Yogananda's *Cosmic Chants.*

October 25, 1947

Dear ________,

We do not want to live in a cloud of delusion, especially where the Master is concerned. If we are not willing to look at ourselves in the mirror of his opinion of us and his wishes for us, how can we hope to reach the Divine Goal? We should always try to tune in with Master by telling him our reasons for something he questions, and studying carefully his objections.

We live, you and I, near a great spiritual power, but what will that avail us if we do nothing for ourselves? The Lord Buddha said: "Whatever a hater may do to a hater, or an enemy to an enemy, a wrongly directed mind will do him greater mischief. Not a mother, not a father will do so much, nor any other relatives; a well-directed mind will do us greater service."

I will close with these familiar words of Swami Sri Yukteswarji to His Holiness, our Master, when he was a sickly boy: "The mind has made you sick. The mind can also make you well."

Gyanamata

* * * * *

August 8, 1940

My beloved Master,

When I stood beside your car and talked the day you left for your retreat, I was quite sure you understood what I said. But now I am not sure I made myself plain, and so I am writing this; because I cannot, even for a moment, endure the thought that everything is not perfectly clear between yourself and me.

I had greatly desired to be alone during the time of your

absence from the Encinitas Hermitage. I need not go into the reason for this. It seems to be my temperament to seek seclusion, and persists in spite of repeated disappointments—still, I do think I have improved a little. When the disciples told me that a trip was planned, they said that you wanted Miss ________ to come and stay with me. To this I said nothing, because if it meant just a little extra feeling of security to you to have someone here, I would not spoil it by any selfish wish of mine. But later, they asked me to tell them frankly which I preferred: a companion, or to be alone. I then knew that I need not hesitate to speak on your account, so I told them I would greatly prefer to be alone. I may say here, in parenthesis, that I had one good reason for this desire. Many people wish to be alone just to avoid work and trouble. I wanted to learn how to use solitude for the good of my soul, for I always feel that solitary days contain a special jewel of realization, could I but find the way to use them rightly.

Then the disciples told me that you would want the Mt. Washington devotees to come down and enjoy the beach.

Lastly, they told me that I must not work for those who come down, that I must let them cook and wait upon themselves. That this was your wish, and that you always told them that if they came down when I was alone, they must depend upon themselves. I knew this already, because they had told me themselves; but I also knew, by experience, that some of them did not take your order very seriously.

Then I began to think of myself, and of how their visits would affect me. I knew that I was unable to make a calm, cold-blooded resolution to let them take care of themselves; either it would be impossible for me to live up to it, since it is absolutely opposed to the character I have tried to build up; or I would become very much disturbed in my mind if I watched for consideration and thoughtfulness and did not receive them. I have been in similar situations many times, and I well knew that the thing for me to do was to use an affirmation I made for myself many years ago: "If I am able, of course I will do it cheerfully and *willingly*. If I am ill, and so unable, nobody will expect the service of me."

So this is what I had in mind when I stood beside your car and told you that I must consider my own state of consciousness which was more important to me than anything else. When you said, "All right," I thought you meant you would let them come, and that you consented to my doing my best to make them happy.

So, after writing this to you, I am dismissing the subject from my mind. I shall not selfishly seek my own rest and pleasure. I will *willingly* do whatever is in my power to make them happy and comfortable. I can hear you say, "Make them an omelette, Sister." That shall be their main dish for dinner.

The only reward I ask is a clear, undimmed consciousness, and your smile. It is entirely impossible for me to have peace or happiness unless I see approval in your face.

With deep devotion,
Gyanamata

* * * * *

My blessed Master,

For this cause was I born and came to this hour: in a humble way to help you and your disciples. How I came to be ready for this work, even in a small degree, is a deep mystery to me. I can only rejoice, and thank God that it is so. But it is marvelous that it should be true of me.

I am very glad you told me that you want me to continue with my duties if I am able, for now I know exactly what your wish is, and need not worry as I have been doing. You had spoken to me several times about resting, and I thought I might be acting in a willful manner in continuing on with all my duties. Now I am free to follow the course that is most pleasing to me—that is, to keep on with everything you have given me to do, as I am able, until you give me the word to stop.

All I know is that I must please you. Somewhere in the Hindu scriptures it says that if the guru is pleased with one, the opinions of the gods matter not at all, and I have exactly that feeling. I do not reason out why it should be so—I simply feel that it *is*.

Whether I have the opportunity to see you or not, I am ever at your feet, taking the dust from them, and pouring over them the essence of my devotion. If I could never see you, this would continue the same, for it is the settled attitude of my mind, and does not cease, day or night.

Gyanamata

CHAPTER 7

Renunciation

Though already along in years when she entered the Self-Realization Fellowship ashram, Sri Gyanamata embraced the monastic life with great zeal and a natural, mature understanding of the renunciant path to God. Though many of the letters in this chapter were written specifically for the benefit of the monastic disciples, the truth they express is applicable to any sincere seeker. Having actively sought God for years before entering the ashram, Gyanamata was well aware that the essential aspect of renunciation—for the householder as well as for the monastic—is inner surrender of earthly attachments, and the cultivation of the one desire to seek God and follow His will.

To all who sought her counsel, regardless of their outer role in life, she recommended the inner renunciation of lesser desires and the practice of the yoga meditation techniques taught in the *Self-Realization Fellowship Lessons.* This, she declared, is the highest path to true freedom.

December 1940

Dear ________,

Happening to know that having to give up your room so often disturbs you, I would like to tell you some of my experiences. It was this same unhappy attitude of mind that brought about the greatest battle of my whole spiritual life. In retrospect everything else seems easy by comparison.

I could understand why I must give up wrong things, but I did not know that the seeker for God must lay all at

His feet, must hold *nothing* back. I do not remember that I ever wanted the best for myself. I was willing to share. This is the way I remember myself in the years that have passed away like a dream, leaving me nothing but peace where I remember that I lived up to my ideal; pain if, when I sit in judgment upon myself, I see that I fell short. What I could not understand was why everything must go; why things that were right, that were mine, that harmed no one, why all the dear little rights and privileges must be taken from me. But they were so taken by God. He was thrusting me out of a life of dependence upon small comforts into one that should be lived for Him alone.

I want to tell you that this matter of a room and place to keep my clothes caused me a great deal of pain—such was my temperament. I had only two little places that I could call my own. These were two attics, one on each side of the house. One was cobwebby and had no window. Here I tacked a sheet to the framework of the walls and hung my clothes. In the other I put an army cot, and there in the early morning I went to meditate. All that I asked in the way of a room was just a little corner that could be mine under all circumstances.

It was during this period that a good teacher came into my life. He had heard of me from mutual friends, and came to Seattle on purpose to see me. He questioned me about my life. I told him everything....His face, as I talked, showed intense feeling, but no pity, no indignation on my account. When I finished, he said quietly, "You have nothing that is your own. You must not cling to phenomena." It was as if a light—clear, white, and very bright—had been turned on in my brain. An unforgettable experience! If he had been sorry for me or tried to comfort me; if he had blamed others and said I was unfairly treated, he would not have touched me. He would not have helped me. But he recognized me as a seeker for God.

He forced me to face the truth proper to my state. He cared not at all whether it was painful to me or not. And from that moment I, who had been blind, saw. I saw that an attitude that is perfectly justifiable for a householder is poisonous for one who has stepped upon the path of complete renunciation, holding the soul in bondage. I saw that God is a relentless Master, never accepting anything short of perfection, never satisfied if only a part is laid at His feet.

We thank Thee, O Father, for Thine inexorable demands upon us. For refusing to listen to the tearful, little, complaining, whining self. And we pray Thee, deliver us from that self, that we may live in Thee.

Gyanamata

* * * * *

Dear ________,

Please take others into consideration in making your decision. One of the dangers that threaten all who take up the life of renunciation is that of becoming too self-centered. We have to watch ourselves, analyze our reactions, acts and emotions, and we may see that the dominant thought is, "How does it affect me?"

His Holiness Swami Sri Yukteswarji's admonition ought to be in our minds constantly: "Learn to behave." It covers so much: Learn to think of others. Learn to treat others as you yourself would like to be treated. Learn to suffer silently and patiently. *Learn to die to self that you may live in God.*

Do not always ask, "What will *I* get out of it?" Say instead, "I wonder how I can help." View the plans of the group from the standpoint of the others, not just yourself—remembering that when "the *I*, the *me*, and the *mine* is gone—then the work of the Lord is done."

With love,
Sister

* * * * *

Blessed Master,

I am a Sister and an old woman. (How natural it seems to write "Sister"; how strange, "old woman.") If the people in the village do not see that the monastic robes I wear are the most suitable and comfortable for me, I am sorry; but their opinions do not touch me. When you initiated me, I turned my back once and for all on the world and its ways.

"If thou forsakest the world, thou comest into That whereof the world is made; and if thou losest thy life, and comest to have thine own power faint, then thy life is in That for whose sake thou forsakest it, viz., in God from whom it came into the body." That I be not disobedient to this heavenly vision is the deepest desire of my heart, however poorly I live up to it.

With changeless reverence, gratitude,
devotion, and love,
Gyanamata

* * * * *

For her sister-disciples, Gyanamata wrote, on December 16, 1934, the following message and "Prayer for a Sister":

Do not judge your fitness for *sannyas* by the things you know or can do. You might be letter-perfect in the philosophical teachings, in the practice of the techniques; you might be able to stand before an audience and deliver a good lecture; you might be ready to instruct a class of students, yet you might not be prepared for *sannyas*.

The test is whether or not there is a fire of devotion burning upon the altar of your heart. If there is, and if it burns steadily through joy and pain, through success and the gratification of your innocent wishes, and through denial and the frustration of your desires, you are ready right now. The rest can be acquired as you go along, for sisterhood is a state of constant striving for higher and higher perfection along all lines.

Prayer for a Sister

Teach me to meditate until I intuit Thee.
Teach me to pray until I find Thee.
Teach me to demand until I receive Thy Kingdom.
Teach me to seek Thee until I find Thee.
Teach me to love Thee whether it is Thy pleasure
  to reveal Thyself or not.
Teach me to meditate until I feel Thy Bliss.
Teach me to seek Thee until Thou dost answer.
Teach me to feel Thy Peace, until Thou dost
  reveal Thyself as Bliss.

Gyanamata

* * * * *

April 12, 1945

My blessed Master,

Thank you for your note. What you say about visiting me draws from me this question: If spiritually you are ever at my side when I need you, and your prayers are ever with me, have I not the highest? Ought I then to desire the lower, the earthly? No.

Among all my regrets for my imperfections, all my wishes that I had been more worthy since I came to you from Seattle, this one ideal stands out—I call it the one perfect thing of my life: If I ever felt a little human wish for something I could not have, this question was immediately presented to my soul, "What did you come here for?" The answer was always, "For God alone." In an instant my vision was clear and unobstructed again. This has been the unshakable, immovable fact of my discipleship. In our relations, yours has been all the merit, mine the great reward, and will be from everlasting to everlasting.

With devotion as unceasing as your blessings,
Gyanamata

* * * * *

Dear Miss ________,

I have given your letter of August 12 careful consideration. You and your cousin have decided that there is no question we cannot answer. But there is one. It is this: "How can one have his cake and eat it too?" Your cousin wants to enjoy forbidden pleasures of the flesh and at the same time possess spiritual peace and security. This cannot be done, for one cannot serve both God and mammon. It is up to her to choose.

She stands at this very moment at the fork of the road, and must make the decision for herself. She may have a truly spiritual career, leading the souls of her listeners to the very gates of heaven, or she may "eat husks with the swine." The sensual life can end only one way—in illness, suffering, and disillusionment. Having done that which places her peace, safety, happiness, and her career in jeopardy, she seeks the remedy from God. He will not fail her, but she will have to face the consequences of her actions in some way or other. And she will have to be stern with herself.

I will pray for her that she be led to the right action that she must do; and that she may, after having passed through a purifying ordeal, find peace in God. In the world lie all the sufferings of the flesh; in God is peace. Whoever would have the one must let the other go.

Gyanamata

* * * * *

Dear Miss ________,

Answering your question about our teachings on the necessity of overcoming desire, they are not out of harmony with Christian teachings. In fact, they are exactly the same. If they ever appear to be different, it is because the same truth may be put into different words. They are intended for those who have turned their faces to the rising sun of Self-realization, who wish to die to the lower self that they may live in God.

You say: "The Christian ideal uses desire as the great motive-power of life." Yes, but desire for what? Is it not for better things, for higher ideals, until the ultimate desire for God is reached? The desires that our teachings tell you to "kill" are those for money, for position, for self-gratification —and even these are allowable in moderation and as aids to development. "Kill" is not a good word to use in this connection, for it implies a force that is neither desirable nor necessary. If you will refer to *The Science of Religion,* you will find that the very heart and soul of the instruction given about desires are contained in these words: "We should put a hedge around our wants." That is, we should control them. Do not let them grow into rampant weeds that will impede your progress and drag down your mind from God.

In your own case, desire led you to the point where you surrendered your will to God, saying, "Thy will be done," and then found in that renunciation the fulfillment of all your desires. This is the very goal to which our teachings on the control of desire will lead the sincere student. The human will is then one with the divine will; and the soul, thus free from entanglements, will make rapid progress.

You rightly say that progress is a matter of application, and this is true, not only of you, but of everyone else. We have no teachings, no techniques, that will in any way take the place of the student's own effort. Personal zeal and hard work are absolutely necessary to success. But the techniques of concentration and meditation, which you have learned, and the technique of Kriya Yoga, will do quickly what surrender to the will of God, devotion, and study of the scriptures take years to accomplish. A burning fire of devotion will bring a sure reward, but why not take the aid of a scientific technique?

Gyanamata

* * * * *

June 16, 1939

Dear _______,

We must go on learning renunciation until we have nothing more of our own. Whether we realize it or not, all the storm of unrest arises from self-will. Accept everything that happens during the day as coming from God. He is always the Giver, both of pain and joy.

Sometimes I glimpse, as a fair land lying just beyond me, a state of consciousness from which all unnecessary and harmful words and feelings are banished—sarcasm, resentment, wit and jokes with sharp points—and Love, which includes patience and understanding, rules.

The entrance to this fair country is barred against us as long as we prefer to listen to the voice of our lower self and be ruled by its demands.

With love in God and Guruji,
Sister

CHAPTER 8

Wisdom From Gyanamata

For many years, Gyanamata was responsible for replying to letters requesting spiritual counsel from the Mother Center. In answering the questions of others, Sister demonstrates her natural ability to penetrate to the core of the most difficult personal problems or metaphysical subjects with her intuitive insight.

The following are extracts from some of her letters, written mainly to Self-Realization students. Also included are some condensed "nuggets of wisdom" from her diary—simple notes she jotted down, which help to reveal the depth and clarity of her thought.

Dear ________,

What you speak of as "the baptism of the Holy Ghost"* the SRF teachings call "the baptism of *Aum* or Holy Vibration." It may come upon the disciple, if he is ready, when he is meditating; or it may be imparted to him by the touch of his master. On the day of Pentecost it came with great power upon the Apostles, who were gathered together awaiting the blessing promised them by Christ.† Theirs was an exceptional case, though no doubt the same thing has happened to other seekers after God-realization. The lives of Jesus' disciples were completely changed after they had experienced spiritual immersion in *Aum*—they became as new men and wrought mighty works.

* John 1:32–34.

† Acts 1:4–5; 2:1–4.

In your own case, I think you should feel that if you are fortunate enough to receive the grace of God in such full measure, it is worth paying any price. In other words, the scorn of some member of your family should not influence you. Pray that God give you what is best for you, and do not fear any consequences.

If you do not receive the blessings of the baptism of the Holy Ghost or *Aum* Vibration, do not be worried or anxious. Keep ever seeking a higher state of consciousness. God will give you the reward in His own good time and way.

Gyanamata

* * * * *

Dear ________,

I believe you will better understand the Master's teaching about the "origin of evil" if you keep in mind that there are different planes of being. On the highest plane of all, there is nothing but undifferentiated Spirit—God. Here Satan does not appear, but neither do men and women. In God there is neither John nor Mary. On the lower plane, the plane of manifestation, Satan appears as a necessity, for this is the field of opposites: light and darkness, heat and cold, joy and pain, laughter and tears, good and evil.

If all men always used their God-given reason aright, Satan would disappear; but they do not, and out of that fact arise two other opposites—love and hate. And from hate springs jealousy, envy, greed, murder, and all the rest of Satan's brood. It is possible that man would not have much strength if it were not for his long fight with Satan; on this plane, strength of character is developed by the fight that must be waged.

Never forget that Satan's abode is in man's own consciousness. A consciousness filled with God—with love and longing for the highest—gives no place to Satan; he flees, vanishing as does darkness from a room when light is turned on.

Gyanamata

* * * * *

Dear Mr. ______,

Your letter of June 9 received. We are sorry to hear of the difficult position you find yourself in. Religious beliefs sometimes separate dear friends. This should not be so, and would not be so if the persons concerned had greater understanding. There is only one God, and He is the Father of us all. Why should His children quarrel about Him?

The trouble with sectarianism in religion is that it places too much importance upon mere intellectual belief. But is mere belief enough? No. To simply hold to a dogma or formula of words will not save anyone. It must be a faith so deeply imbedded in the soul that it brings Christ to birth in the consciousness of that man. A member of any denomination may have this living faith, or may be without it; the mere fact that he subscribes to a certain creed does not necessarily prove its presence in his heart.

We are trying to help you deepen your actual realization of spiritual truth. Earnestly ask yourself whether our teachings have helped you or not. If the honest answer to this question is yes, then be faithful to them; and at the same time, you will prove to others—by the uprightness of your life and your increasing spirituality—that you have a living faith in God and the Lord Jesus Christ.

Very sincerely yours,
Gyanamata

Dear Mrs. ________,

You ask for a list of the benefits that Yogoda* gives. It teaches you to keep your body strong, fit and free from pain by proper exercise. It tells you the effect of food, and advises you what kinds to eat if you wish to be well. It frees you from all kinds of fear—fear of poverty, of sickness, of loneliness, of death. It will explain to you that you need not be a failure—that you may have success in your chosen work, and may find true and congenial friends.

It will teach you how to think positively, and will provide you with mental nourishment that will turn your mind into a storehouse of jewelled thoughts. It will teach you to look forward to the future with calm certainty.

Best of all, it will teach you by the practice of the lessons on concentration and meditation to turn religious belief into certainty. It will turn "God" from a word of three letters into a glorious realization, a well of calmness, peace, and bliss. Under the guidance of my Master it has done all this and much more for me, and many students all over the country can bear testimony to the truth of these words.

What are you prepared to give in return? Will you give steadfast loyalty, patience, and earnest endeavor till the goal of Bliss is reached?

Very sincerely yours,
Gyanamata

* * * * *

Dear ________,

The mind of man is really *one,* though when we analyze

* A term used by Paramahansa Yogananda to describe his teachings when he first founded his work in India (from Sanskrit *yoga,* union with God, harmony, equilibrium; and *da,* that which imparts). In the West, he later translated these meanings into the name Self-Realization.

its functions, we divide it into three parts: conscious, subconscious, and superconscious.

It is the conscious mind that you are using when the things connected with the senses of sight, hearing, smell, taste, and touch engage your attention. This mind sleeps at night. You contact or use the subconscious mind when you remember past events during the day, or dream at night. So-called forgotten events, even of our past incarnations, are not really forgotten; they have merely slipped out of our conscious mind into the subconscious, and may be brought up again. The state of superconsciousness is above both. It is the realm to which we ascend during meditation. It is here that we realize ourselves as souls independent of the body, and it is here that we contact God as deep peace and Bliss-consciousness.

Gyanamata

* * * * *

Dear ________,

You ask, "What vocation should I follow to increase my income?" We are asking Paramahansaji to pray for you. By the power of his prayer may you be guided to the position and work for which you are best fitted.

Since you have been a Self-Realization student for several years, you no doubt know that prayer, when offered by a master, is not the mere repetition of words. It is the sending out of powerful vibrations that draw toward the person prayed for the desired good. You must do your part by holding a receptive attitude of mind, being firmly convinced that the power of his prayer can help you.

Also, you must surrender your will to the Divine Will. The fact that you want a certain thing does not prove that it is the best thing for you, nor that you may have it immediately.

You may have karma to work out first. But if you will persist in holding the right attitude, practice meditation, and keep your eyes and ears open, your own *must* come to you. The practice of the techniques that you have received in the lessons will give you the power to draw to you what your needs demand, and will also raise your consciousness to a plane where you shall desire only those things that contribute to your highest good.

You further ask, "How can I change the attitudes of others?" This must be accomplished by your kind treatment of them, and by sending vibrations of love and goodwill to them when in meditation. You must not feel resentment because this position, to which you say you are rightly entitled, is withheld from you. Resentment is disastrous in its effects, both upon the character and upon the circumstances of one's life; and is a very effectual barrier, shutting out both material and spiritual benefits. If you can completely banish resentment from your mind, then you will automatically be able to treat this person in such a manner that his attitude toward you will be changed. There is no other method of changing the attitude of a person than this: kindness and faith in the good qualities he possesses (these you must manifest when you contact him), and the use of prayer vibrations.

We would like to answer the thought that seems to underlie your letter. There is no quick way of acquiring yogic powers, an expansion of consciousness, or a high degree of spirituality. It is a step-by-step process. The techniques must be practiced patiently and persistently, with the firm determination *never* to give up until the desired goals are reached. What you are in this life is the result of your past lives. Begin, then, at once; and build for yourself better than you have in the past. You are your own law giver. You are not being offered just beautiful theories, but techniques that are based upon scientific principles, and that have been discovered, tested, and proved by the masters of India. Be faithful, be determined; and you shall prove their truth and value for yourself.

Gyanamata

* * * * *

Dear Mr. ________,

Remember that relaxation is of utmost importance in meditation. In your case, because of your physical disability, relaxation may not be perfect; but do not be discouraged on that account. We all have something to overcome. Just hold a steady, unwavering determination to succeed. Say, "The sky may fall, but I shall never give up."

Your other question is regarding the Master's teachings about the importance of a healthy body. One should strive by every means in his power to gain physical health, if he hasn't already achieved it; and if he has, to keep and maintain it by obeying the laws of health. No one can deny that a strong, healthy body, with a straight back and spine, is a very great asset in any walk of life.

But though illness is undesirable, it is not an insurmountable obstacle. The only obstacle is the failure to learn to concentrate and meditate upon God. This means the turning of the whole mental and spiritual life toward God; it means filling the mind and consciousness with thoughts of God. I would like to suggest that Paramahansa Yogananda's book *Whispers from Eternity* would aid you greatly in doing this. In studying the *Lessons,* if the meaning of any paragraph is not clear at first, return to it again and again, and at last you are sure to grasp it.

The thing for you to do at the present time is to render

yourself receptive to our teachings and help by meditation, by prayer, by study, and by following your doctor's orders. Perhaps someday you will be able to visit Mt. Washington and have the inspiration and help of a personal interview with Paramahansaji. The eagerness with which you read books on the Hindu philosophy and absorb the truth of its teaching proves that your soul, after many incarnations, is awake, and ready to commence the return trip to God.

You are fortunate to have a natural appreciation for one of life's most beautiful pleasures: music. It is the language of the soul, and you can sing your prayers to God. As you say: "Beautiful music can lift one out of the mire of the humdrum everyday life; it can talk to the soul." I have told you to follow the orders of your doctor, but do not listen to any doctor when he tells you that you will never be able to sing—or do anything else—again. Nothing is impossible to God, and He performs miracles of healing every day. Just stand by, and do your part.

That "something" which has urged you on, telling you that you *can* be happy, is the God dwelling in your soul, the Self you are trying to realize. Be of good courage. He will lead you through all to the Goal.

Gyanamata

* * * * *

Dear Mrs. ________,

You will remember that over a month ago, when you told me some of your undesirable phenomenal experiences in meditation, I promised to write to you, because we did not have time then to talk. Then, a little later, we spoke on the same subject and you said that the experiences had kept up; and because they had, you thought it indicated that "that was the way you were intended to be."

Ever since then I have wished to express myself to you; however, many things have kept me from doing so. But I know that since I have the idea that *possibly* I may be able to help you, I will have no mental rest until I try to do so.

1st. I want to remind you of what Paramahansaji said to you when you told him about these peculiar experiences. He said, "Resist them." These two words ought to have prevented you from entertaining the idea that you are *intended* to experience such things; and they contain all the advice you really need if you will only follow it up. When I write as I am about to do, I am only enlarging and explaining what the Guru has already said to you.

2nd. We cannot say that because a thing happens to us, and happens persistently, that this proves it to be a necessary experience. That idea would justify all the follies that distort and mar our lives! Under that theory a drunkard could say: "The craving for liquor comes daily. Why do I have it if I was not intended to drink? I am sure God *intended* me to be this way." No! A thousand times no! The victim of a terrible temper could say: "I was born this way. When I am annoyed, when my will is crossed, I see red and want to kill someone. I am sure I was intended to be this way."

A little thought will show you that this is a silly idea, and that the underlying principle of self-control applies to you. This life is not a bed of roses, dear Mrs. ________; it is a field of battle in which our constant effort must be to become something which we are not "naturally." All of Paramahansaji's teachings and techniques have the one end of showing the beauty of holiness; they teach the natural, average man or woman how to become a saint.

3rd. It may be that your particular temperament, or something in your karma, ordained that you were to begin the process of spiritual development by going off temporarily in the wrong direction. But if you take the wrong turn when on a journey, you must immediately rectify it as soon as your mistake is pointed out to you—otherwise you never will reach your destination. So it is with you.

4th. What must you do, then? The whole process is indicated by Paramahansaji's words to you: "Resist it." When the peculiar feelings and manifestations come, shake yourself out of them. Calm yourself. These experiences are not caused by, nor are they a part of, true meditation. Fill your consciousness with thoughts of God. Consider what the desired goal of meditation is. It is pure God-consciousness. Stillness. Above all, do not encourage the manifestations in any way. Do you know that a drunken man may, if he wishes, "pet" the symptoms of drunkenness and make them worse? Or he may sober himself by an effort of the will and calmly wait for the symptoms to disappear. You may do just the same thing. You *must,* if you want to enjoy the bliss of God-realization.

5th. Has anyone told you how Paramahansa Yogananda's body becomes when he goes into *samadhi*? It is motionless—heart, lungs, muscles, the whole frame. *But his soul is with God, drinking the nectar of the Spirit.* Does not that thought thrill you? Do you not want this very day to commence to use his techniques as they are intended to be used—with common sense, discrimination, and will power—in order that what he is, you may someday be? Then follow his advice: Resist the follies you told me of, and learn to meditate properly.

6th. Consider how fortunate you are. You have found the Guru. He has called to you; and not to you alone, but to your husband and daughter. "We are all of one mind," your husband said to me one day. God has ordained that you three shall move toward Him hand in hand, but you must patiently rectify your mistakes, and never give up, no matter what happens.

May God bless you, and if I can help by making suggestions, please let me do so. It will make me so happy.

With love in God and Guruji,
Gyanamata

* * * * *

Dear ________,

In regard to your sex troubles I want to ask if you have a copy of Swami Yogananda's *Scientific Healing Affirmations*? In it he gives advice to those troubled in this way. I suggest that you also practice concentrating at the point between the eyebrows, thinking that the sex force is being drawn up to the brain, where it can be used for mental and spiritual purposes. Do this as many times as you like, or as often as seems necessary, always holding firmly to the thought that this force is being drawn upwards.

Consider what a difference is made in a man's character by a change in the object upon which his desire fastens itself. You will see that you can give up your desire for lower pleasures and attach that same desire to a higher object, if you will to do so. A little illustration will make my meaning quite plain:

As long as a man has no goal for which he is working, he spends his money easily and carelessly. He hardly knows what it goes for. But what a change takes place if he commences earnestly to desire something that he can obtain only if he first saves up a certain sum of money! Perhaps he wants to go to college, or to travel, or to marry. He now saves every possible cent.

As with the man above, so with you. Your physical infirmity and your desire for self-development are the means that God is using to awaken your soul—to call you from the lower to the higher life. In order to answer this call, you must endure and work, study, and practice, always with firm determination never to give up, no matter what obstacles you encounter upon the path.

The life energy is the very instrument with which you work for spiritual awakening. It is the fund you have saved in the bank. If you spend it, dissipate it in excessive sex pleasure, you will have no strength to fight for the higher life. But if you will save it, hoard it, and lead it upward to the brain, you may use it for creative work and for Self-realization. A thrilling thought, a glorious possibility!

Gyanamata

P.S. Do not be discouraged. Many great saints have had to fight the same battle. St. Francis of Assisi is an example. He fought, and he won the fight.

* * * * *

Notes, in Gyanamata's handwriting—points she intended to cover in writing to a student:

1st. Teach yourself to think of God as a loving Father, then you will not fear Him.

2nd. Human fathers and mothers are sometimes cruel; God is never cruel, because He is divine, perfect.

3rd. Our sufferings do not come from Him. They are the result of our ignorance. We suffer because we love wrong things, and suffering comes as a result of our actions.

4th. Children born in rich, comfortable homes, who have kind parents, often run away, because they are willful and think they will be happier if they are "free."

5th. Likewise, we have run away from our Heavenly Father.

6th. He lets us suffer because He knows that the suffering will teach us to be good and to return to our heavenly home.

7th. You need not fear good spirits. You yourself are a spirit in a body of flesh and blood.

8th. You protect yourself from bad people by keeping away from them. Protect yourself from bad spirits by thinking of God. They do not like to come, cannot come, where God is. So fill your mind with thoughts of God.

* * * * *

Nuggets of wisdom—provocative thoughts from Gyanamata's diary:

Sleep

The human body is a lump of flesh. Sleep is a passive, unconscious way of approaching the soul. Condition of sleep: pseudo attempt of soul to reach Spirit. Soul connected with body is called ego. The omnipresent bird of life is imprisoned in a cage of bones and must be made free. Rest does not mean unconsciousness. Consciousness is never tired. Nature is the body of God. He works in it all the time. He never sleeps. Rest is nothing but a relative state of the mind. Constant sleep drugs the soul. The more meditation, the less sleep needed. It is vital to control the desire to sleep.

Pain

Harmonious thoughts do not produce pain. Pain comes from one thought contradicting another.

Detachment/Happiness

The ego loves change. Love of change must not be applied to principles. No one shall ever speak the "last word" that gives the standard of life; the best standard is Truth, which gives happiness. That which gives unhappiness is bad. Both conscious and unconscious habits must be broken up. We are all the victims of certain vibrations of matter. If we desire, we can change these habits. Sensory relaxation means not only detachment from the senses, but from habits. We always deal with subconsciousness and consciousness, rarely with superconsciousness. Enjoy, but do not be attached. Say: "I need only Spirit to live." Nothing really "gives" happiness, it is merely the gratification of desire. When desire is gratified, happiness comes.

Light/Energy

Sensory relaxation from eyes. Closing eyes produces darkness. Converged eyes, half light and half darkness. Eyes only intended for certain vibrations. Anything that hides light is darkness. First step: Concentrate on middle horizon seen with converged eyes. Why do we see light most in the head? Because brain is filled with light current. The light seen is the life force. When eyes are converged, nerves squeeze out light. People of understanding talk little. Eyes have wonderful power and current. Material light and darkness have blinded us to the light of life force. Light seen through two causes: will, and the withdrawal of energy. Spiritual eye contains all perceptions of universe. All is made of consciousness and energy.

Work/Ambition

We want to work here as princes, not as beggars. Between activities, be relaxed. Never dwell upon what you cannot do or have. As the Master says, "Child busy with play, youth with sex, old age with worry. Who weeps for God?" To be unknown, but beloved of God, should be the highest ambition. Earthly experiences a process of destruction of delusion. In God wildest dreams are realized.

Teachers' Training

Love consists in usefulness. Parents, companions, God—loved for usefulness. Every teacher must strive to increase degree of usefulness. Must know laws of etiquette, and yet have a tremendous sense of independence. Teacher must have experience, but must be above all, and able to express himself clearly and to the point when necessary. The more you are one with God, the more useful you will be. Do not seek greatness, seek spirituality. Increase your conviction. Be just to yourself. Do not deceive yourself. Meditate at night, and pray till God answers. Try to feel the Father in your students.

CHAPTER 9

"More and Better"

Through her words and especially through her example, Sri Gyanamata made it explicit that once a spiritual aspirant has set his feet firmly on the path that is right for him, the sole desire becomes simply to do "more and better" in following it. Whether giving of herself in service to others, or quietly practicing the presence of God within, Gyanamata's efforts reflected perfect attunement with the spirit as well as the letter of her Guru's counsel: "It can always be deeper."

May 10, 1946

My divine and blessed Master,

The poet Browning said that courage was courage only when you felt the serpent of fear writhe beneath your feet. I believe I understand this. It was what I meant when I said to you that if you sent me out into the darkness, and I went without hesitation, though afraid, that was courage. For if one never knows the sensation of fear, can one be called courageous?

I well understand the goal that you wish me to dwell upon and finally reach—complete forgetfulness of the body in the thought of God and in His service. I try to overcome my weakness by dwelling on your life in which there is never a thought for anything but the salvation of those who have taken refuge with you. I spent years reading and rereading the lives of the saints who "climbed the steep ascent of heaven in peril, toil, and pain." Now I seldom read.

I don't need to, for in my hour of need their words float on the surface of my mind, like leaves on a pool. I pick them up and "feed on them in my heart, by prayer"—and upward look—"with thanksgiving." Daily I put forth my God- and Guru-given strength to adjust myself to life in this completely changed body. In hours of concentration, or perhaps weakness, when I need them very much, the words of the holy ones come to me.

Just now I am reading a most wonderful book. The title is: *The Saints that Moved the World.** They are St. Anthony, the saint of renunciation; St. Augustine, the saint of the intellect; St. Francis, the saint of love; St. Ignatius, the saint of will power; St. Teresa, the saint of ecstasy. The author puts something into his book that he has gained by profound study and discipline. I thought I knew all about the life of St. Francis, but I found I did not know the half. At times when reading I am stopped by the thought that the best I have ever offered God, can ever hope to offer Him, is but a teaspoonful of water compared to the ocean that lies outside the Hermitage. But though my own smallness is thrown into such strong relief by these saints who reached God by hewing footholds in the solid rock that towered above them, my joy is so great that such giants, such things can be, that I walk around the Hermitage in a dream of happiness.

As I look back over the years, I am reminded of something I said to ______ long ago: "If I were younger and stronger, I would show you!" "What would you do, Sister?" she said, laughing at me. I believe she thought I would say, "Teach" or "Lecture on the platform"; but my answer was, "The same things I do every day, only more and better." That is it. That is my only ambition. *More and Better.*

Gyanamata

* By René Fülöp-Miller (New York: Thomas Y. Crowell Company, 1945).

Dear______,

There is a mistake that we all need to guard against: A few days of happiness, of bliss, do not mean that the fight is over; it has to be waged again and again against our only real enemy, the self.

You have endeared yourself so much to me that I cannot bear to think of your losing ground. So fight on, and never think of giving up, even for a minute. Take firm hold of the Guru's robe, and let nothing unclench your fingers. In one of the initiations, he says, "Ask the help of the Guru again and again." Obey this order to the limit. Be with him all you can—remember, he is "up there" as much, if not more, than he is here. His company can save you. Constantly ask him never to stop praying for you until you are safe. May God bless you—and I know He will.

With love in God and Guruji,
Sister

* * * * *

July 1, 1949

My divine and ever-blessed Master,

The 20th of this month will be the seventeenth anniversary of my initiation into *sannyas.*

The years pass in review before me, and leave me with two thoughts: The work performed by me—it could have been so much better done. My devotion to God and Guruji—it could have been so much deeper. The flame burning in my heart could have burned so much higher, have been so much brighter, so much more intense, if my only and constant prayer had been: "Change me."

Opposite: Paramahansa Yogananda and Sri Gyanamata on the grounds of the Encinitas Ashram Center, 1941

So long Thy power has blest me, sure it still
Will lead me on,
O'er moor fen, o'er crag and torrent, till
The night is gone.*

Gyanamata

* * * * *

July 10, 1948

Divine Master,

"Kabir says: Verily he has no fear, who has such a guru to lead him to the shelter of safety!"†

I wish I could remember your exact words to me on Thursday night. They pointed me to the pathway not only of safety, but of peace; and I knew it was the voice of God speaking.

But the spirit of them sank into my heart, and awakened the recollection of words spoken by you to me several years ago. Whatever I am, or am striving to be, they apply perfectly: "It can always be deeper." I have not only the exact words, but the spirit of them, too.

"Kabir says: It is the Spirit of the quest which helps; I am the slave of this Spirit of the quest."‡

Gyanamata

* From the hymn "Lead, Kindly Light."

† *One Hundred Poems of Kabir,* trans. Rabindranath Tagore (London: Macmillan and Company, 1915), extract from poem XXII. Kabir was a great sixteenth-century saint of India.

‡ Ibid., from poem III.

Opposite: Self-Realization Fellowship Hermitage, Encinitas, California. Gyanamata resided here from 1937 until her passing in 1951.

From Sri Gyanamata's personal diary—sometime in the early years of her sadhana *(spiritual discipline):*

November 14.

This morning I had the happiness of going a little deeper in meditation than ever before. The points I noted were unusual calmness and yellow light, more steady than heretofore. Breath slower and slower...."I" watched these things, also seemed to watch my mind, one part of which I thought was quiet. Once I watched the active part so intently that I forgot my meditation. Returning to it, I was surprised to find it undisturbed and even stronger. Again, as I have thought and written over and over, the experience seems wonderful while I am in it, but nothing when I try to put it into words. What will it be like by and by when I arrive at *real* meditation?

When I think how my Guru came over land and sea, into my very house, to bring me the blessing I had waited so long for—as truly *to* and *for* me as if I were the only one in all this land who needed him—tears come to my eyes, and the emotions of gratitude and devotion well up strongly in my heart. This morning I searched within for some such feeling, only to find perfect calmness, and the thought, "He would say, 'go deeper.'" At such moments I feel that if I only could bring a very strong effort of the will to bear, I would go much deeper.

CHAPTER 10

Loyalty and Receptivity to Truth

Paramahansa Yogananda wrote: "It is not a pumping-in from outside that gives wisdom; it is the power and extent of your inner receptivity that determines how much you can attain of true knowledge, and how rapidly." In the short essay that follows, Gyanamata shows that, practically speaking, receptivity comes as a result of being loyal to a guru and faithfully practicing his teachings.

To seekers who did not understand this vital point, her letters offered sympathetic but straightforward counsel: Realization of Truth comes only from holding steadfast to one's chosen path, not by giving up or seeking another teaching when the way seems difficult or when one's spiritual efforts are not immediately rewarded. "Patiently, faithfully practice," she urged, for loyalty to a true guru—the channel through which God works to liberate His children—automatically attunes the consciousness to God himself.

A Priceless Jewel

*"Pilate saith unto Him, what is Truth?"**

Many there are who put this question. Much time is spent in searching for the ultimate Truth. And yet the blessed fact is: It is ever present with us. It is not here nor there. It is not the exclusive property of any person. It is universal like air and light, and like air and light it does not have to be

* John 18:38.

searched for. As air and light stream into a house through the open windows, so if the windows of the soul are thrown open, Truth will flow in and illumine the man according to his ability to recognize and receive it.

Apply the tests to self that usually are reserved for abstract Truth. Apply the acid test to your own character. Have you faith? Not, "What have you faith *in,*" but "Have you faith?" Are you capable of loyalty? How far will it carry you?

The "gentle Dauphin" to whose person and cause Joan of Arc was devoted, was, in himself, worthless—and yet, not quite, after all; for he inspired Joan with such a passionate loyalty that she, a simple peasant girl, freed France, and was faithful, even unto death, to the Voices that inspired and directed her. Deserted by the unworthy Dauphin, now king through her loyalty, is she to be pitied for having mistaken base metal for gold? No, and Charles only obtained a temporary good, while she, in her own loyalty, the attribute of her own character, possessed a jewel of such worth and brilliance that we may envy her. The good cause justifies the fight, Nietzsche said; but I tell you that the good fight justifies the cause. Think on these things.

Above us stand those great ones who have won their palms in Bliss, who, beginning on the plane of loyalty to a master, to a teaching, to their fight for self-mastery, "subdued kingdoms, wrought righteousness, obtained promises, stopped the mouths of lions, quenched the violence of fire, escaped the edge of the sword, out of weakness were made strong, waxed valiant in fight, turned to flight the armies of the aliens. Women received their dead raised to life again: and others were tortured, not accepting deliverance; that they might obtain a better resurrection; and others had trials of cruel mockings and scourgings, yea, moreover of bonds and imprisonment: they were stoned, they were sawn asunder, were tempted, were slain with the sword; they wandered about in sheepskins and goatskins; being destitute, afflicted, tormented (of whom the world was not worthy); they wandered in deserts, and in mountains, and in dens and caves of the earth."* O world, unworthy indeed!

To some one of these great ones you belong. Trust God and your good karma to lead you to him. Where placed, think on Joan of Arc, and give. Give, not carefully, prudently, grudgingly, but freely and generously with both hands.

O blessed ones, bestow upon us a little of your courage, faith, and loyalty to a cause, to a master, that there will be no time, no need, to search for the Truth, for it will live in us, manifest through us, and lead us to unimagined heights, since "The race is not to the swift, nor the battle to the strong,"† but the victory is unto him who is faithful.

* * * * *

The following is from a Self-Realization student, and is answered by Gyanamata's letter, immediately following it.

September 23, 1935

Dear Self-Realization Fellowship,

For over twenty-five years I have been searching for the truth in regard to survival [of consciousness after death]. I thought I had found the path through your organization.

But some weeks ago I read in the press what a swami said—that it was ridiculous to think one could experience God or Cosmic Consciousness through the written word, through lessons. Also, I received a long letter from attorney Clarence Darrow, in which he states he had tried for years to prove immortality and God—but without result. He says we are cosmic orphans. He has had a long life in which to learn

* Hebrews 11:33–38. † Ecclesiastes 9:11.

the truth and a great deal of experience among spiritualists—and he has no belief in and no hope of immortality.

What is the real truth? Do the religious and "occult" methods merely result in building up in believers a great suggestion of God—to such an extent that these individuals *create* their own God? I think Voltaire said that if a God had not been created for man (by the priests), it would have been necessary for man to create a God—or something to that effect.

Do you personally know for certain that life persists after death?

Sincerely,
W. C.

* * * * *

October 21, 1935

Dear Mr. C_______,

You will remember that last May some letters passed between us. You told me of how your soul hungers for God, for the constant realization of His presence. Also of the blissful state you have enjoyed at intervals during your life, and still more frequently since you began to study Swamiji's teachings.

Can you imagine, then, my surprise when your letter of September 23 was handed to me to answer? What a change in a man to whom God had revealed Himself as Bliss! And what had brought about this change? A few words in a newspaper have meant more to you than the testimony of generation after generation of holy saints, who renounced all that the world could offer and counted it nothing in comparison to what they gained in God-consciousness. You also state that Mr. Clarence Darrow writes you that for years he has tried to prove "God" and "immortality" and has failed.

Again, one man's word against so many, and against the blissful experiences of your own soul. You conclude by asking if we personally *know* that life persists after death.

A very great saint who lived in the fourteenth century wrote: "Some simple folk fondly imagine that they are going to see God, as it were, standing there and they here. Not so. God and I are one in knowing." I think your whole trouble is indicated by these sentences. You ask that proof of a life beyond this, a life that is all Spirit, be given you in terms of material existence. You ask that we prove God and the higher realms in the same way that we would prove the existence of the President of the United States, and the Capitol, Washington, D.C. This cannot be done, any more than a man can prove by the multiplication table that he loves his wife.

The proof we have to offer you is the testimony borne by the great yogis who are our spiritual preceptors. By reason of their high development they are able to enter the astral plane, follow the souls of the dead, and give them aid. You must either accept their word, or wait until death or your own development gives to you proof that cannot be gainsaid.

As to God—why, according to your own testimony, He has been closer to you than hands or feet all your life, but because you cannot sit down opposite Him in a chair, or receive a typewritten letter from Him as you have from me, you don't know whether or not He exists.

First of all, what do we mean when we say "God"? Who, what, *is* He? I will give you Swami Yogananda's answer to this question, in his own words: "God is Universal Intelligence, Absolute Existence, Eternal Consciousness. He is Cosmic Vibration and ever-conscious, ever-new Bliss. In the beginning was the Word, or Cosmic Vibration; and the Word was God. Vibration is the cause of all things, therefore Vibration is God. God is manifested as Cosmic Vibration."

Is not this stupendous, awe-inspiring? And is it not obvious that such a God cannot be "found" in the usual meaning of that word; nor can He be expressed through any assertion, but can only be *directly experienced*? "God and I are one in knowing." That is, He is experienced in the deep places of the soul.

Mr. Darrow is searching everywhere for God. He will surely find Him if he persists in his search. But this God that we hunger and thirst after is only found after endless incarnations. At present, Mr. Darrow is probably looking for Him everywhere except in the right place. Jesus said: "The kingdom of God is within you."* Where is a king to be found but in his own kingdom? However long the search lasts, it is never in vain. At last the light shines, and God reveals Himself as He is.

What better answer to *all* your questions can be offered than the life and teachings of Swami Yogananda? As a child he searched for his teacher. Having found him, he remained with him for ten years, receiving instruction in meditation and other yogic practices, and discipline for the developing of his character. Then, having renounced name, family, money, and all desire of personal joy save in God, he went out into the world to give to others what he had himself received. Jesus said: "If any man will do His will, he shall know of the doctrine, whether it be of God, or whether I speak of myself."†

Please, dear Mr. C_______, put Swamiji's teachings to this test: Ask yourself if you think it is likely that he is offering teachings, the truth of which he has no proof; if it is possible that he is giving us stones for bread? Faithfully, patiently practice, praying to God to give you the only proof of His existence that is worth having—personal realization. Cry to

* Luke 17:21. †John 7:17.

Him: "The stars may fall, the heavens be shattered, but never will I cease to cry until Thou revealest Thyself to me!"

If you care to write me further, and receive letters from me in regard to this deep subject, please do so, and I shall be very happy to respond, if you are willing to be patient with me.

Very sincerely yours,
Gyanamata

* * * * *

To a student of the Self-Realization Lessons who had ceased practicing the teachings, Gyanamata wrote:

Dear Mrs. ________,

Replying to your letter of March 7: First you say that you gave up work in the teachings because there were so many unexplained problems. Life itself is somewhat of a problem; would it help to stop living? One cannot apply the rules of the classroom to life. In the school of life, each day's work is not finished before the next task is commenced, and it sometimes happens that a lesson which we thought was completed and laid aside forever is presented anew to us, with "unfinished work" written on it by the Great Teacher.

The Guru-Preceptor of all students in Self-Realization Fellowship is, naturally, Paramahansa Yogananda, the founder of the work in this country. Why then do you ask to be directed to some other master? You are in direct contact with him when studying the *SRF Lessons.* These teachings embody what he learned from his Master. He has enriched them by his own meditations and realization, and presented them for the use of his followers worldwide. Raise yourself to his vibration by meditation and other spiritual practices, and contact him in the Spirit. Some students have wonderful contacts in this way, and see in meditation the Master whom they have never seen in the flesh.

In the lessons you are getting the *personal* instruction of a Master, which is what you say you desire; yet you stop his lessons, and ask him to direct you to someone else. This is inconsistent. The relation of guru and disciple is a deeply spiritual one, and does not depend wholly upon personal contact. Paramahansa Yogananda's students are to be found in several different countries. They have never seen him, yet are his faithful followers.

There is nothing in Paramahansaji's teachings that contradicts the opening verses of St. John's gospel. It is merely a question of from which plane of existence, or being, the matter is considered. On the transcendental plane, God, the Absolute, alone is found; but on this earthly, material plane, Satan is very evident. He is the independent cosmic vibration, which is cut off from God by choosing the downward path; he is not the Creative Word—the Christ. The things that are made by this satanic vibration are the evil desires—everything that tends to drag a man down and keep him in bondage. Christ Consciousness through the Holy Ghost comes as the savior of his soul, frees him, and leads him to God. This is the Word, which was with God from the beginning.

You say you want things straight and in accordance with the teachings of the yogis. Truth is always one. Doubts and questionings are a part of duality. In the highest state of God-consciousness there is no Satan, no man nor woman, neither Conrad nor Henry can be found there, for all is One.

Anything you find in the lessons that is not quite clear, put aside for the time being, returning to it again later when you have gained more understanding and light. In the meantime meditate, and fill your mind with thoughts of God, for in God-consciousness all problems and perplexities dissolve.

Gyanamata

July 12, 1944

Dear ________,

I have three anniversaries this month: my birthday; today, the day the Master had dinner at my house in Seattle 19 years ago; and some time this month the year before that (I've lost the day) was the first time I saw him—so I have been his disciple for 20 years now.

Do you know, I have come to feel something fantastic in the praise I receive for being "loyal" and "devoted." But what else *could* I be? I felt this first when Dr. Lewis* told me that he talked about me to his class, telling them how loyal I was. I answered, saying that "I am loyal" implies a possibility of disloyalty. One does not talk of being loyal to the sunshine, or the flowers, or the beauty and grandeur of the ocean or a mountain; nor does one receive praise for it.

I am glad that you keep my letters and find my example inspiring, but if you would look into your own true heart—look deeply—I think it would guide you aright without me. You have your Self and you have him, the Master and all he is and all he means to you. You have had much more than I ever have had. How puny my letters and example appear in comparison!

With love in God and Guruji,
Sister

* Dr. M. W. Lewis was a devoted disciple of Paramahansa Yogananda from the time of their first meeting in 1920. He served as a Self-Realization minister and, from 1952 until his death in 1960, as vice president of Self-Realization Fellowship.

CHAPTER 11

Devotion

Sri Gyanamata often liked to quote the Lord Buddha as saying that the essential goal of the holy life is to deliver the mind from the everyday habits of thought that keep it bound to the duality of worldly consciousness. In the letters that follow, most of which were written to her Guru, Sister tells of the original and unique ways she employed to raise her mind from the mundane thoughts of the world into the awareness of the presence of God and Guru.

By continual deliberate actions—keeping mementos of the Guru, mentally following him as he traveled around the country, writing to him, stopping to think of what he had done for her—she came to fill her mind with the lofty realization of the blessings of God that flowed continually through him to her.

New Year's Day, 1940

To my blessed Master,

I thank you for your Christmas gift—the little lacquered box. I have not decided what to keep in it yet, but I like to look at it.

After you left Seattle I asked myself what method I could take to be receptive to you. I could think of no other way than by keeping you before my mind by deliberate acts. So, at seven o'clock each morning, I stopped whatever I was doing and concentrated for a moment, saying, "He is praying, for *me*." I mentally followed you around the country as you went from city to city on lecture tours.

Do you remember my taking you upstairs to my room when you came to my house in Seattle? Silently you looked at my pictures of holy men; and then, turning your back to the long row of windows, you prayed for me very softly and gave me my first blessing, the one that enabled me to hear the *Aum*. After that, as long as I remained in Seattle, a vase of orange flowers (that were sometimes fresh blossoms and sometimes artificial ones) stayed on the floor to mark the spot where you had stood.

In my room now is the rosary from the Mount of Olives, together with *Kriya* beads, and the little white stone you blessed for me the last time I was ill; all were given by you, so all are sacred. It would make this letter too long to write all the things I have done that you might be a real presence with me in my room, in my mind, and in my soul.

The path by which you reach me is now a well-beaten one. I no longer need external aids (but I like them just the same, and add another to the list whenever one occurs to me).

I never think that anything you give me is a reward. I am not a hireling, but your own. The difference between you and me is one of degree, not of kind; the goal I long for, work for, pray for, is the same goal to which Your Holiness has attained. So this work of yours is *my* work. I do not mean that I do not appreciate the golden words of praise you speak to me from time to time. I repeat them over and over to myself, feeding on them in my heart with prayer and thanksgiving.

On the card that came with your gift, you said that I must remain here on earth to be with you to serve the work. That thought was in my mind before I received your gift and card. As I contemplated the year just commencing, I said to myself, "Perhaps I have another year in which to be near him." That was what I came for—to be near my Guru.

So I am not trying to get away. In the first place, I couldn't. You support my life. I have no power to reject your healings even if I wanted to. But I don't want to. How thankfully, how gratefully I accept them when they come! In the second place, to try to get away would be a despicable act, after the blessings you have poured out for me. God forbid that I should so requite you!

O blessed Master, how did you manage to give me so much time during this, the busiest season of the year? Perhaps it does not take time so much as intensity of effort. For three mornings the healing vibrations came; the body was relieved and comforted, and the mind lifted up to God. Without your help I could not have succeeded at all in making my Christmas the kind I wanted it to be.

You gave me another glorious morning today. I was wrapped in power, with flashes of golden light.

Guru-Lord, remember me—the poor Sister—when thou comest into thy kingdom.

Gyanamata

* * * * *

August 25, 1946

My blessed Master,

You often say: "In thought you rise above the body." I did this yesterday, when I talked to Virginia about your life—that divine life which we daily see unfolding before our eyes: the weekly trips between San Diego and Hollywood, the sermons, the classes, the guiding and inspiring interviews, the prayers to God for those who suffer or are in need, the instant response to every call; year in, year out, it goes on, with no time for personal rest, refreshment, or pleasure—save the greatest of all, which comes to you from God.

Virginia said to me something about myself which made me glad. I told her, with regret, that I am not naturally a worker. She said, "Well! No one would suspect it!"

Gyanamata

* * * * *

Sunday, February 4, 1945

My blessed Gurudeva,

I try each day to lift my mind to God and to keep it with Him. Every morning I first make this effort between the hours of three and seven. If an inspiring thought occurs to me then in the ordinary way, I know it comes through my mind; but if it appears suddenly, like a flash of light, I know it comes straight from God through intuition.

This morning I happened to hear over the radio the words, "Flesh and blood hath not revealed it unto thee." Nothing more. An instant realization came to me: "That is how you know about the Master!" I looked up the whole quotation: "He saith unto them, But whom say ye that I am? And Simon Peter answered and said, Thou art the Christ, the son of the living God. And Jesus answered and saith unto him, Blessed art thou, Simon Barjona: *for flesh and blood hath not revealed it unto thee, but my Father which is in heaven.*"*

In the same way I know you. God has told me, hath revealed it unto me; and like Simon Peter I am blessed.

Gyanamata

* * * * *

January 2, 1948

My divine Master,

Your Christmas gift made me very happy. My special

* Matthew 16:15–17.

thanks for the amulet that bears your likeness. When you look at me at our rare meetings in the Hermitage kitchen I see a shadow on your face which I interpret as a doubt, a fear that I am depending too much on the material aid the doctor gives, and not enough on what comes from God alone. O Master! After all these years *must* you feel a doubt of me? However far I have fallen below the ideal in other particulars, in this one I have not so fallen. As the needle in the compass points ever to the north, so my heart and soul have ever pointed—without swerving—to God and Guruji, to God through Guruji. All else belongs in the same class as eating when I am hungry and going to bed when I am tired.

The anniversary of that day when the Word was made flesh in the holy land of India, for the sake of all the world, is very near.* Glory be to God in the highest, and on earth peace and goodwill to men!

> Yea, thou shalt answer for us, righteous Lord,
> Thine all the merit, ours the great reward!
> Thine the sharp thorns, and ours the golden crown,
> Ours the life won, and thine the life laid down!

Gyanamata

* * * * *

August 1949

My ever blessed Master,

I am told that records are being made of your voice, chanting. I wish that records could be made of the smiles that sometimes flash on your face in response to some secret emotion. The smile you gave me lately was as truly a blessing as a touch of your hand on my head.

So God smiles on me through you.

Gyanamata

* A reference to Paramahansaji's birthday, January 5.

Thank you, O blessed Master, for the spray of flowers from your garland, which came to me with your blessing. The blessings come anyway, have come for years and will continue to the end.

It is strange how the human heart loves to have some outward object to treasure. How dear to me is any sign that I have found favor in your sight!

Gyanamata

* * * * *

Saturday noon

My blessed Master,

When I greeted you, you said: "I seem to be a stranger to you." I was much puzzled, and did not know how to answer. Now I think that you must have said it because I did not come down immediately upon your arrival.

So please let me tell you the reasons. This is one of the days when I do not feel well. I did not want you to see me when I was so conscious of feeling and looking ill. So I said: "I will wait a little. There are so many things to claim his attention, he will not notice my absence. When I look better, I will go."

There is another reason—one I don't think I have ever mentioned to you. All my life I have had to train myself to stay in the background. *Always* I had to do this with those I loved best. I was patient, and waited until they were free to give me their attention. Otherwise, I would receive some sort of rebuff. So now I do not mind the background at all.

Surely you know—you who know *everything* about me must know this—that my devotion and love rush to greet you wherever you are, whenever you appear! *Always* I am standing invisibly before you, humbly and patiently awaiting the moment when I will receive a word and a smile from you. For sixteen years I have followed you from point to point, until now I do not feel your absence—for where you are, there I am also.

Please forgive me. It shall not happen again.

With deep devotion,
Gyanamata

* * * * *

My Gurudeva,

I have found a beautiful way to direct the mind to God. It is your poem "God! God! God!" Just the repetition of the Holy Name. How simple, and just suited to my present state.

Gyanamata

* * * * *

Saturday afternoon

My blessed Master,

I did not come to offer *pranams* to you when I returned to the Hermitage because of Mr. Lynn's arrival. I feared I would be in the way. Indeed I tried to get into the Hermitage unseen.

I feel as if I had been away a very long time. I suppose this is natural, the result of not being away from the Hermitage for over two years.

I deeply enjoyed the few hours at Mt. Washington. Memories rushed upon me as I opened the front door and stood in the reception hall....I looked at all the changes and improvements. And your room—I wanted to stand in that hallowed shrine a moment and think of the times when you were away lecturing, when I used to go there every night and sit on the floor to meditate. The ashram was very silent, as nearly everyone was out, so I got the full effect of the poignant memories that seized me at every turn.

This morning I had just enough time to look at the pepper trees, and the nearby surroundings, such as the wishing well, where my name stands under yours [*see photo facing page 185*]. I asked myself with a rush of astonishment how it had ever happened that you wanted to put my name there!

Everything looked so neat, so beautifully cared for. It made me so happy to see it. Indeed, if I could have stayed just a little longer, I would not have wanted to come away at all. I realized as never before that there never could be another Mt. Washington—first in my heart always.

With deep devotion,
Gyanamata

* * * * *

Sunday morning
Hermitage

Divine Master,

We expect you today, and I, the Solitary, have no way of showing my joy at your coming, save a few words of devotion.

But perhaps you will not come. We cannot tell. Please stay with us more. Of what use is this beautiful place without you?

> Unutterably dim,
> Our bright world lacking Him.

Our lives hang upon yours. As for me, you know that I depend upon you in a special sense. This morning when I commenced to meditate, I knew at once that I was going to have to get through my Sunday work without your especial support.

Are these words selfish? Then it is selfish to love you, to draw strength from your strength, to watch for your smile, and try to cause it, to be ready to come and go at your bidding!

I have learned, while writing this, that you *have* come! My spirit lifts because you are here.

Gyanamata

* * * * *

Dear ________,

How shall devotion be stimulated? What fuel shall we use to replenish the fire upon our altar? The Gita says that the Lord will not reject the smallest offering—a flower, a fruit will do. Ask your heart. It will guide you. Perform regularly whatever act makes devotion burn to heaven in a clear, bright flame.

As the seeker grows in devotion he arrives at last at that stage wherein he can say, when enduring the pains of discipline, "Father, whate'er Thou dost lay on me, I deem it altogether done of Thee." Ultimately, the devotee does not know when he is being disciplined, because all distinctions are done away with—all is One.

Just before I came to Mt. Washington I was listening one day to a program on the radio. My attention was caught by the following words:

> I am but a simple maid,
> Foolish and unheeding;
> Yet I follow, unafraid,
> Where my heart is leading.

These were just the words of a song from a light opera, but I copied them down, because I recognized that they described the path that I have been following. From point to point, from one object of love to another, I had followed *unafraid* until at last the twin stars of love and devotion led me to Paramahansaji, to Mt. Washington, to "God alone."

God lures us from one object of desire to another until we understand that it is He Himself that we have been longing for all the time, and in Him our restless hearts find rest. "I brought with me the thirst for the Infinite, and I have come for the meeting with Him."

Gyanamata

CHAPTER 12

"Suffering Can Be a Pathway to Greatness"

Physical pain provides a formidable test for anyone trying to realize his true nature as a soul, because when the body is demanding attention, it is much more difficult for the mind to transcend material consciousness. Even so, many saints have risen above great suffering and reached their Goal. Such a one was Sri Gyanamata, who was tested with tremendous physical suffering and yet emerged supremely victorious.

It is said that one never knows his or her spiritual strength until faced with adversity. Through her trials—physical, mental, and spiritual—Gyanamata developed heroic perseverance, endurance, and an unconquerable attitude; she found that these tests strengthened her character as nothing else could have. In the letters that follow, Gyanamata shows others how to cultivate that same positive spirit and healthy spiritual perspective by which they also could come to experience that "suffering can be a pathway to greatness."

Dear ________,

There is more that may be said about the bodily trouble you are undergoing. Illness has many causes—physical, mental, metaphysical. But it is always a test. Bear it bravely or conquer it. The Master said that suffering can be a pathway to greatness.

Not long ago Paramahansaji remarked: "The dream will break, and you will be free!" And he said it with a smile. Do not make the mistake of holding on to your condition by mourning over it. Stress the points in which you have gained. Remember that part of the cure lies in forgetting the illness. We have to *affirm* health when we do not feel it. This helps us to experience the truth.

You know that the state the devotee most desires is to feel consciously at all times the presence of God. To aid in bringing about this blessed consummation, we must affirm that it is so (even if we cannot feel it) and must magnify and give thanks for each mark—tiny or great—of His presence or favor.

I always believe that if I will try just a little harder, I can bring about the conditions that seem just out of my reach. Remember that no one, not even a master, can do *everything* for you. You have to do much yourself. So if you want to be well, start now and affirm health with all your heart. Count your gains and blessings; skip the rest. The law of attraction will do all that is needful.

A poor Sister, but a loving one,
Gyanamata

* * * * *

Dear ________,

I have come to measure spiritual advancement, not alone by the light that surrounds one when he meditates or by the visions he has of saints, but by what he is able to endure in the hard, cold light of day. Christ's greatness was not only that he could go into meditation and gloriously realize his oneness with the Father, his absolute identity, but also that he could *endure.*

Perhaps I might have forgotten this truth but for what

Paramahansaji said of it. "That is an ultimate realization," he told me. "All saints have had it." So, by practicing the intellectual method of meditation, mentioned in *The Science of Religion,* I had arrived at a realization that what the Master says is a true and ultimate realization.

I always remember this truth when I mentally try to find a way to escape from something that seems too hard for me. I think then: "I am escaping, not overcoming."

With love in God and Guruji,
Gyanamata

* * * * *

February 3, 1949

Dear ________,

Your letter touched my heart. The words our Master wrote me when I had been in the hospital a few days apply to you at this time equally well. They are paraphrased as follows: "All the devotion, wisdom, and faith that you have acquired are being now tested by God. You must now use all your spiritual acquirements to pass the test of God. Keep your wisdom-light ever burning during the darkness of this test. And this is what I pray for you, that you ever remember and love Him and forget the body."

Then Master reminded me of the sufferings of the saints, and of the soldiers in the war, and he gave me no sympathy at all; sometimes it seemed he did not even understand me. When I thanked him for help he had given me, he replied shortly, that I ought to be able to help myself. Thus God spoke to me through him.

I advise you to read the lives of the saints, considering what they suffered—yes, even imposed upon themselves—that, dying to self, they might live in God. Consider especially Saint Teresa of Avila, and the glorious example she left behind her. You reminded me once that you are not Saint Teresa. True. But there are ways in which we can imitate her. It is said of her, "She considered that much of the time of the saints of the desert was passed without any consolation whatever." She was continually reminding herself of God. And God said to her, "During this life the true gain consists not in striving after greater joy in Me, but in doing My will."

This ties in with what you have often heard me say, that the degree of our realization is proved not by the lights we see in meditation, or the visions we have of the saints, but in what we can endure in the hard, cold light of day. Think on these things, dear, and rely on God—who is within you as He was within Saint Teresa—to support you to the end.

With love in God and Guruji,
Gyanamata

* * * * *

Dear ________,

The Bible says that God never puts on us a burden above what we are able to bear, that there is always a way of escape. In other words, there is some way—concealed, but not beyond our powers of discovery—of escaping by rising into a clear, pure atmosphere that lies above the plane of stress and strain. I have methods that I use in my own case, and *always* I have the positive assurance within myself that I could live permanently upon that higher plane if only I would constantly put into practice the spiritual knowledge I have. So, dear, you must discover which method of meeting this condition is best for *you*. Only thus can you gain the benefit of this experience. Any other "escape" would only mean a postponement—you would have to face the same sort of conflict some day.

I often think how strange it is that I should have had to come into a Hindu organization in order to understand the meaning and value of Christian teachings. Probably the outstanding Christian teaching concerns the value and necessity of suffering: that without being thrown into a fiery furnace of suffering, we do not attain to union with God. On the contrary, the Hindu teaches that man makes his escape, discovers his own divinity, through the bliss of meditation. Since I have lived and served at Mt. Washington and the Hermitage, these two seemingly contradictory teachings have revealed themselves to me as parts of a whole. Fitted together they form a complete picture of the path man must tread on his upward march.

With love in God and Guruji,
Gyanamata

* * * * *

Dear ________,

My heart overflows with sympathy and love. Yes, I am sure that one cause is the war. Think what the world vibration must be at the present time. I listen to the lovely sound of the ocean and the birds, I look from my window at the pink and red hibiscus—but I do not forget that intangible dark shadow, like the feeling that there is something with you in the room. It's not so intangible, either, if you go to San Diego or some other point of danger!

Long ago, before we entered the war, or even feared much that we would have to, I happened to see a letter that the Master wrote to someone. This person had been complaining that she did not progress spiritually. He told her that many people had the same feeling, and that it was caused by the dark and heavy vibrations of the war on the other side of the world that they had picked up unconsciously.

You write of your "spiritual lassitude," and this may be one of the reasons.

I believe that there is another cause for your feelings. Even those who know of a surety that there is no real joy except in what comes from God, and that the innocent pleasures of the world only divert their minds for a little while, are sometimes assailed by days of just such weariness as you are experiencing. In education not enough stress is laid upon the need for courage in the character. We must learn to *endure.* And the only way to learn is by enduring. In courage one sees the brilliant triumph of the soul over the flesh. "Heroism is the dazzling and glorious concentration of courage."

Then too, remember the words of the Lord Jesus: "Father, save me from this hour: *but for this cause came I unto this hour.*"* As with him, so with us; how can we expect to escape that which we were born to endure?

Of course I do not think it would be wrong for you to go off by yourself for a day. But it will only divert you a little. Would you not rather ask in meditation to be given what you need? Then if a free day comes, you will know that it is from His hand. The truth is, that which you want is with you all the time, closer than hands or feet. Any moment it may lift you above the world and personal depression. Wait patiently for Him.

No outward trial really matters. We should become stronger and stronger through our experiences, until we are able to stand among those of whom it may be said that their conquest of self has been final, needing no further testing.

Gyanamata

* * * * *

* John 12:27.

July 26, 1938

Dear ________,

I thank God and Guru that today I am free from sickness and pain. These trials come to all at times, and should be borne with whatever fortitude we are able to summon to our aid, while striving at the same time to work our way to a state of consciousness in which sickness and pain are unknown.

But do you believe that anyone who comes to this earth-plane of existence, whether for the sake of his own development, or to aid others in attaining emancipation, is ever exempt completely from all forms of suffering? The masters all hang upon some kind of cross—can the disciple expect to go scot-free? I think not. In this world all must suffer, either because of their own karma or because of that of others. When he faced his agony Jesus said, "Father, save me from this hour." Then he added, "But for this cause came I unto this hour." He saw that he could not escape, that he must live it through to the end.

I am writing because I want to assure you that you did not disturb me when you came to me at the cave.* And that my earnestness (my vanity prefers to call it that, rather than excitement) was not caused simply by what you said to me. It was because what you told me was so exactly like many instances I have observed since coming to California, instances that have led me to this conclusion: The practice of meditation *alone* does not perfect the character; one may have some wonderful results of a phenomenal nature, and yet be lacking in the basic virtues.

We must, as Swami Sri Yukteswarji said, learn to behave, and that means the will must be purified and put in control

* One of two meditation caves built into the bluff overlooking the ocean at the Encinitas ashram.

of the daily life. We must learn that "sacrifice" means going without something that we would like to have, for the sake of a person or a cause. That "renunciation" means the giving up of some pure pleasure or right for the sake of a higher good that we perceive before us—possibly in some far distant incarnation. We must aspire not only to stand beside the Master on the Mount of Transfiguration and share his bliss of God-consciousness; but we must aspire also, with equal ardor, to aid him in bearing his cross of Calvary.

I thank you and Mr. ________ for your good wishes. My heart holds the same for you both.

With love in God and Guruji,
Gyanamata

* * * * *

Dear ________,

When I lived in Seattle, I had a complete view of Mt. Rainier from my dining room window. It was wonderful when illuminated by the rising or setting sun. But the sun was not always rising or setting. Then, too, for days and even months the mountain was hidden by clouds. Perhaps I did not see the mountain all winter, but I never felt afraid that I had lost it.

St. Anthony* in his cave had a visit from the Lord Jesus and reproached him for having gone away. "I have never left thee," was the Lord's answer. Many of the saints lived in the desert for years without any consolation at all. Can you expect better treatment than a saint? Mr. Lynn said to me once, speaking of those touches with which God favors us: "I see that you cannot have it whenever you want it." There are many other instances that might be cited, but I have said enough.

* A fourth-century Christian saint; one of the "Desert Fathers."

You were taken up to the Mountain of Transfiguration. But you had to descend into the valley to be tested, and to work under most painful and difficult circumstances. Be glad that you were on the Mount, if only for once, and remember that He is beside you, for "Where to us God seems least, He is often most."

Gyanamata

* * * * *

Christmas 1945

My divine and ever blessed Master,

At this time I am moved to tell you how I have tried to meet the test of illness about which you warned me. I knew I ought to have enough power, after long years of seeking God, to help myself at least a little. I began by following this line of reason: I thought of the many sufferers this world contains, especially of the soldiers, many mere boys, who have had to adjust themselves to a long life without hands, or perhaps eyes, arms, and legs. If I were to be included among the world's cripples, I could only say, "The judgments of the Lord are true and righteous altogether."* So I accepted, and attained some measure of calmness.

When things became worse, and I no longer knew what it was to awaken out of sleep in physical comfort, I called to mind the comforts that the mercy of God, and the grace of the Guru, had provided for me.

Something you wrote me soon after I was taken ill has been a great source of consolation and strength to me. You referred to "the darkness of this test." In moments of great need these words have come to me, and in their wake followed acceptance and peace. I have wondered why. This

* Psalm 19:9.

morning I knew. It is because God is in the darkness. Dionysius the Areopagite, a Christian mystic of the fifth century, says that this darkness shines brighter than light, and that there are mysteries revealed to "the soul that sees not." Bless me and pray for me, that if I must dwell in darkness, it may be that divine darkness which "He hath made His secret place." And that I may be "united in my higher part to Him who is wholly unintelligible, and whom, by understanding nothing, I may understand after a manner above all intelligence."

All my life I have fed my soul with the sayings of the saviors that God has sent to the world. Now, in my time of need, I do not have to depend upon a book. If I keep very still and listen, something comes to the surface of my mind that calms and strengthens me. There are the blessed words that God spoke to me Himself one night before I was taken ill. I was looking at the picture of Christ, and considering his sufferings. I felt a peculiar, indescribable movement within me. It was as if I were deciding to make suffering for myself, though such an act is very far from me. A Voice spoke to me. It was not my own voice. I was not talking to myself. It was not my mind. It was clear and distinct and separate. It said: "Endure what I shall send. That will be enough."

Gyanamata

* * * * *

December 13, 1940

My blessed Master,

Yesterday, for the second time, you spoke of the suffering of the good, as if, though you knew the reason, you could not help feeling surprise. I answered that I was not good, therefore I suffered. As soon as I had spoken I felt ashamed of having done so for the second time. My words must have sounded like an affectation of humility. In reality they were a sincere and simple statement of the way I feel. I am sure that what I do suffer is not half of what I deserve, but I am deeply thankful that through the mercy of God and the grace of the Guru, I escape so much more than I can ever know. Jesus said that no one should be called good except God.* That must mean that no one can be called good who is not God-conscious.

I write all this just as if you did not know the answers to these questions. Really what I am doing is allowing myself the happiness of expressing myself to Your Holiness. Suffering has never constituted any problem for me. We cause our own suffering, building it up bit by bit—except, of course, the God-men, the saviors of the world. They suffer because for man and his salvation they have come down from heaven onto a plane of manifestation where suffering is the rule. When you visited Ramana Maharshi† in South India, in order to draw him out you put to him several questions, one of which was, "Why so much suffering?" He replied by asking, "What suffers?" It is the self, the ego. If it did not suffer, would it not grow very strong and powerful? And if I do not die to self, how can I live in God?

It is said the whole life, like a panorama, passes before the eyes of the dying. I wonder if it might not be that I am

* "Why callest thou me good? There is none good but one, that is, God."—Matthew 19:17

† An Indian sage whom Paramahansaji visited in 1935.

Opposite: Gyanamata meditating at "spiritual wishing well" on the grounds of the SRF Mother Center, 1935. In the cement base, near the hand- and footprints of her Guru, are Gyanamata's handprints and the motto she lived by: "God alone" *(see also photo facing page 121).*

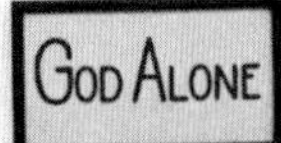

Altar niche in wall of Gyanamata's room at the Encinitas Hermitage, with pictures of the Self-Realization line of gurus: Mahavatar Babaji, Lahiri Mahasaya, Swami Sri Yukteswar, and Paramahansa Yogananda. Her motto, "God Alone," hung in her room throughout her years in the ashram; each year, on the anniversary of her taking the final vows of dedication to God, she would inscribe the date on the back of this sign as a renewal of those vows.

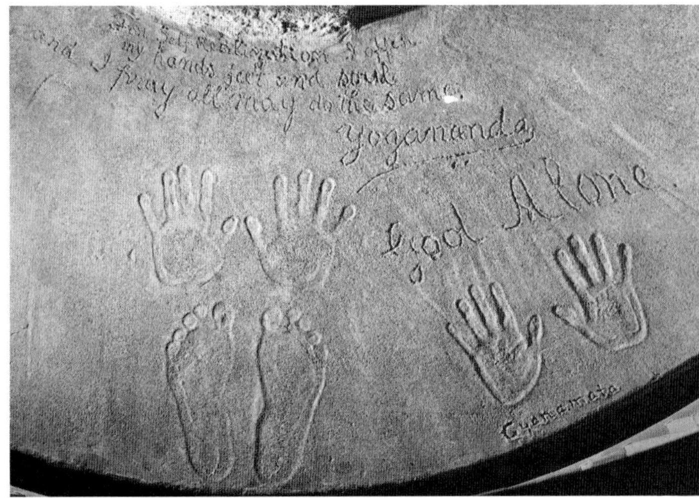

Base of spiritual wishing well at SRF International Headquarters. When the wishing well was installed on April 9, 1934, Paramahansa Yogananda made impressions of his hands and feet in the cement, and inscribed: "For Self-Realization I offer my hands, feet, and soul, and I pray all may do the same." At Paramahansaji's request, Gyanamata also made handprints, and wrote her motto, "God Alone."

(See also photo facing page 121.)

undergoing this experience now, before the event, in order that later on I may be free to give myself up to the joy of that moment? Anyway, daily I sit in judgment upon the deeds done in the body, and sometimes memory is like a knife driven into my heart. That is why I cannot feel that I am good.

What greater joy could I ask than what flows from my acceptance by you? Therefore, though not good, I am blest. All these years I have counted myself fortunate if I could but hear the sound of your voice. God has granted that I hear it calling to me in the early morning, during the day, late at night; and so, though stripped of everything, I am a blessed Sister, made so by your grace.

With deep devotion,
Gyanamata

* * * * *

October 27, 1942

My divine Master,

If we never had anything painful or alarming to face, if it were just joy in God all the time, what would we be? Spiritual cream puffs. Of course I know that this is not the case if the foundations of character are deep and strong, if they cannot be shaken by anything. Then one may wish to spend night and day in His joy.

Something happens, and the mind throws the worst possible light upon it. It is not what happens, but the mind that makes me suffer. The circumstance [about which I questioned you] kept presenting itself to me again and again, until this morning it dragged me down to the lowest point. I did not want to go on. We want to quit when it stops being fun. I certainly wanted to quit this morning! But I must be willing to carry on my fight on all fronts, and not expect to enter into the Peace before I wear the laurel wreath of the conqueror. I prostrate myself before you, who received me, and kept me, and held me to what I needed.

With profound devotion,
Gyanamata

* * * * *

September 16, 1942

My Master—ever blessed and beloved,

There was something you said that took me a long time to understand. You said, "Do not think so much of the other world. Think of this one." When anyone speaks of "the other world" I always think of higher levels of consciousness, and at once I thought that if I could lift myself entirely above this world how much more valuable I would be to you. But what you meant was, "Do not think about death." I do not feel that I exactly *think* about it, but the thought certainly is present in my mind. I hold my karma, and certain aspects of my physical condition that drag my mind down, responsible for this. It is not my will. I never expected that it would be so with me.

Waking in the night or early morning, I always used to find joy present within me. I have changed. I regard it as a trial, a test sent by God for the good of my soul. If one can delight in God only when He comes as joy, what is he? But suppose God comes only as pain? That it takes a spiritual hero to endure. If, in the darkness, the mind never wavers, if love and longing never grow weak, it is then that you prove to yourself that you really have the love of God.

The thought of death comes as a temptation when in suffering. And you made it *very* tempting in your sermon on Sunday [in which Paramahansaji explained the peace, freedom, and joy experienced in the afterlife]. I was reminded of a poem that has lived in my mind since girlhood. A dying person speaks. The poem begins, "How still the room is!" and ends with the words, "O death! the loveliness that is in thee, could the world know, the world would cease to be!"

Gyanamata

* * * * *

July 12

My divine Master,

All my life, no matter how ill I was, I never believed that I was going to die, not even when my family despaired of my life. I always said, "I will be better in the morning." If I ever said, either then or after I came to you, that I would like to die, it was the expression of the desire to escape from suffering.

It was not until after I came to the Hermitage that the thought of death definitely came to me. You once referred to that time as "the breaking-up period." Of course I did not dwell upon the idea—it just came to mind once in a while. I read, long ago, that one could not prevent birds from flying over one's head—but one need not let them make nests in one's hair.

I think it was about two years ago that the idea came in a more permanent form to me. It was as if I had been sitting quietly in my room and the door had opened for an unexpected visitor. This was repeated many times. It seemed natural to me to think, at my age, that I *might* be going to leave the body. I don't remember wishing to die, but if I did, it was only at some moment of weariness or illness, as a means of escape. I *never*—and this I earnestly ask Your Holiness to believe—I never *tried* to die; I never refused, or tried to refuse, your blessed healings when they came. I was ever receptive to you, and tried to be more so all the time. I am not capable of such black-hearted ingratitude towards the one with whom I have taken refuge. This is one of the basic thoughts or ideals that is always with me, unchanging, fixed.

And now I come to what I most wanted to tell you. In your sermon two weeks ago you said: "If you think you are bound, you are; but if you think you are *free,* you are free—what can bind you?" This acted upon me instantly. And later I reasoned with myself and made it stronger. I said: "Meditation burns the seeds of karma, and my great Master has meditated for me for years. *I am free!*" I am holding to this liberating concept.

Daily I put forth my God- and Guru-given strength to adjust myself to life in this completely changed body. In hours of concentration, or perhaps weakness, when I need them very much, the words of the holy ones come to me. I thank Thee, O God, because Thou hast spoken to us by the mouth of Thy holy prophets and saints, which have been since the world began. A mighty sound going up from all people, blending in one cry, "God! God! God!"

Your glorious sermons! To listen is to be drawn by golden cords, very fine, but strong as steel—up, up, from the earth and body to heavenly places.

With deep devotion,
Gyanamata

P.S. Sometimes the thought of what you are, and what you are trying to give me, of your meaning and value in my life—of how the weeds that have been allowed to grow in my character too long are finally pulled up—comes over me like a tidal wave, and I wish I had new words, something more worthy of my feelings, to tell you of my reverence, gratitude, devotion, love. Then, for I can find none, I say, "Surely, surely he knows!"

To a devotee who had questions about how to cope with physical suffering:

Dear _______,

One answer will cover all your questions: Turn to God and fill your consciousness with the realization of His perfection. Let your weakness be dissolved in the worshipful thought of His strength. It is not necessary to explain things to God, for He knoweth your need before you speak, and is more ready to give than you are to ask. When you meditate, turn away from everything except the one absorbing thought of His overshadowing Presence. In this way you will become receptive, and healing will flow through body, mind, and soul.

When not meditating, if you wish for an intellectual understanding of the laws that govern healing, read and reread with concentration what Paramahansaji has written in *Scientific Healing Affirmations.* Note that he says: "Matter does not exist in the way we usually conceive it; nevertheless, *it does exist as a delusion.*" Do not, therefore, strengthen the delusion by allowing your consciousness to dwell on the body. When you meditate, let not the thought of your physical needs come between you and Him who is Author of your being—the Giver of every good and perfect gift, including that of healing.

With love in God and Guruji,
Gyanamata

P.S. The best time to use healing affirmations is just before meditation. If you earnestly and deeply repeat them, you will find that you have become concentrated, and have passed from affirming into meditation.

* * * * *

To a woman whose brother was experiencing mental suffering:

Dear Mrs. ________,

Did you notice that in the next-to-last paragraph of your letter you answered your own questions? I quote: "After all that has been said, deeply I feel that I am being watched over and loved and the Plan is being worked out for my growth and his (your brother's). There has been no failing of Divinity."

It may be that your brother-in-law was right in thinking that your brother needed more drastic treatment than yours, but it is seldom that relatives are able to give such treatments successfully. It needs the hand of a friend who stands apart from the life of the one who is mentally ill.

Men who are failures, who find themselves a burden upon those they love, often suffer deeply, dreadfully, before they awaken to a realization of their weakness and discover that nothing except their own effort can give them the joy and safety of success. A man is expected to succeed. If for any reason he can't, his shame may show itself in unreasonable and even unkind actions to those he is dependent upon. Remember this, and if you must err in your treatment of him, err on the side of kindness.

Remember that there is no situation in life that cannot be endured to the end if met with courage and determination. Of course everything is easy if one wears a "cap of Bliss." But do not expect to obtain this "cap" too easily. Remember,

> Sleep *after* toyle, port *after* stormie seas,
> Ease *after* warre, death after life, does
> greatly please.

But first come toil and storm and war and life.

Gyanamata

* * * * *

Dear ________,

You are just passing through a painful moment, in which you are putting the question, "What good does it all do? What does it get me?" When you decided to leave the world and enter on the path of renunciation, you commenced a long and difficult climb—than which there is no longer and more difficult one in the universe.

When I was a little girl I heard the saying, "Those who want to see the monument mustn't give up on the stairs." It refers, I think, to a monument in London, to see which one has to climb a very long flight of stairs. It made a deep impression upon me because of its significance, and I always remember it when thinking of some long and difficult undertaking. I thought of it the other day when you seemed so discouraged.

Gyanamata

* * * * *

Dear ________,

To your question as to why we must suffer, I would answer that we are on the wheel of life. As it turns, we are hurt; and it is the part of our mind or psyche that responds with pain that indicates the shortcomings that God wants us to rise above.

As I pass my life in review, I cannot recall a time when I thought it necessary to ask the above question. Yet I did not want to suffer—I wanted my own way, O yes! Answers have come from time to time, however, without my questioning. The one which has given me the most satisfaction, as I remember, is the one which the Master drew from Ramana Maharshi, who put a counter question, asking: "What suffers?"

In these two words, as in a nutshell, lies the whole subject. The answer is obvious—that which must die if ever we are to reach the Goal. The little self grasps the Self by the throat; it must be put to death if ever we are to live in God. But will the little self ever die if it does not suffer? Will Self-realization ever come if it [that little self] does not die? There is no suffering in God. In God, in Peace; out of God, out of Peace.

What really matters can be put in a few words: complete surrender to God, to the Divine Will. If we did that one thing perfectly, what else would we need to do? What else would we need to know? Doing, knowing, in one divine act, we would find Him on any plane, and would enter into Peace—for "Thou hast made us for Thyself, and our hearts are restless till they rest in Thee."*

Think on my words the next time your heart aches over some favor withheld which you think ought to be granted. Remember that it is God who is both the Giver and the Withholder of favors.

Once I heard Master say, "If you shut me out, I can't come in." All the masters say the same thing. Jesus said, "Behold, I stand at the door and knock: if any man hear my voice, and open the door, I will come in to him, and will sup with him, and he with me."†

But we shut them out. We shut out God, and then ask, "Why does God permit suffering?"

Remember, then, that no matter what one's deprivations—no matter if one must ever press the nose against a window and look in at happy company from which one is debarred—there is no suffering if God stands at one's side.

May you have a joyful Easter.

My love in God and Gurudeva,
Gyanamata

* *The Confessions of Saint Augustine*, Book One.

† Revelation 3:20.

CHAPTER 13

Divine Healings and Spiritual Experiences

Sri Gyanamata did not dwell on the spiritual experiences and healings that came to her, for she realized that it would be a hindrance to concentrate on anything of a phenomenal nature at the expense of the Goal—God alone—which she kept ever before her. Therefore, as stated in one of her letters, she channeled her efforts exclusively toward "the greatest accomplishment—to abide by the will of God."

She perceived it appropriate, however, as part of the guru-disciple relationship, to acknowledge such experiences to her Guru and to express her sincere gratitude for his intervention on her behalf. She humbly fails to mention that her attunement and faith were the devotionally plowed soil in which the Guru's healing seeds were able to sprout. And when others were healed through her, she emphasized that in these instances she was only being used as a channel for her Guru's powerful vibrations. Through her spiritually attuned consciousness, she experienced many inspiring visions and healings, a few of which are recounted in the following letters.

January 13, 1940

My blessed Master,

Yesterday morning when it was time for me to meditate, my mind was full of sad thoughts. I struggled, but it was impossible for me to drive them out. They mastered me.

Then came your beautiful, powerful vibrations. They took firm hold of my being, and instantly I was free! I had that nameless joy, the joy without any "because." And it stayed with me all day.

I do not like to tell of it, because to speak of it seems, in some way, to spoil it. It makes me feel as if it had never happened. Such experiences are intangible; they are to feel and rejoice in, not to talk about. But I think I ought to tell you. I want to make acknowledgement. Nothing exactly like it has happened to me before, during all the years in which you have been helping me.

While I draw this fleeting breath,
When mine eyelids close in death,
When I rise to worlds unknown,
And behold Thee on Thy throne,

may I remember what you have done and are doing for me.

Gyanamata

* * * * *

Written before Sister came into the ashram, when she was living in La Jolla:

Beloved Master,

I believe you saved my life in order that I might have a deeper realization of God. I must endure my karma, while never ceasing to work against it. If I can realize God, then my heart problems, and the arteries, the left kidney, etc. will not matter. Even if I don't, they don't matter.

I am at a loss for words to express my appreciation and thanks for the days spent with you at Laguna. It is all written in my heart, but I don't think I can express it. Many times I shall live over and over again those hours—with you on the beach, watching you stand over the stove cooking that wonderful Indian food—how good it is!—serving us with your own hands, telling us amusing stories, and the beautiful, beautiful chanting!

The broken bone in my hand gave me a still richer experience. I was actually *near* you when you sent out healing vibrations. I was awake and waiting. Then came the vibrations, and the tiny but sharp pain when the bone slipped into place. Then peace and sleep.

Lord, bless me again with your golden touch before you leave the Center. Touch me with the divine fire, taken from the altar of your meditation, that the smoldering embers of my devotion may burst into flames, for you are the vehicle of God to me. Without your blessing I cannot succeed; with it, I cannot fail. Do not refuse my prayer-demand.

With gratitude, devotion, and love,
Edith D. Bissett

* * * * *

June 2, 1942

My blessed Master,

I want to tell you something that may not interest you—but I justify my action by the fact that you have always willingly read the many, many letters I have written you during the last eighteen years of my life.

For a long time I have considered myself as a storage battery of your holy vibrations. Many happenings have confirmed me in this belief.

I had asked for a special blessing from you on an anniversary of my initiation into the sisterhood, whose date fell during the time you were in India (1936). The blessing came strongly all day long. I was on the edge of ecstasy.

Last summer when you were away so long visiting the SRF centers, Mrs. ________ came to me one Sunday morning and said, "Will you help me, Sister? I am so tired that unless you help me I cannot get through the service." I have found that it is best to say "Yes," even when I am in doubt of my power. When I want to pray for anyone, or to commend him to God, I have a simple method. Plotinus says that "the flight of the Alone to the Alone" is a short one. I interpret this to mean that those who turn to God with love and longing are quickly with Him. Of course I do not apply this to those who like yourself can go deeper and deeper into God, until they leave behind all save His glory. Plotinus just intended it for lesser devotees like me, whose love is such that God cannot quite refuse to recognize them.

So I sat down at the dining room table, made that inner turn to God, and then thought of Mrs. ________. I held to the thought of her until the service was over. She came and thanked me, saying, "I felt your vibrations all during the service. Without them I could not have got through. Oh, Sister, you are wonderful!" The vibrations *were* wonderful—but they were yours.

Monday of this week I went to San Diego to have my shoes fixed. When I got home little ______ told me that Mrs. ________ had hurt her foot, and that the hurt had "gone to her stomach," meaning no doubt that the accident had made Mrs. ________ feel sick. So I considered that I ought to go and see if I could help her in any way. At least she would have the comfort of knowing that someone cared. I found her sitting with her foot in hot water. She told me about the mishap; that a flowerpot full of stones had fallen on her toe. We talked a little, and I came back to the Hermitage. The next morning I went again to see her. She was wearing her shoes, and looked happy. "I have had a wonderful healing. I am so thankful. And it came to me through you," she insisted. "As soon as you came into the room it began." You, Master, had healed her, using me as the medium.

I am strong only in one thing—devotion to my Master. In all else I am weak. "But God hath chosen the foolish things of the world, and things which are despised, hath God chosen, yea, and things which are not, to bring to nought things that are: That no flesh should glory in his presence."*

My glory is in God himself, and in that Master who has taken my weakness and turned it into a channel through which his grace may flow to others.

Gyanamata

* * * * *

My blessed Master,

I want to tell you why I asked that favor this morning. I never see the light of the spiritual eye† perfectly—that is, if I close my eyes when sitting in the sunshine, quickly I see the circle of gold, and the beautiful blue center, but not the star. I only see the star in the darkness, and then I do not see the colored circles. You may remember that the day you left for your trip, you touched me between the eyebrows just before you went down to the car. Thinking intently of you, I closed my eyes, and there was the light, all the parts together and in place. Small, but perfect. It was the very first time I had seen the light as a whole.

Gyanamata

* I Corinthians 1:27–29.

† The single eye of intuition and omnipresent perception at the Christ (*Kutastha*) center (*ajna chakra*) between the eyebrows. The deeply meditating devotee beholds the spiritual eye as a ring of golden light encircling a sphere of opalescent blue, and at the center, a pentagonal white star. Microcosmically, these forms and colors epitomize, respectively, the vibratory realm of creation (Cosmic Nature, Holy Ghost); the Son or intelligence of God in creation (Christ Consciousness); and the vibrationless Spirit beyond all creation (God the Father).

Sunday, August 2, 1936

Divine Master,

This morning after meditating and receiving the blessing of your vibrations, I went out under the pepper tree to raise my arms over my head in the exercise that Mr. Lynn loves so much. He advised me to practice it three times a day, and I do when I feel physically able. This morning, as I lowered my arms slowly, I first saw a golden light; then that dimmed and I saw a small, deep blue circle. In the middle was a large eye, looking at me. That widened, and I saw a section of your face. Your eyebrows, eyes, and the upper part of your nose.

It is enough, O God—a light touch, a faint whisper, a tiny ray of light—if the meaning is that Thou art near.

On the back of my "God Alone" placard I wrote this prayer—my prayer, on the fourth anniversary of my initiation into *sannyas*. It was written by St. John of the Cross, but I changed "Mt. Carmel," where he lived, to "Mt. Washington," where I live.

> On Mt. Washington God alone and I—
> God alone in my spirit to enlighten it,
> God alone in my acts to sanctify them,
> God alone in my heart to possess it.

With deep devotion,
Gyanamata

* * * * *

My blessed Master,

This morning the power of God flowed from you, and His finger touched me. I saw the clear white light which Mr. Lynn says I ought to see. As God comes to me in feeling and not in phenomena there is nothing else to say. And I know no new way of telling you of the physical relief and rest, the deep spiritual joy, the gratitude, devotion and love that comes to me at these times.

With deep devotion,
Gyanamata

* * * * *

Golden Lotus Hermitage
October 7, 1941

My blessed Master,

Your note from Boston came yesterday, filling my heart with joy, as any words from you ever must. But it is not just selfish thoughts of my own happiness, nor of my dependence on you—from whom I draw support for body and soul—that are filling my mind just now. I am thinking of this wonderful tour and of the many disciples who have not seen you for so many years, who are being refreshed and inspired by your presence.

I am also thinking of something you wrote Mr. Lynn when you were in India (in 1936): "We shall never be Yogananda and Mr. Lynn in any other incarnation. Let us do as much as we possibly can for the world while this incarnation lasts." I thrilled to those words then. I shall never cease to feel wonder and astonishment that I am connected with your Order and this great work, even in the humble capacity of a poor Sister.

I am deeply thankful for the freedom I have here in the Hermitage to move about and do things for myself in my own way, for my quiet room, and for the visitors—many of whom hear their first words of the truths of SRF from my lips, and who thank me with unmistakably sincere gratitude.

I have been having short meditations during the day on the veranda outside the dining room. When I meditate in the light I see beautiful changing colors. At first I thought these effects were due to the sunlight upon my eyes; but often, when I open my eyes, both sky and ocean are cold and gray. Occasionally I see faces. It is curious to see a face in profile, then have that face turn slowly and look at me.

One day I saw a glorious ruby cross. It did not hang perfectly straight before my eyes; it was tipped a little, so that I could not see the end of one arm. At first the stones were dark red. As I looked, the stones became lighter in color and seemed to burn, until at last they glowed like pigeon-blood rubies. Yet they were really more beautiful than any other stones I have ever seen, because they seemed to be on fire within. The cross remained for some minutes. I opened my eyes several times, but when I closed them again, it was still there.

With the devotion of the poor Sister,
Gyanamata

* * * * *

October 3, 1943

My blessed Gurudeva,

The book [*Autobiography of a Yogi*], the work on which you are pressing to a conclusion, I have longed for since first I knew you were writing it. In imagination I hold in my hand a copy, fresh from the press. I do not commence to read it at once. I hoard it. When I do begin to read it, I do so very slowly and carefully, thinking of what you have given to the world. I think of this, also, when I read the *Praecepta.** All the great masters have told men to seek God. But never before has there been given a complete technique by which men can carry on that search day by day. You came on earth to give that detailed instruction.

* Paramahansaji later changed the name of the *Praecepta* to *Self-Realization Fellowship Lessons,* the name by which this home-study series is known today.

I told you of the meditations I used to have on the veranda outside the Encinitas Hermitage dining room. It was two or more years ago. The best time was when the sun was setting....It seemed I shut my eyes to this plane and immediately opened them on another. There was a regular program: First I would see the white light; then a big jewel, cut perfectly with facets, like a diamond. It was purplish-red in color. Then clouds and clouds of golden yellow light. Then faces....On one occasion I saw you, wearing a turban, as you did when you first came here from India. Your face was in profile first. Then you turned, and I saw your full face.

Twice, in visions, I saw your Master Sri Yukteswarji. His hair and beard made a white halo around his face, and his eyes were encircled with blue light.

Recently you let me read something Dick [Wright] wrote describing his first sight of Sri Yukteswarji: "His dark eyes are haloed by an ethereal blue ring." So I, *I*, saw the same blue light around his eyes that Dick had seen years ago, when he stood before Sri Yukteswarji! As Dick described him, so I saw him, twice!

I, an unworthy disciple of Your Holiness, walk the path that leads to the heights where you and he—two, yet One—dwell!

With reverence, gratitude, devotion, and love,
Gyanamata

* * * * *

My blessed Master,

Something very sweet, a beautiful though small spiritual experience, came to me while you were away. In the early morning, the day after I commenced to take the doctor's medicine, I felt too sick to meditate; so I took the little stone you gave me, and holding it in my hand, went to sleep. I had two reasons for asking you for that stone—the first one being that I wanted something from your room in my hand; and the second, because all my life I have had a very peculiar feeling: After the worst of a sick day is over, I always wish that someone would hold my hand. I do not know why. But it is very strong. The feeling even comes in my right hand, not just in my mind. I held the little stone all the night I was sick, without opening my hand.

The morning I am writing about, as I slept, holding the stone, I thought I was standing somewhere outside the Hermitage, in my Sister's dress. I had the stone in my hand, and kept the hand behind me. Suddenly the feeling of the stone left me, and the feeling came that someone was holding my hand. I turned to see who it was, and found behind me a shadowy, draped figure. I felt awe and joy, and said, "It is the Lord!" I woke in peace and joy. At other times when I have wanted someone to hold my hand, I have always felt that there *was* Someone near who could hold it.

With deep devotion,
Gyanamata

* * * * *

May 26, 1945

Blessed Master,

I hope my silence speaks my deep gratitude as eloquently as the most beautiful words could. But sitting up in bed this afternoon, trying to rest—I say trying, because resting involves as much effort as does anything I am faced with the necessity of doing—a tidal wave of thanksgiving flowed over me for the relief that God gave me through you on Thursday night. I dare not say more, because my life ought to match my emotion and my words, and it never, never can.

I was sitting up in bed at the time. It is the most comfortable position I can take when I feel the worst. Suddenly the divine benediction came. The finger of God touched me. Just the very first touch was enough in itself, if there had been no more.

Blessed Master, I would like to say to you words I have said before:

> I give Thee back the life I owe,
> That in Thine ocean depths its flow
> May richer, fuller be.

I will try to live a life that corresponds to these words. Do not reject it because of its weakness and imperfection.

Gyanamata

* * * * *

February 22, 1946

My divine Master,

I felt as if I were on a Mount of Transfiguration. Like the disciples of Jesus, I did not want to come down. I do not think I am quite down yet; I am not sure. I wish I might stay a little higher up the mountain than I was before.

The first night that your vibrations came to me, I was sure that the flood of golden, glorious, holy, prayer-vibrations were intended for Mr. Lynn—that you were using me as a channel through which they could flow to him. Though I have never mentioned this to you, I have always thought that sometimes you use me in this way—the first time being when Rex injured his leg so seriously before I came to Mt. Washington from Seattle. "I am the bulb and Thou art the Holy Light gleaming within it."

So, when you told me to pray deeply for Mr. Lynn at night, whenever I meditated, and all day long, I took your meaning to be that I was to turn my full concentration upon him that I might render myself the clearest possible channel for the power that flows to you from God. So I took the simple, easy means that are all I am able to use for such work. I called up his image before me, and tried to hold it. That was for the mind. I called to my remembrance my wonderful contacts with him in the days when he was always in ecstasy; his spiritual generosity to me when—as he expressed it—he "was conscious" of me. This was for my heart. This morning I have the feeling that you, O son of God, have healed him.

So do Thou, my Lord,
Thou and I never apart;
Wave of the sea,
Dissolve in the sea!*

I am the bubble; Thou art the Sea.

Gyanamata

* * * * *

February 11, 1945

My blessed Master,

For years I have wanted to know something about the astral plane—something authoritative. I would not buy a book on the subject (if indeed there be any), because I could not judge if it were truthful and gave the facts or not.

Nor would I ask you. I do not ask you such things. I simply take what you give me. I know it is better for me to concentrate on God and on my duty in this plane than to ask curious questions about the next.

Now the desired information comes to me, from God

* From "I Am the Bubble," in *Cosmic Chants,* by Paramahansa Yogananda.

through you, in your recent talk on the astral world.* You said, in one place: "The greatest accomplishment is to abide by the will of God, not by our own will." And, glad as I am to learn all that you told about the astral realms, I know that that sentence conveys the greatest truth. If I could follow that counsel perfectly, my Goal would be reached.

With deep devotion,
Gyanamata

* The material in this talk was similar to that which appears in *Autobiography of a Yogi,* chapter 43.

CHAPTER 14

Gratitude to God and Guru

Sri Gyanamata once wrote to Paramahansa Yogananda: "I am embroidering this last chapter of my life upon the fabric of your will. When I do not see the pattern of that will before me, then I do not know how to place my stitches." By thus humbly attuning her life to the will of God and Guru, she opened the door of receptivity to the divine grace that flows to the sincere disciple. Experiencing these supernal blessings, Sister naturally felt immense gratitude welling up within her heart. The letters in this section—of which many are just short missives of appreciation to her Guru on Christmas, on New Year's Day, or on his birthday—are outpourings of the spontaneous gratitude, love, and devotion that she felt so strongly for her God and Guru.

Christmas Day, 1941

To my blessed Master:

For recognizing me in Seattle as one of your disciples from the past—for receiving me when I had no one else to turn to—for holding me to the path, when, bewildered by an agony of pain, I knew not which turn to take—for everything that has come since, up to the present day—for all you are that I know you to be and for all you are that I cannot know—I offer you reverence, gratitude, devotion, and love. But not enough, oh, not enough! It can never be enough.

Gyanamata

Christmas 1948

To my blessed Master:

During the Christmas season, I do not think only of that great master who lived and suffered twenty long centuries ago, I think of that great one who is living and suffering with and for us now.

To your students and disciples, who are scattered over the whole world, you have given the key that will enable them—if they are faithful, and however remote they are from your presence—to attain ultimately the highest peak of realization.

But Master, we do not appreciate you as we should; that is manifestly impossible. You will forgive us—not weighing our merits, and pardoning our offenses.

Sometimes, during the night or in the early morning, I hear your step outside, and think, "He is alone with God."

Gyanamata

* * * * *

New Year's Day, 1941

My blessed and beloved Master,

You gave me a star of great brilliance in the words you wrote on my Christmas greeting card. You said that I have given "divine cooperation" in "countless" ways. This star will shed a consoling, uplifting, and inspiring light on my heart forever.

With deep devotion,
Gyanamata

* * * * *

Sunday evening

My blessed Master,

When you say wonderful things to me, I am unable to

give you any sign of what I feel. I am speechless; so I have to write. You said that I am near to you, that I always have been, and that nothing will ever come between us. You looked straight at me when you said it. I felt such awe! that you could say such words to *me*! Such a priceless gift, beyond the power of princes or kings to bestow! Then a feeling of expansion came, and is with me yet.

You have often said that I have great faith. But if I can feel the power of God flowing through you to me, is it not more than faith?

Gyanamata

* * * * *

My ever blessed Master,

Tomorrow will be the fourteenth anniversary of my initiation into *sannyas.* Fourteen years unmarred by anything except my errors and lack of understanding. I ask myself, "Do I even dimly understand the power that has been expended for me, the prayers sent up to God?"

O blest communion, fellowship divine, to which you have admitted me!

So long Thy power—God's, yours—has led me; sure it still will lead me on.

Gyanamata of Yogananda

* * * * *

May 8, 1940

My divine and blessed Master,

For many years—I think from the very first time I saw you—I have wanted to offer you, as the outpouring of my own heart, the poem I am about to copy. But I thought I had no right to do so, until I had had certain experiences. All these years I have waited. On Monday afternoon I was thinking of you, and of our relationship—but when do I think of anything else? This poem came to my remembrance, and the wish I had had so long to write it to you.

I do not think things out. Suddenly an intuitive flash shows me some truth, whole and complete, which has been hidden from me before. I know with sureness. So, in such a flash, I saw that the poem* conveyed exactly what has been taking place between Your Holiness and myself wordlessly, and that I had the right to copy it and offer it to you:

> It is the mercy of my true Guru that has made me to know the unknown;
> I have learned from Him how to walk without feet, to see without eyes, to hear without ears, to drink without mouth, to fly without wings;
> I have brought my love and my meditation into the land where there is no sun and moon, nor day and night.
> Without eating, I have tasted of the sweetness of nectar; and without water, I have quenched my thirst.
> Where there is the response of delight, there is the fullness of joy. Before whom can that joy be uttered?
> Kabir says: "The guru is great beyond words, and great is the good fortune of the disciple."

This is the true expression of my heart, but if I were to try to explain or talk about it, I would spoil it.

Gyanamata

* *One Hundred Poems of Kabir,* trans. Rabindranath Tagore (London: Macmillan and Company, 1915), poem XXVII. Kabir was a great sixteenth-century saint of India.

Thanksgiving Day 1938

Blessed Master,

On this and every other day, you are my deepest cause for thankfulness. But if, through having forgotten the past, I do not properly understand the present, and therefore fall short of offering you perfect service and devotion, please exercise your divine prerogative—and forgive.

Gyanamata

* * * * *

July 24, 1945

My divine and blessed Master,

I've no words to thank you for the wonderful gift of the gold cross! It is too delicately beautiful to be appropriate for me, but very dear and precious because you gave it to me. My surprise was great; for a while I was bewildered, and said to myself, "It cannot really be for me!" I wanted to write you at once, but I could not; my heart was too full.

But if I can't find words for the gift, what words are there for the note that came with it? I thought of my twenty-one years of discipleship, and felt as if you had placed a golden crown upon them. You were pleased with what I had said in the note I had written to remind you of the anniversary.* To please you has been the central wish and only desire of my heart since first I saw you. The crest-jewel of my golden crown was your assurance: "I am ever with you." In that promise I rest secure. I repeat it over and over to myself.

I thank you also, from the deepest part of my soul that I can reach, that you do not leave me in suffering; but, when

* The anniversary of Gyanamata's taking the final monastic vows of *sannyas* on July 20, 1932.

God wills, lift me to heavenly places, where "He shining, all shines after Him."

Gyanamata

* * * * *

Saturday morning, March 22, 1941

My ever blessed, ever beloved Master,

I have attained to the gratification of a desire that has been ever present with me since you found me in Seattle—to have upon my body something which need never be taken off, and which would be a constant reminder of my Goal and you. Now upon my arm is the bangle given me by you.

The strange thing about my entertaining the above desire, and the foolish ones I confessed to you in my last letter, is that I well know, and have known all along, that I do not belong to the type that profits by such things. External aids, rituals, symbols, tokens, do nothing for me—yet I have sought them persistently. It is possible, I suppose, that since they were always directed to you, they have made me more receptive to you. But the only things that really help me upward are the daily lifting of mind and heart to God, and the help that comes from you.

How delicious is the sensation of liberation! I experienced it a year ago last Christmas while meditating. For a few minutes—perhaps it was only seconds—I was entirely released from all downward drags. It was like having a window opened when one is sitting in a stuffy room and feeling a cool breeze blowing in.

But when I am tired, and I *am* very weary (sometimes it seems as if I could not go on, though I do not feel the desire to stop, either), I hear the voice of Jesus, speaking in a Christian hymn:

> Well I know thy sorrow, O my servant true,
> Thou art very weary, *I* was weary too!

or,

> The cup which my Father hath given me, shall I not drink it? (John 18:11)

Then I lift my eyes to your divine life and contemplate it. As Jesus went up to Jerusalem to be crucified, so you came here and have been crucified upon a cross of suffering as well.…All this you endure.

As I watch, I see you "waking, eating, working, dreaming, sleeping, serving, meditating, chanting, divinely loving."* I watch you going back and forth every week from Encinitas to Los Angeles to give the Sunday services, though this must surely take its toll on your body. I see you giving interviews to those who come to you for help, denying yourself to none, inspiring, comforting, reproving, and uplifting the fallen and sorrowful. No opportunity to extend the work is overlooked by you.

I see that wherever the rain of your heavenly vibrations falls, flowers of marvelous beauty spring up, diseases are healed, rest and peace are substituted for pain. There are countless people who never realize from whom health and prosperity have come. Your brain, tongue, and heart are ceaselessly busy sowing the seeds of faith, understanding, and aspiration, where darkness and ignorance reigned supreme before; your beloved voice inspiring the hopeless and weary; your blessed energies bringing light out of darkness, and order out of confusion, working tirelessly on the erection of a "world city"—one not made with hands, eternal in the heavens.

* A line from Paramahansa Yogananda's poem, "God! God! God!"

I try feebly to place my feet in the prints made by yours, and know that my *real* tokens and treasures are the gracious glances that your eyes bestow upon me sometimes; the sound that I hear underneath your voice when you speak to me; a word said, or written upon a card, that sinks into my heart and is never lost or forgotten. Having them, why have I ever desired anything else? I cannot tell. Life is a paradox, as you said to me some weeks ago.

With deep devotion,
Gyanamata

* * * * *

Sunday, September 17, 1939

My blessed Master,

Mr. Lynn says that what one feels, but cannot describe nor talk about, is realization. Then what I received from you this morning was realization. If I wish to speak, what is there to say?

They say you "spoke as one inspired" at the temple this morning. I, too, have knowledge of your inspiration, but it comes to me another way.

With deep devotion,
Gyanamata

* * * * *

This is possibly the first note that Sister wrote to Paramahansaji following her coming into the Mt. Washington ashram in 1932:

Mt. Washington Center, Saturday

Dear Master,

To look at you is meditation. Sometimes when I am meditating, the memory of some moment when I have come upon you unexpectedly in the halls or rooms of the Center comes to me, and tears flow from my eyes at the wonder and glory of your finding me after my long years of waiting.

In gratitude, devotion, and love,
Edith D. Bissett

* * * * *

My ever blessed Master,

I see now that you do not want me to deface in any way the image of my life, which you have been holding up for the inspiration of the other disciples. I do not *think* I have talked complainingly to the young women disciples, but I shall watch myself more closely hereafter. I have said a great deal about what has befallen me* in an attempt to awaken in them thankfulness for their physical blessings. Their hands, for example. They all have smooth, pliable, strong hands, suggestive of service. I have reminded the disciples not to accept such hands as a matter of course, but to be thankful to God for them, and to remember that bodily blessings, which young people often take as a matter of course, can be lost.

This incident has given me a much clearer vision and deeper understanding of what you want my life to be—the ideal you are holding up before the eyes of my soul.

"Lord, Thy word is a lamp unto my feet, and a light unto my path."†

The great relief your healing and prayers gave me next morning I can feel but cannot describe. Your hand took away the pain at once.

How many times you have bought and paid for my life! How deep my guilt if I do not bend every effort to the attainment of the goal you have placed before me, how

* Gyanamata was at this time troubled by crippled hands, a result of neuritis.

† Psalms 119:105.

double-dyed if I do not divert all thoughts of self to God and you!

Memories of the years during which you have stood apart from me, yet have been ever with me, dissolve my heart in devotion, gratitude, love, and unspeakable reverence.

Gyanamata

P.S. I want to tell you how kind and sweet Virginia is to me. If she finds me in the kitchen, even at four o'clock in the morning,* she takes everything out of my hands into her own, carries all I need to my room, and stays until she is sure there is nothing more she can do; then she leaves, telling me to call her if I need help.

* * * * *

My divine Master,

This year, 1947, I have been your disciple for twenty-three years. The twentieth of this month, next Sunday, will be the fifteenth anniversary of my initiation into *sannyas.* I never fail to call your attention to this date.

Would that I could express the emotions of reverence, gratitude, devotion, love, and deep unworthiness that burn in my heart....

When you were in Tucson you wrote me, "I am deeply praying for you." And, "I ever pray for you within." Also, "I am ever with you in God and unceasingly praying for you." I copied these words from your letter on a piece of paper and keep them by my bed. They are the Bread of Life to me. With thanksgiving, I feed on all that comes to me from you in my heart by faith.

Gyanamata of Yogananda

* Gyanamata customarily began her day by rising at three or four a.m., and warming some milk to drink before her several hours of meditation.

Sunday, April 13, 1947

My divine Master,

I have always found that when I have something I want to say to you, but do not feel equal to the effort of writing, if I wait patiently, just exactly the right day comes. So it is now. The subject I have on my mind is THE BOOK [*Autobiography of a Yogi*].

After you gave it to me at Christmas, for months I was content just to possess it. To have it beside me on the bed, to know that it was mine, and that I could take as long in reading it as I wanted to. Then, when I was ready to begin, a still longer time passed because I was only willing to read it on my best days.

I am so glad that picture of you was chosen for the jacket. Of all your pictures, it is my favorite. I thank you for the beautiful words you wrote about me in inscribing the book to me [*see page 264*], but still more for those written on the Christmas card that came with it. "With unending love," you wrote. That you could say such words to *me*! I treasure them, and they come to me with sustaining power in moments of great weariness.

In going over in my mind what you have given to the world in this book, I see it illumined by the light that shines from the glorious figure of His Holiness, your Master [Swami Sri Yukteswar]. In my Mt. Washington days, I listened with rapt attention to the descriptions you gave of your life with him—of his power, but especially of his method of training and discipline, his arrows of reproof, tipped with barbs to pierce the ego. I thought how wonderful to be able to stand before one's master and say, "I accept anything you mete out to me, anything at all, however hard and cruel it may appear on the surface, anything that will shape me into what *you* are." To so desire God that no pain, but only joy, is felt in the process!

I am reminded of a book about a number of masters of India. I had never heard of them before, and cannot now remember anything in the book except one incident: There was a rather unique holy man who had a high temper and often would not allow his disciples to come near him. If they persisted in pressing upon him, as they often did in spite of his angry shouts, he would pick up stones to throw at them. But those disciples who—out of reverence, devotion, and eager desire for God—picked up and kept those thrown at them, found when they got home that the stones had turned into golden nuggets!

Reading the chapter on the resurrection of "The Lion of God" [Sri Yukteswar], I thought of how the Hindu scriptures say that the teacher must be wonderful; and the disciple must be wonderful, too. Here it was before my eyes! The wonderful teacher, the wonderful disciple—together a perfect whole. And I know where to find you both: You have ascended into the heavens. One may *look* toward a place where one longs to be; so each day I look to where you live in the glory of God, and try—oh, such feeble efforts—to thither ascend and dwell with you continually in heart and mind, in understanding and spirit.

You know what I have to contend with, also what fate would be mine did not the prayers of Your Holiness ever plead with God for me. From New York, from Mt. Washington, from India, from Encinitas, your holy vibrations have come to me—sometimes like a powerful wind, sometimes just a gentle touch. I wish I had some golden words to express what I feel—but it is not necessary, since you know all about me, including the things I do not know myself.

I am prostrate at your feet,
Gyanamata

* * * * *

Saturday evening

My blessed Master,

Unfitted as I have always been, even on the very best day of my life, to render personal service to a master, and utterly and completely unfitted as I now am, I want to thank you for sometimes letting me have the joy of doing some small personal thing for you.

These small acts, to me, are outer symbols of the deep devotion of my heart, little rituals that thrill me as no church or temple service ever has. How is it that these joys have come to such a one as I? Surely it is through the mercy of God and the grace of the Guru.

With deep devotion,
Gyanamata

* * * * *

Friday, May 7

My Gurudeva,

The words you spoke to me the last time we met go up and down in my mind. You said you expected more of me than of others. I know you have the right to expect more of me than of any of your other disciples. Those who are given much and loved much—from them much may be expected. But whether I will be able to measure up to your expectations is another matter. It seems possible that owing to illness I may fail. Still, the same God who has been with me all these years (74 in July) will support me *through you* to the end.

In spite of your perfect knowledge of me, of your God-consciousness and wisdom, I doubt if you know to what extent I depend upon you and am supported by you. In the morning, if I am depressed and weary, and you speak to me over the telephone as you almost always do, recognizing me and speaking very gently, since you are just out of meditation, immediately my consciousness is lifted. From the sound of your voice I receive some of the vibrations you have brought with you.

When your eyes look at me, still more when I hear your voice, when I dwell upon you in consciousness—all fear leaves me. My soul rejoices!

With deep devotion, ever and always,
Gyanamata

* * * * *

Christmas Eve

Blessed One:

Rex and Hughella unite with me in presenting this gift. To us it is more than a Christmas present. It is an offering from deep down in our hearts, one that we lay humbly at your feet. I have the special favor of being every day, waking and sleeping, under your protection. And they, from time to time during the year, ask the help of your prayer vibrations, which are always graciously granted, at we know not what cost to you in terms of time and effort.

I have never been overly curious about my past incarnations. It seems sufficient to know that I am the essence of all of them, and that in this one I can have neither more nor less than I have earned. But I *do* confess that I would like to know what good act, or group of good actions, gave me the honor and happiness of striving and working beside you, here at the headquarters of the great work. My body knows sickness and weariness, but my mind, *never.* Willingness never fails me, and wings grow upon my heels at the sound of your beloved voice.

I wish, for your sake, that I were a man, young and strong, ready to live a long life of unceasing effort to aid you in spreading the truth over the whole world. I do not, however, spend much time in wishing that things were different, but rather in praising God for bringing me to this last estate. To quote the words from a card that came to me the other day, and to twist them a little to suit my purpose, "The morning of my life spoke of His glory, and its evening re-echoes it."

Your name will be lovingly known to posterity; and because I am Gyanamata, disciple of Yogananda, it is just possible that mine too may be mentioned. May it be said of me that I lived out my life with undaunted courage, determination, and fortitude, content if able to serve you in the humblest capacity, thankful if I can lift a feathersweight of the burden from your shoulders. Daily I make the effort to go deeper in understanding, and to pour over your feet the perfumed water of a devotion untainted by the least thought of self.

Graciously accept our gift, offered in all humility. I kiss the hem of your robe in gratitude, devotion, and love,

Gyanamata

* * * * *

August 4, 1941

My divine Master,

The check I am enclosing requires some explanation. It is the second half of our offering to you. When I wrote Rex that I wanted to offer to you the down payment on the books, I called to his attention the many times during the past seventeen years that you have poured out your divine power for us—when you have been our only refuge, our only hope. Replying to me he said that he felt a little hurt that I had thought it necessary to remind him of those times. We may never be able to do this again; but this once, at least, we know the supreme joy of giving you an outward, visible sign of the deep gratitude and devotion of our souls.

As for me: "I have made Thee the polestar of my life."* The delicately poised needle of the compass shakes and quivers. But the needle of my devotion has been immovable since that first day I met you in Seattle, when you made a little weighted toy lie down upon the tablecloth, afterward imparting to me by the light touch of your finger the power to do the same thing on the following day.

Even if I can never again offer you money, the flow of reverence, gratitude, devotion, and love from my heart shall never cease. When I think of my death, and wonder how it will be then—and afterward—I think our relationship can only be greater; because when the veil of the flesh is removed I shall see you as you are and will therefore adore you as I ought.

Gyanamata

* * * * *

Friday

My divine Master,

I will write to Mr. ________. I intended to; I do not need help. I have written with the first finger of the right hand ever since my hands began to give me trouble. I can use only that finger on the typewriter, but it is better than trying to write with a pen—I don't know why. I am writing you that way now.

But I have to wait for a good day—I mean a day when I feel physically fit to write and to express the devotion my heart feels for you. But even under the best conditions I will not be able to tell him the half of what I feel for you, of what I know about your life. What then is to be said about all that lies outside my knowledge?!

I thank you for the grace you have just shown me.

Gyanamata

* A phrase from one of the chants in Paramahansaji's *Cosmic Chants.*

Sunday, November 12

My divine Master,

There is something I want to tell you about the time I thought I was going to die—the thought keeps recurring to me, no matter how many times I push it away. It is that I planned to go consciously.* I never thought that I would go unconsciously—yet I almost did, and but for you I would have.

I have never been deeply concerned because I do not remember my incarnations. I am the essence of them all; surely this is the most important memory. I would like to have a feeling of continuity. You gave it to me once by saying that I had meditated a great deal in my last life. I felt a thrill of joy because you tied these two lives together and made them one. I can scarcely write about this subject. It overpowers me. But the process does not matter. What matters is the end in God.

I came from Seattle to be near you, and now I am absorbed in you through THE BOOK [*Autobiography of a Yogi*], in which you give your life to the world. I am following you through the years as you have revealed them.

Gyanamata

* * * * *

Gyanamata lived at the Self-Realization Hermitage in Encinitas from 1936 until her passing in 1951. In 1941, Paramahansaji arranged for her to spend a day at Christmas with him and the other disciples at Mt. Washington.

January 11, 1942

My divine and beloved Master,

I am a little ashamed because I have written to you so

* And so she did—she left her body consciously, at the appointed time, just as she had "planned."

much lately, but I cannot be happy until I have thanked you for my wonderful day at Mt. Washington. It was indeed happy from the moment when, to my astonishment and joy, I recognized that you were welcoming *me* with flowers, to the last word of your farewell blessing.

I am so different from everyone else in my reactions, and I don't believe that any of the other disciples knew how happy I was to be with you while you and Mr. Lynn .were having your Christmas celebration together. Sitting very still and saying nothing does not mean that I am not enjoying myself. Quite the contrary. But perhaps you know this—you, who I think must know me through and through.

My personal Christmas joys begin with the cards you write me. Of course I like what you give me, but what is the most marvelous gift compared to the proof, given by the cards, that I have pleased you? And your approval means God's, too.

I had the happiness of examining every nook and corner of the Mt. Washington Center. The lovely views from the windows have been etched upon my heart since the years I lived there, I suppose because of the intensity of my devotion to you, and the agony I was in after the death of Mr. Bissett.

It will be a long time before I am with you again in the same or in a similar way, and perhaps I never will be. But if it does happen sometime, please let me just sit in a corner of the room and drink in the joy with which it is filled, and I will have the most wonderful Christmas that the heart can imagine.

For what you are to me, my reverence, gratitude, devotion, and love,

Gyanamata

My divine and blessed Master,

The King of Love my Shepherd is,
Whose goodness faileth never,
I nothing lack if I am His,
And He is mine—forever!

Where streams of living water flow,
My ransomed soul he leadeth,
And where the verdant pastures grow,
With food celestial feedeth.

Perverse and foolish oft I strayed,
And yet in love he sought me,
And on His shoulder gently laid,
And home rejoicing brought me.

In death's dark vale I'll fear no ill,
With Thee, dear Lord, beside me,
Thy rod and staff my comfort still,
Thy cross before to guide me.

And so through all the length of days,
Thy goodness faileth never,
Good Shepherd, may I sing Thy praise
Within Thy Courts forever.

I do not know to whom credit should be given for this anthem,* but I am sure that could the author know the inspiration that has come to me by using it in meditation, I would be excused for quoting it.

"I am the good shepherd," said the Lord Jesus, "and know my sheep, and am known of mine" (John 10:14). The masters, the Good Shepherds of this world, come down from their high places and give their lives to searching for disciples who are lost in the darkness. They find them in

* Music by J. B. Dykes (1868), words by H. W. Baker (1868).

desolate and dangerous places, arouse them, lift them to a divine shoulder, and bear them with rejoicing to a safe place in the fold. They feed them with celestial food and give them living water to drink, of which, if a man eat and drink, he shall live forever. They give them power to become the sons of God. They give their own lives, to the last ounce of flesh and the last drop of blood, for the redemption of the sheep who know their voice.

Lord, evermore give me this heavenly food and drink!

Good Shepherd, may I sing Thy praise within Thy Courts forever!

Gyanamata

* * * * *

May 3, 1935

Divine and blessed Master,

Enclosed is a little gift from Rex, Hughella, and me. It is an offering, on the eve of your departure for India, thanking you for your many favors—those we know of, and those that must forever remain unknown.

It is not intended for the temple in India. It is for you. I offer it for the temple of your body, from which blessings and healing flow constantly to me. I do not ask to have my picture or name preserved in the temple in India. That would not be enough; it would not satisfy me! I ask that my name be engraved on your memory; that I sometimes be in your thoughts when you meditate; and that occasionally, when you pray, my name arise from your lips to God.

I ask that when the incense of your prayers soars to God, and when you make a place for me, you will pray that love and devotion burn like a fire in my heart, consuming in its heat the petty, the trivial, the unworthy, the selfish—all that now remains like a dark stain on my soul. I ask that you pray that this fire of love and devotion in me be not only a cleansing and consuming force, but burn up to heaven, and be a tower of strength in me, enabling me to stand entirely alone if necessary—unmoved, undaunted, thankful that at least I have seen the shadow of His shadow! Pray, Lord, that nothing but He may ever satisfy me, that life to me may continue to be a dry and barren desert, until I can live night and day, night and day, forever in His joy.

As for him whose gift to us you are—Swami Sri Yukteswarji—I am prostrate at the feet of His Holiness.

Gyanamata

* * * * *

Tribute to Swami Sri Yukteswar

Upon the mahasamadhi *of Swami Sri Yukteswar in 1936, while Paramahansaji was in India for a last visit with him, the following tribute was written in his honor by Sri Gyanamata:*

Let our thought of Swami Sri Yukteswar be deep and strong, that whatever is lacking in this our outer expression, the inner memorial of our souls shall be rich with gratitude, devotion, and love. We have thousands of students, all of whom owe the knowledge they have gained of the soul, of God—and of the techniques that will, if practiced faithfully and with deep devotion, lead to Self-realization—to this great Master, who trained and sent to us Paramahansa Yogananda.... We have listened spellbound to the account of those years from Paramahansaji's lips. When they were concluded, Sri Yukteswarji said, "Now you must do something for the world!"

Our Gurudeva tells us that his Master liked practical people very much, those able to plan and carry out work for the good of humanity. It was no doubt this idea that made him, when Guruji became lost in meditation, shake him out of it, and say, "Take this broom and sweep the floor." Think of his joy when the work was started in this country!... "Child of my heart, O Yogananda!" he wrote. "Seeing the photos of your school and students, what joy comes in my life I cannot express in words....I am melting in joy to see your Yogoda [Self-Realization] students of different cities. Beholding your methods...I cannot refrain from thanking you from my heart. Seeing the gate, the winding hilly way upward, and the beautiful scenery spread out beneath the Mt. Washington Center, I yearn to behold it with my own eyes."

O blessed Swami Sri Yukteswarji, our humblest and profoundest *pranams* to you! We do not feel that you have withdrawn from us, but that you have come nearer, and that your passing was but in preparation for greater service to mankind.

* * * * *

A poem written by Gyanamata to her Guru, upon his return from India in 1936:

Salutation!

When you left us long months ago,
Our hearts were heavy with unacknowledged misgiving.
Would the dear, holy land,
The land of your birth that you call "My India,"* hold you?
Would its needs appeal to you as more pressing than ours?
At the end of our waiting would you say:
"I have given you fourteen years of the labor of my hands,
The blood from my veins, the wisdom of my mind, the love
    of my heart.
Now you must give me up to India"?

* A reference to Paramahansaji's poem by this title.

With deepest interest we received the reports of your
triumphal march from city to city.
Of vast audiences that received you with acclamations and
hung upon your words,
When the clarion tones of your voice rang out,
Telling them that man must work if he wishes to win
Salvation—Liberation,
And offering them anew the teachings and techniques of
their sages,
Enriched and expanded by your meditations.
With surprise and joy we heard of the new centers that
were being opened in this faraway land.
Of students who flocked to you to enroll under your banner,
And of our own *Praecepta* being translated into their native
tongue.

At last we understood.
Our selfish demands were stilled.
Our souls and hearts expanded to welcome our new
brothers,
And we said: "He does not belong to us, but to the world."
And so, uplifted and purified, we are welcoming you upon
your return,
Saying, as did Simon Peter of old to the Christ:
"Lord…Thou hast the words of eternal life."
Anew we offer you the service of our hands and hearts,
with the words:
"Here am I, send me."
And we lay at your blessed feet fresh flowers from the
garden of our souls,
With the gratitude, devotion, and love of

YOUR FAITHFUL DISCIPLES

CHAPTER 15

Rajarsi Janakananda

It is difficult for most people to imagine the beauty of the relationship that can exist between two saints. Such friendship, as Gyanamata points out in one of her letters in this section, is not dependent upon outer contact—it is a communion of souls. In the following letters, one is given some insight into that unique relationship—in this case, the ideal friendship between two of Paramahansa Yogananda's foremost disciples: James J. Lynn (Rajarsi Janakananda) and Sri Gyanamata.

Mr. Lynn met Paramahansaji in Kansas City in 1932—a few months before Gyanamata entered the Mt. Washington ashram. A self-made millionaire, Mr. Lynn found in the Self-Realization teachings and the guidance of his Guru the means to reach life's highest goal—conscious, unshakable union with God. In 1952, following Paramahansaji's *mahasamadhi* [a yogi's final conscious exit from the body], Rajarsi became the president and spiritual head of Self-Realization Fellowship/Yogoda Satsanga Society of India, a capacity in which he served until his passing in 1955.*

Paramahansaji once publicly stated: "Of all the women I have met in America, I think the one who has found highest favor with God is Sister Gyanamata. Of all the men I have met here, I think the one who has found highest favor with God is Saint Lynn."

The letters that follow were exchanged before Parama-

* His inspiring life is described in *Rajarsi Janakananda: A Great Western Yogi* (published by Self-Realization Fellowship).

hansaji gave Mr. Lynn the monastic name and title "Rajarsi Janakananda" in 1951. Gyanamata therefore often addressed him as "Saint Lynn," as her Guru did.

From Gyanamata to Paramahansaji, written while he was traveling in India, in which she talks about Rajarsi:

Mt. Washington Center
September 5, 1936

Divine Master,

On Sunday, August 30, I had the great happiness of feeling the uplifting vibrations of your presence. They grew stronger as the day passed, and at my meditation time on Monday morning I floated in a sea of peace and joy. I looked down the dark tunnel of eternity* with awe at the thought of the relationship of guru and disciple. I have never become accustomed to these occasions. Each time I marvel at the joy and well-being that come upon me when you draw near in Spirit.

Mr. Lynn, whose only wish is to be a channel through which your power may flow to us, sends me his wonderful spiritual vibrations frequently. On the morning I have mentioned, he asked me to come up and meditate with him before he took his sun bath. He always meditates before and after *everything*, except this one thing. His visit to Mt. Washington was going to end that day, a Sunday. Knowing that he would be gone before my return from our church services, I went upstairs to meditate with him and to say goodbye....

No words of mine can adequately convey to you Mr.

* A reference to the spiritual eye of intuitive perception. Through this "single eye" the deeply meditating devotee may behold, as through a telescope, the vast vista of the universe, the spheres of heaven, and the realm of Spirit—tier upon tier. The guru helps the disciple to open the spiritual eye and behold the omnipresence of God and of the soul (a reflection of God).

Lynn's unselfish devotion. His one thought, during these visits, is to pour out his wonder-power for our sakes. One night he stopped at my door to give me his blessing. He added a word of personal praise, which I have now forgotten; and then, looking past me he said suddenly: "And there behind you is Swamiji! God bless you, Sister!" The fervor in these words of blessing made them sound more like thanks; as if some credit were due me for the vision he had had of you.

Blessed Master, *I* cannot see you, but I can feel the vibrations of your presence. The joy it gives me each time is so great that I would not exchange it for the wonder of a vision.

I am prostrate at the feet of Your Holiness,
Gyanamata

* * * * *

Four notes from Rajarsi to Gyanamata:

Blessed Sister,

Do not concern yourself with the thoughts of others or what might be their reactions to you. You are a remarkable person, and in you Mt. Washington has just the presence of power and strength it needs.

Surrender thoughts and feelings to God. Know Him to the exclusion of all else and you will swim in that perennial joy and bliss of Spirit. And how wonderful is your spirit—only one who can feel knows fully.

* * * * *

Saturday, 14th November

Blessed Sister,

You will be lonesome. This short note is to let you know, as you will feel, that I am with you.

My meetings with Swamiji here* were filled with divine bliss. I told him that I had arranged with a dear friend for a place on the ocean near San Diego for us to stay awhile. He had already seen a house [in his inner vision] and so may know something about what we have done; but not all, possibly—and there still is a good chance for a pleasant surprise. Durga Ma told me last night how well the building is progressing.†

My plans are to come December 4 when I hope the Hermitage will be ready.

I so much miss Swamiji today and am looking forward to being with you and him soon.

* * * * *

Hermitage, Thursday

Blessed Sister,

Just to convey the message that I am praying for you—and my love and blessings. Be brave and calm and know that God is with you and His will be done.

The Hermitage is not complete without you. You are

* Kansas City, headquarters of Mr. Lynn's business, which included the world's largest reciprocal fire-insurance exchange (of which he was president), vast oil operations, citrus fruits, railroading, and substantial banking interests. Paramahansaji stopped here on his return trip to Los Angeles from India to see his beloved St. Lynn, through whose generosity it was possible for him to journey to India to see his guru, Swami Sri Yukteswar, before Sri Yukteswarji's passing.

† Here Rajarsi is humbly referring to his purchase of a large tract of land in Encinitas where he had constructed the Self-Realization Fellowship Hermitage, while Paramahansaji was away in India and Europe (June 1935 to October 1936). It was indeed a "pleasant surprise," as Paramahansaji lovingly recounts in his *Autobiography of a Yogi,* Chapter 48.

Durga Mata, secretary and member of SRF Board of Directors, was one of Paramahansaji's earliest disciples. She passed away in 1993.

missed in many ways. For example, I miss meditating with you. When I next come, you must be here.

* * * * *

Blessed Sister,

Your note brings a word of testimony to the wonders and love of Spirit. Such results are only of and by His power. The grace of the Great Ones be upon you.

* * * * *

From Gyanamata to Rajarsi:

August 12, 1937

Blessed Saint,

I well know that with you words are entirely unnecessary, you being in that state in which all is known through Spirit. While I am not so fortunate as yet, I can feel the approach of that blessed condition in which two people, no matter what their relationship, seek only the consciousness of that holy vibration, to which you referred the other evening when you said, "Do you feel how strong the Presence is?"

It is already true of me that never do I yield to the temptation to speak to you in words without later reproaching myself after you have gone, saying: "You have wasted some of the few precious moments that he spent with you, in quite unnecessary words."

Since I am writing, I would like to say that the meaning of the advice you give me, and the necessity of it, is well understood by me. Deep down, I *know* that all my strained efforts are not helping me at all—that if I could make an absolutely complete surrender, God would then flow into my soul as I desire. Yet in spite of this knowledge, every now and then a dark cloud of frustration and despair of attaining my chosen goal in this incarnation settles down over me.

Your most gracious and generous help, which from the first you have poured out for my benefit, gives me greater assurance of success than anything I have had since I first began to practice meditation, and through that help I know that I am going to find strength to make the surrender.

As to what you said about limiting myself, that I must think of myself as going on and on forever: I cannot remember the time when I did not know this. The knowledge seems deeply imbedded in my soul. But I cannot *think* about it. For the present it does not seem to concern me, and gives me no consolation. The goal that I see just before me is a gentle flow of Bliss, or, an occasional touch of Bliss. *Then* I shall say, "Lord, I don't care how long I have to wait for the rest."

With love in God and Guruji, and with deepest gratitude and devotion,

Sister

* * * * *

Sunday morning

Blessed Saint,

Entirely for my own satisfaction I want to try to express to you my deep gratitude. It was heavenly that first night to feel again the waves of peace that always come to me when I stand before you, and the effect lasted for twenty-four hours.

Last night my body was so weary that I had little hope that I would be receptive to you, but this morning when I commenced to meditate, I fell at once into deep peace and rest. Tears flowed from my eyes as I remembered how, in the midst of the joy that you must feel at being here, you never forget me, and my need of your blessing. I wonder also at how spontaneously and instantly I am receptive to you.

I thank God for the mercy He shows to me, who am so unworthy of such favors.

Sister

PART III

Letters to Sri Gyanamata

CHAPTER 16

From Sister-Disciples

It is said that truly good and saintly persons are most appreciated by those with whom they associate on a day-to-day basis. These people can observe daily the flawless example, the unfaltering continuity of character in such godlike souls.

The short letters that follow are a few from some of those who lived with Sri Gyanamata during her years in the Self-Realization Fellowship ashram at Mt. Washington and Encinitas. Included also is one of the many letters received from other SRF students and friends who wrote to express their sentiments upon Gyanamata's passing.

April 15, 1936

Dear Sister,

Your letter has made me so very happy. I know you understand me—even better than I do myself—and that is why I look up to you for counsel and understanding. What I feel in my heart—that you know, and I am content.

Your little talks mean a great deal to me, and I always like to have you come to sit and chat with me. I enjoy your putting your ideas on paper, too, because I can save them and in the years to come, I know your letters will help to create anew in me those ideals and the thorough understanding that your little talks always do arouse.

You have helped me throughout these years more than words can express, and I have grown to depend upon your counsel and to love you, oh, so very much, in my own little way. Bless me always, dear Sister, that I may ever be living only to serve my Guruji and the Masters.

* * * * *

My dearest Sister,

_______ gave me your loving greeting this morning. Thank you, my wonderful Sister, for thinking of me. When I learned you were ill, my first impulse was to rush down to assist in nursing you.

Dear Sister, I wanted you to know that I long to be there if I can help you in any way, and hope that you will ask for me if there is anything I can do. I can always get away from my work now that _______ is able to give me greater assistance. Above all, you know how much you mean to me, and will ever mean to me through eternity—what a great inspiration your life and love are to me every day. Always I can recall some words of wisdom that you have said to me. Or when in a tight spot, I ask myself, "How would Sister react to this?" or, "How would she handle it?" So you see you are never very far from my thoughts, nor from my heart.

I add my humble prayers for your welfare to those of all your younger sister-disciples living here and in Encinitas. When I was ill in the hospital, Master told me, "Keep your mind on God." I did so as much as I could, as much as my body would allow me, and much of the time I could feel that great bliss and peace resting upon me. I pray that you may feel His presence also—and that feeling Him, you may find freedom from all the human weaknesses that try to attack the soul, the real You.

I love you, my dearest Sister, and pray that you will continue to hold me in your thoughts.

* * * * *

July 20, 1941

Dearest Sister,

There are so many things I want to write to you on this memorable, holy day [the anniversary of your *sannyas* vows].

You have often said to me, "I don't think the Master realizes how great he is." Dearest Sister, I know you don't realize your own greatness. So it must be with all those true, selfless devotees of God.

When I think of your wonderful qualities, your boundless devotion to our Guruji, and your uncomplaining willingness even when the body rebels, your enduring patience with all of us—oh, how truly good you are, dear Sister! If ever I can reach even a tenth part of the goal you have attained, I shall be grateful.

Pray for me; always correct me. More than you realize you are, next to Master, the greatest inspiration in my life.

* * * * *

Dearest Sister,

Mr. ________ wrote Master a beautiful letter, and spoke specially of you. He said he would never forget how "beautiful and lovely she looked sitting at the end of the table at dinner—just like a heavenly visitant."

Master wrote back that you are the greatest of all women disciples, as truly you are.

* * * * *

Dear Sister,

You certainly have a gift of analyzing people rightly and most justly. I have meant so often to write to you regarding your letters. Will you please, when you see me do something wrong, please tell me—for your judgment is always correct.

There is no one like our Sister.

I pray that I may be of some help to you—you who always consider others first. You are so sacrificing and patient and humble. I pray that you are well. We miss you.

* * * * *

Dearest Sister,

In a rush I write to tell you that Master says it is all right to have meditation in his study.

Were your ears ringing Sunday? They say the ears ring when anyone talks about a person, and Master said a lot of things about you—that you are the greatest woman disciple he has, a real saint. How truly blessed we are to have you, Sister dear.

* * * * *

Saturday, December 24, 7:30 p.m.

Dearest Sister,

We just finished a beautiful December 24 meditation. Master spoke of St. Lynn, then of you. He said: "Sister is already freed. Her feeble body means nothing. She has already been liberated."

So, blessed Sister, please pray for all of us disciples.

* * * * *

July 1944

Dearest Sister,

Many happy thoughts for you on your birthday. I have had many deep realizations lately, and among them is the understanding that true devotees of God like yourself are very rare in this world of *maya*.

It gives me inspiration to try to follow in your saintly footsteps.

July 21, 1939

Last night at lecture, Paramahansaji mentioned you as "the most godlike sister" he had ever known.

* * * * *

Dear Sister,

I was overwhelmed to receive your note. My dear little Sister, a beautiful soul like you reminds us of cathedrals and mountains and all great and beautiful things. You are the one whose example makes us all want to be Sisters of the Order—that is, like you!

Having heard that you have a picture or two which you are going to give to ________, I'd like to beg one for myself (a picture of you, I mean) if you do not mind my having one. If having it where I could see it often would help me to become in any way like you, it would have been of great service not only to me, but to God and our Guruji.

* * * * *

Beloved Little Sister,

As I sat in your room a moment last night I saw your life as a very fragile little flower, yet so rich in the fragrance of Spirit. How much you have given me! When problems have weighed heavily, and I have been in your presence, your inspiration has so lightened my burden.

Time nor space can ever erase the essence of the life you have given us. You have been such an example for those of us who struggle to be more like you. How blessed I am in knowing you and in our service together with Master. No one can take your place within my heart. The love you have shown my children has been a precious gift to me; your life, a constant inspiration. God bless you always.

* * * * *

From an SRF student, written shortly after Sri Gyanamata's passing:

God showed His love for me in permitting me to see, speak to, and touch the beloved Gyanamata before she was allowed to rest in the arms of the Divine Mother. She left such a deep and lasting impression in my heart and soul, and she has been constantly in my thoughts.

One night, I feel certain it was the time she passed away, I was lying in bed and I could not go to sleep for thinking of her. So I turned on the light and talked with her, writing down what I wanted to say. I felt her very, very close, but the following day I could not bring myself to send her the letter. I felt something had happened and yet I did not want to believe it.

However, I feel the spirit of Gyanamata in my life stronger than it has ever been since meeting her. As the Master mentioned, when I looked on her face there was no pain in the eyes, but a love full of ineffable sweetness and understanding that leaves me, even now, inadequate to express. Even her death has brought greater wisdom and light into my life through the words of the Master in the *Self-Realization* magazine.* How can it be death when I feel her spirit so alive all around me, with a greater intensity than ever before? I know that at the present time she is guiding me very strongly through the beautiful example of her life and the wisdom pouring from her letters in the magazine.

I wanted to write you this letter to thank you for the privilege of having met Sister face to face. When I first met you all in August I spoke to one of the nuns at India House,† and I mentioned that one of the things I desired most on

* Excerpts from Paramahansa Yogananda's memorial tribute to Sri Gyanamata were published in *Self-Realization* magazine.

† SRF Hollywood Ashram Center.

my visit was just to look even once upon Gyanamata and to thank her for all that she had imparted to me through her letters. I never realized how soon my desire was to be fulfilled. I was amazed when later, in Encinitas, someone took me by the arm, and before I knew it I was standing at the foot of her bed. If it had been possible I would have given her every ounce of my strength then and there, but when I looked into her eyes, it was I to whom she gave strength and love.

I could go on trying to express what is in my heart, but all I can say is that I shall try to pattern my life as even a tiny example of that great example of devotion and love of God set by this saintly woman.

CHAPTER 17

Letters From Paramahansa Yogananda

More than anyone, Paramahansa Yogananda understood and appreciated the spiritual stature of his devoted "Sister." Her faithfulness and cooperation with the desires of his heart, not only for the good of Self-Realization Fellowship, but for the further elevation of her own soul, were ever a comfort and joy to him.

Because of his many responsibilities, the Guru was unable to write often. "But," he wrote, in one of the letters in this series, "I do write to you ever in my heart and spirit." Just as she would often leave a short note of greeting or gratitude at her Guru's door, so the Master would sometimes do the same for her. Characteristic was this note he once left along with a small gift-remembrance: "My deepest blessings to our angelic Gyanamata, whose seat is reserved in heaven." Such purity and intimacy was demonstrated in this ideal relationship of guru and disciple! One can feel something of the deep love, understanding, and mutual regard shared by the Guru and his beloved disciple. Also included are statements that the Master made to others about Gyanamata.

The first three letters in this group were written by Paramahansaji in the years immediately following the first meeting between Guru and disciple in 1925, prior to Sister's entering the SRF ashram:

October 23, 1926

Dear Mrs. Bissett,

I am glad to receive your letter and hear of your recovery. I was very much pleased that your spiritual realization was so marked, and that you remember all the things that transpired while I was with you. Many follow but few are chosen*—those who choose themselves by being deserving.

Give Rex my blessings and love.

Very sincerely yours,
Swami Yogananda

"The Lord be with you." S. Y.

* * * * *

May 13, 1927

Dear Mrs. Bissett,

I received your interesting and warm letter, and thank you for your kind thoughts.

It makes me very happy that you have improved; do not be discouraged if traces of the condition do occur occasionally. Just press forward with stronger faith than before, determined to win. As you know, there are new cells forming in our bodies each day. By affirmations impress upon these new cells life, health, perfect manifestation.

You are progressing in your concentration and meditation. Don't become discouraged. Sometimes it requires a long time to get results, but the joy of the realization when it does come is worth all the efforts spent.

I appreciate your co-operation in securing new students in Yogoda.

* Cf. Matthew 22:14. "For many are called but few are chosen."

I have prayed for you.

With blessings,
Very sincerely yours,
Swami Yogananda

* * * * *

September 15, 1928

Dear Mrs. Bissett,

Your letter and beautiful extracts from your spiritual diary were received.

Yes, you were one of the reasons why I came to America, and it is a great joy to me to see the faithful ones who do not allow time and space to dim their interest. The little star you see in meditation is the "door," and as you continue you will sometime pass through it and progress far.

With blessings,
Sincerely yours,
Swami Yogananda

* * * * *

July 4 [Sister's birthday; year unknown]

Dear Sister,

Your letters ever touch me deeply. They are profound and inspiring. I wish your health were better that you could inspire thirsty souls for years to come....Please adopt everything necessary for your health.

I have never seen such unselfish, noble examples in the West as in you and St. Lynn. I never write, but I do write to you ever in my heart and spirit. I don't talk, but I do ever talk to you in silence. You understand me more than most, so I don't talk to you [outwardly] though I have always wanted to do so.* Forgive my outward negligence. I am ever with you and ever will be afterward in God and Guru.

With blessings of God,
S. Yogananda

* * * * *

December 9, 1933

Dear Sister,

It is overwhelmingly difficult for me to write, as I don't get even two hours of rest per night. Please let everybody know that in my absence you are the spiritual head of the institution, and everybody should obey your wishes, for I know they are impartial and God-directed. Since you represent me and my wishes as truly as ever anybody has done, I have implicit confidence in your actions and judgment. You have satisfied all the critical scrutiny of my divine standard. I follow my Father's will, you carry out my wishes, and we both follow the Father's will—for it is that alone which satisfies me and will ever content me. May the ever-burning One illumine every altar of your thoughts, feelings, and activities.

Boundless blessings,
S. Yogananda

* * * * *

May 13 [circa 1933]

Dear Sister,

Thank you for your very kind letter. I am so happy that the foundation stone is being laid right, but it is only God who can really solidify things [here the Master is referring to

* Paramahansaji refers here to his lack of time, owing to his heavy schedule of teaching, traveling, and guiding the younger disciples.

Mt. Washington]. I deeply appreciate your divine motherly interest. I am so happy to feel I can send devotees safely to one who helps them and inspires them with my ideal. I cannot tell you what a relief it has been since you have been there. I needed somebody at Mt. Washington to interpret me rightly to those who cannot contact me. Heaven will bless you for this. Your salvation is an accomplished fact. Your bridge of faith you have built; and you will soon cross the chaos of delusion and become a shining star in His bosom, to show others the way that leads to God.

Deepest blessings,
S. Yogananda

* * * * *

At this time, Gyanamata was in charge of Mt. Washington; and in this letter, Paramahansaji—who was then on a lecture tour in Indianapolis, Indiana—is referring to the financial and housing responsibilities that were being incurred at the SRF Headquarters:

October 27, 1933

Dear Sister,

I wish you and a few others were here to help with this tour. You don't know how I appreciate you all—the real ones through whom God's sincerity and power flows.

Though we have to go through poverty experiences, we must never think ourselves poor and limited. We are rich with Infinity, unlimited, all the treasures—material and spiritual—which belong to God. We will take whomsoever necessary, at the same time of course exercising economy. There is no room for extravagance, but there is room for taking everybody who is sincere and harmonious—all the world if that is necessary and is the will of God—and He will provide for us. He could long ago have ceased making it possible for us to exist there, but He is supplying our needs.

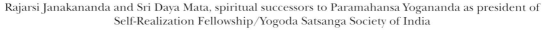

Rajarsi Janakananda and Sri Daya Mata, spiritual successors to Paramahansa Yogananda as president of Self-Realization Fellowship/Yogoda Satsanga Society of India

Paramahansa Yogananda meditating in the Temple of Leaves, an outdoor shrine on the grounds of SRF International Headquarters. Gyanamata kept this photo on the bedside table in her room.

Why should we worry, except to do our own parts to the best of our ability.

Unceasing blessings,
S. Yogananda

* * * * *

Written from the Mysore Palace, India:

November 24, 1935

Dear Sister,

Eternal greetings of Christmas and New Year reach you as deeply as ever when I was near you. I am happy to know that you are there as the guardian angel of Mt. Washington. May God keep you there as long as possible for my sake and for the sake of Mt. Washington. Rejoice, for we have almost twice as big a place in India as Mt. Washington. I am very happy. Eternally you are protected by God and Guru's blessings.

Yogananda

* * * * *

Written from Ranchi, India:

January 6, 1936

Dear Sister,

A million thanks for your dear, dear letters. Please look after your health. You must stay well as long as possible and not leave us. Mt. Washington needs you—I need you. Heaven waits for you here and hereafter. I am with you always, now and forever.

Deepest blessings,
S. Yogananda

* * * * *

Kashmir, Srinagar
May 19, 1936
1:20 a.m.

Dear Sister,

Your letter deeply touched me. God is ever with you. Twenty years of your loyalty has become loyalty for eternity given to God. You are blessed.

S.Y.

* * * * *

Encinitas Hermitage
July 10, 1938

Dear Sister,

______ wrote me a very unpleasant letter saying that I was trying to throw him in servants' quarters here. A spiritual teacher is the servant of all. What a difference between your spirit and his! Gladly you slept in the laundry room.

* * * * *

October 21

Dear Sister,

Just a line to tell you how much I enjoy your letters and your impartial analysis of every situation. What I intuitively realized about _______, I was so glad to get verified by your intuitive observation. They see clearly, those with whom the impartial God and His love remain.

So happy God is with you always, and through portals of devotion you behold Him always.

Life is coming and going—nothing is permanent except God. All else will be washed away by the waters of time. But it is a good thing that during sleep time our troubles vanish. All the waves of life ultimately will melt in His one bosom in eternal awakening. For to sleep in Him is to be awake.

All alone so can't write much or regularly. I am with you always, for our mutual Beloved God is in us always.

With boundless blessings, I remain,

Very sincerely yours,
S. Yogananda

* * * * *

August 31

Dear Sister,

Our path lies through the entrenchments of meekness, forgiveness, love, giving good for bad, no matter all the fierce and deadly bullets of evil. We are nearing the Goal. Nothing can stay us. You have done your duty, and God and the Gurus are waiting for you.

I remain,

Very sincerely yours,
S. Yogananda

* * * * *

December 24, 1942

Dear Sister,

This Christmas what gift shall I give to you but the gift of my perpetual blessing—you who have been constant like a polestar in devotion and kindness to me. I want you to know, though I have not been demonstrative, ever in spirit I have blessed you measurelessly and unceasingly.

Your seat God has kept for you in heaven. Your life has been so well lived. Only I pray God keeps your body well that you may easily serve all, for you are ever willing. This is my wish for you for the new year.

Blessings of Christmas and New Year,
P. Yogananda

The next four letters were written at times when Gyanamata was experiencing severe physical suffering:

January 28, 1943
Encinitas, California
Hermitage

Dear Sister,

You have always depended on me for guidance, so I write this, as I feel you need me now more than all other times.

All the devotion, wisdom, faith, that you matchlessly acquired are being tested now by God. Look how the soldiers are suffering [in World War II], and how Christ suffered on the cross, and how Ramakrishna suffered with the most painful of all human diseases. Christ never forgot the Father. Ramakrishna never prayed for healing or relief. You who are so highly advanced must now use all your spiritual acquirements, that before my eyes you pass this test of God. You are an example to all; so do not be overpowered by suffering or have self-pity, but smile away all your troubles.

Many years ago, I begged your life from God; so do not throw away what God gave you by wishing to give up your body. To wish to die is to evade the examination of the transcendental soul as to what it has learned from its experiences with the painful flesh. You must finish all the lessons that God wants you to study in this school of life. So smile and remember we all want you to live and be of service—to God, to me, and to all, who are so much benefitted by your contact.

Do not tie my hands by negative thoughts, but cooperate and wish to live and be of service to this work as long as a drop of blood remains in your veins.

My faith in you is ever unshaken. I deeply feel the impact of your test. But no matter how severe your suffering is, you can endure, as have others who had even more severe tests with their bodies—day and night in horrible pain. So be thankful to Him who is the Maker of our lives. Do not wish to throw away before your time comes what He has given you. Remember what Draupadi prayed to Krishna, "Lord, I care not what pain or test of punishment you give me, but do not test me with forgetfulness of Thy love." And this is what I pray for you—that you ever remember and love God, and forget the body. Draw closer to the Divine Mother, even if She beats you with pain.

As befits your name, keep your *gyana,* wisdom's light, ever burning during the darkness of this test.

With deepest love and blessings, and prayers that you soon become well.

I remain very sincerely yours,
P. Yogananda

* * * * *

Encinitas, Calif.
June 17, 1943

Dear Sister,

Please remember, all your spiritual acquisitions are now being put to the test by physical illness. It grieves me if I see you worry about the physical body. It belongs to God and not to you. Let Him do with it what He wants.

Why give *your verdict* to the Great Healer our Father and to me that your body can't get well any more?

Well or ill, your concern should not be at all about the body, except to take reasonable care of it. What I like to see is your even inner attitude—to be pleased and happy no matter what the Lord does with your body.

With unceasing blessings,
P. Yogananda

May 16, 1951

Dear Sister,

Please do not grieve about the weakness of your body. Help yourself as much as you can. Exercise even a little by walking around while holding to the back of the wheelchair. God must be attained, life or death—all obstacles must be removed by yourself through the help of God and the Gurus.

With boundless blessings,
Very sincerely,
P. Yogananda

Don't give up. Your presence helps others.

* * * * *

July 8, 1951

Dear Sister,

I am very pleased with you, as you are striving more towards your former natural self, surrendering not to illness, but to God and the Gurus.

May God keep you ever near Him, oblivious of all His tests of suffering.

With deepest blessings,
Very sincerely yours,
P. Yogananda

* * * * *

October 6, 1943

Dear Sister,

Received your blessed, balanced letter....No matter what happens, at all times in death and life we are on the lap of Divine Mother. Life is waking on Her lap, and death is sleeping on Her lap. So you see we can never part, for in life and death through eternity we will be waking or sleeping on Her ever-living bosom. I always enjoy reading and rereading your letters. They are so balanced; they are perfect photographs of situations.

Very sincerely yours,
P. Yogananda

* * * * *

December 1, 1945

Dear Sister,

I always receive your thoughts, and that is why I have so little even seen you [to talk to] during my busy life. But I always regret that I haven't discussed much in person with you except through your spirit.

Miss _____ wrote, "Sister reminds me of a lily personified and spiritualized, because of her fairness, her caressing voice, and delicate mannerisms." I fully endorse that and say unto you that God is ever with you through the Gurus, and ever will be, and They are waiting for you when your work here is done. And whenever I join you there, we will talk about everything unsaid in this life, and there will be happiness unending, and I won't regret about not talking with you for lack of time [here on earth]. Your thoughts I ever treasure.

Unceasing blessings,
P. Yogananda

* * * * *

Paramahansaji said the following about Sri Gyanamata to some devotees:

"Remember me to Mrs. Bissett. She is an old devotee of incarnations. When first I saw her I knew she had known me before, and I commended her to God. That is why, from our first meeting, her devotion has been a steady flame."

During the last year of the Guru's life, he sent the following message to Gyanamata through one of the other nuns:

"Give Sister my blessings, and tell her to accept all things as being God's will—as I know she does—and to continue to do this. Tell her to remain positive, and to use the body as much as possible. Tell her not to give up, think of God, as she always does, and my blessings to her.

"Remember that life is God's play, and the last chapter is the most important. The hero and the villain, health and sickness, joy and sorrow, are all part of His drama of light and shadows. In a movie house, the beam of light from the booth, passing through a film, projects pictures on the screen. In life, God is the beam, duality is the film, and we are the pictures. Become one with the Beam, and there is no more suffering."

* * * * *

On another occasion, the Master wrote to a devotee:

"I enjoy just as much being with people without talking as talking. For example, there is Gyanamata, one of my greatest disciples. She and I never talk, but we always understand each other. She always writes in response to the thoughts I send to her. Our thought-letters contain the answers to the other party's questions."

* * * * *

And the Guru wrote to another:

"There are some souls I know who have been sick more or less and have never committed any sin in this life—like Gyanamata. Her body was very frail; she was to have gone long ago, but she has carried on for many years. She has committed no sin in this life. But suffering has brought no change in her eyes. I see the sparkle of God there just the same. She has the same characteristics as Saint Teresa. What a wonderful spirit! Suffering means nothing to such souls."

* * * * *

"I have seen that all those who come in contact with Gyanamata have the highest regard for her. I am very happy because she is of God, and God is with her. I hope that you might all have a little of the understanding that she has. You will make your lives completely different. I can tell her anything that I want, and she does it exactly as I want it. She never misjudges me. She knows what I am doing. That is why that divine flow is with her, because she is harmonizing with me.

"And she was to have gone long ago, but God keeps her here for this work and to help me. I wish you all had that understanding. That is what I want in you. When I don't have to say, but you will understand my wishes. If anybody deserves my company, it is Sister, but many times I have practically ignored her; yet she has always remained steady and true-blue."

* * * * *

In a lecture on December 20, 1942, Paramahansaji said:

"The more you tune in with me the more I will be with you in spirit. Sister Gyanamata, whom I mentioned earlier, I talk to by sending thoughts to her through the ether. Many souls I guide that way. As soon as you reach a certain point of development, then you will see I am directing you. My Master guides me more now than when he was alive. This is the truth I am telling you. Whenever there is a fog in my mind about some decision to be made, I behold him there directing me. You have to be developed, as Gyanamata is, in order to receive this kind of guidance; otherwise, you may say, 'Guru is guiding me,' when instead it is merely imagination or the desires of the ego telling you what you want to hear."

* * * * *

"She is a great yogi. She is always even-minded, always kind and understanding. Even if her body is falling apart, you ask her to do something and she will do it without a word, willingly. That is the beautiful spirit. She has never been out of tune with me all these years. She is far ahead of many renunciants I have seen. She is always with God."

* * * * *

"Follow Sister's attitude in everything. She is my ideal. I am so happy you appreciate Sister. She is a goddess. She and I are one. Think how she understands me—never misunderstands."

The following are handwritten letters from Paramahansa Yogananda to Sri Gyanamata. Virtually all the personal notes and letters from Paramahansaji to Sister were handwritten by him. For publication most have been typeset, but it was felt that the reader would appreciate a sampling of the Guru's handwriting to his disciple.

Dear Sister,

Your very dear letter I read with tears.* O yes many times I wish you were a young man—living here—for I feel you could have done so much. I feel you have done a hundred times more than my expectation, and of all my dear ones here, Mr. Lynn, you and a very few others have fully lived up to my expected standard of highest spiritual life. I never look for more. I am happy for all cooperation I have received—and not only you are honorably mentioned but your impartial and most difficult work of serving others is engraved in the pages of eternity and in my heart. And that you are living by His grace. I pray His grace continue that we may continue to rejoice serving the cause with you with the greatest joy, as it has been.

With blessings to eternity to you, Rex and H[ughella].

I remain,
Very sincerely yours

* The letter referred to appears on pages 219–220.

To Sister Gyanamata, April 11th - 1945 Encinitas Calif.

Dear Sister,

I am so sorry I have not visited you physically - but spiritually I am ever at your side whenever you need me - and my prayers are ever with you. Sahly must have told you why I couldn't see you. Anyway I am very happy you are better to-day - and may God who is our common protector in life + in death - be ever your guardian. There is nothing to fear you are in His good All-accomplishing hands

with unceasing blessings

very sincerely yours

Paramhansa Yogananda

April 11th, 1945
Encinitas, California

To Sister Gyanamata,

Dear Sister,

I am so sorry I have not visited you physically—but spiritually I am ever at your side whenever you need me—and my prayers are ever with you. Sahly* must have told you why I couldn't see you.

* Later known as Sraddha Mata; a member of the SRF Board of Directors and resident of the Encinitas Ashram Center until her passing in 1984.

Anyway, I am very happy you are better today, and may God who is our common protector in life and in death be ever your guardian. There is nothing to fear. You are in His good, all-accomplishing hands.

With unceasing blessings
Very sincerely yours

* * * * *

Dear Sister, Nov 16th 1935
God is invisible also, you need no manifestation. He is ever present with you in darkness & light with my presence - for I am in Him! Christmas & New Years blessings to Eternity.

Nov. 16th, 1935

Dear Sister,

God is invisible also, you need no manifestation. He is ever present with you in darkness and light with my presence—for I am in Him. Christmas and New Years blessings to eternity.

Sincerely yours

* * * * *

The following two short notes were written on cards that accompanied Christmas gifts from Paramahansaji to Sister:

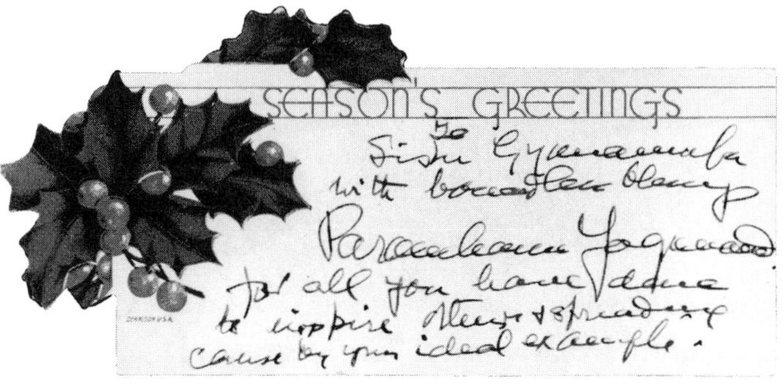

To Sister Gyanamata

With boundless blessings

For all you have done to inspire others and spreading [the] cause by your ideal example.

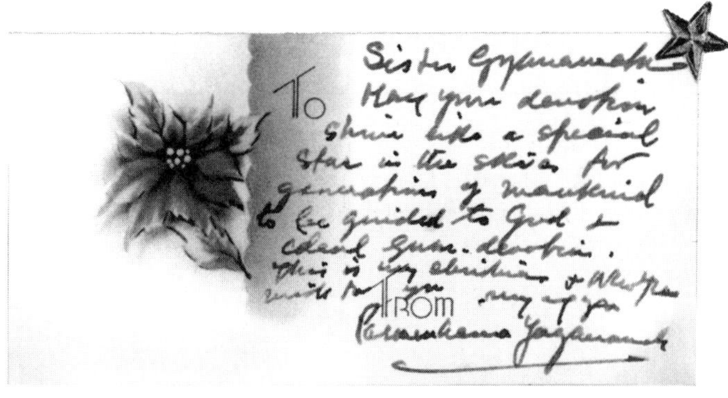

Sister Gyanamata

May your devotion shine like a special star in the skies for generations of mankind to be guided to God and ideal Guru-devotion. This is my Christmas and New Year wish for you.

Very sincerely yours

Inscription from Sister's copy of Paramahansaji's Autobiography of a Yogi:

To Sister Gyanamata
Your exemplary life, like the
morning dew, is blessed by
God to quench the thirst of
seeking souls. God & the gurus
have kept a seat for you in
Heaven.

To Sister Gyanamata

Your exemplary life, like the morning dew, is blessed by God to quench the thirst of seeking souls. God and the gurus have kept a seat for you in Heaven.

* * * * *

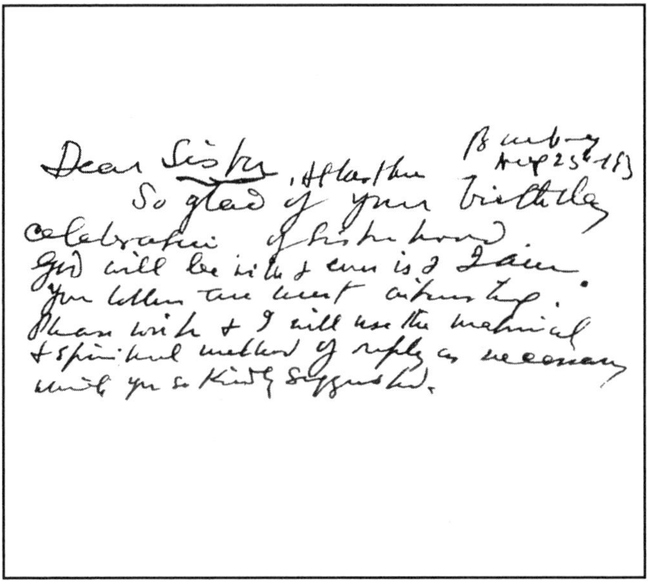
Bombay
Aug 25 – 1935
Dear Sister, At last here
So glad of your birthday
celebration of Sisterhood
God will be with you & ever is & I am.
Your letters are most interesting.
Please write & I will use the material
& spiritual method of reply as necessary
which you so kindly suggested.

Bombay, Aug. 25, 1935

Dear Sister,

At last here [i.e. arrival in India]. So glad of your birthday celebration of Sisterhood. God will be with you and ever is and I am. Your letters are most interesting. Please write and I will use the material and spiritual method of reply as necessary, which you so kindly suggested.

* * * * *

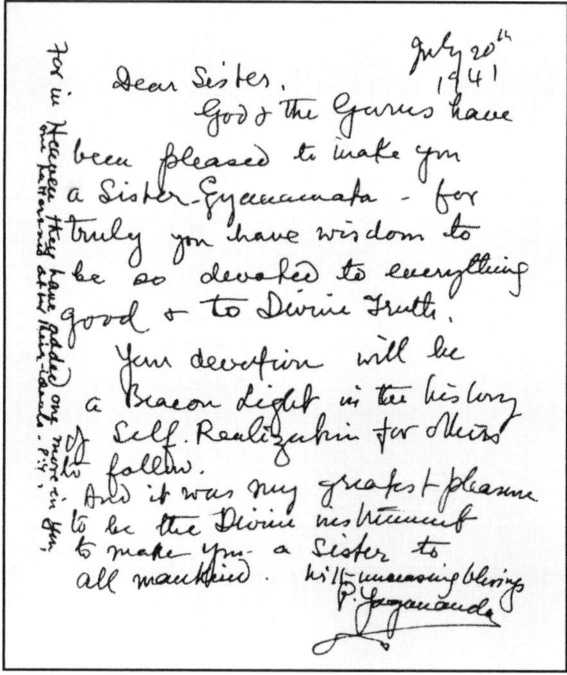

July 20th
1941

Dear Sister,
God & the Gurus have been pleased to make you a Sister-Gyanamata - for truly you have wisdom to be so devoted to everything good & to Divine Truth.
Your devotion will be a Beacon light in the history of Self.Realization for others to follow.
And it was my greatest pleasure to be the Divine instrument to make you a Sister to all mankind.

With unceasing blessings
P. Yogananda

For in Heaven they have added one more in you one patterned after their ideals. P.Y.

July 20, 1941

[*Anniversary of Gyanamata's formal vow of renunciation*]

Dear Sister,

God and the Gurus have been pleased to make you a Sister—Gyanamata—for truly you have wisdom to be so devoted to everything good and to Divine Truth. Your devotion will be a beacon light in the history of Self-Realization for others to follow. And it was my greatest pleasure to be the divine instrument to make you a sister to all mankind.

With unceasing blessings

For in Heaven They have added one more in you, one patterned after Their ideals. P.Y.

PART IV

Sri Gyanamata's Personal Diary and Meditations

CHAPTER 18

Personal Diary

The following selections are from Sri Gyanamata's diary, written during the years 1926–29, in which she included notes to herself, often analyzing her meditations and her thoughts; quotations of Paramahansaji; selections from others' poetry and prose that she found inspiring; questions she asked her Guru, and his answers. Through these writings one can feel Gyanamata's insatiable fire of desire for God alone, her inherent optimism, the clarity, positiveness and purity of her innermost thoughts, and the iron will and perseverance that enabled her to follow fearlessly the truth that was shown to her.

Sunday, October 3, 1926.

Last night ordered myself to wake at 3 o'clock. Waked promptly on the hour, feeling fine inner vibrations. Commenced to meditate at 4 o'clock. At once the vibrations became very strong…it seemed as if something wonderful was very near—so near that surely I must soon touch it. Glory to my Guru, who is opening the door for me! Meditated for 3 hours.

I note that when the vibrations are upon me, it is difficult, sometimes impossible, for me to read. Spiritual reading has been a form of meditation for me. Sometimes I feel that the new meditation is pushing out the old.

* * * * *

Friday.

Commenced meditating at 4 o'clock this morning without result till 6 o'clock. Then suddenly it came. I often compare my attempts at meditation to pushing a boat down the beach onto the water—one pushes and pushes, till suddenly it is afloat and the current catches it. I can stay a long time in this state.

Everything speaks of meditation, suggesting hope of success. Yesterday morning, on the hydrangea bush I found one large flower—though it is mid-October. Why should not I, though it is "mid-October" with me also, put forth the flower of perfect meditation?

* * * * *

November 12.

Last night, reading Swamiji's "Intellectual Recipes," I was surprised and delighted to find a practice advocated that I commenced long ago in my childhood. "When you are worried or grieved, take a book and bury yourself in it. Listen to the comforting and inspiring words of the great minds of all the ages." How many times, with aching nerves, have I followed this recipe! And not once, that I can recall, has it failed me.

In one never-to-be-forgotten moment of agony, I took up *The Wisdom of the Hindus** and came upon this sentence from "The Wisdom of Tuka-Ram": "Thou, O God, givest to each his fit and meet position; and I, acknowledging it to be good, gladly receive it." Simple words, but for me, charged with the realization of him who spoke them, and peace flowed from them into my mind and body.

This recalls the pleasure that I felt over two years ago, when I first read *The Science of Religion* and found my method

* By Brian Brown. Published by Brentano's, New York, 1921.

of reading among the "four methods characterizing religious growth." I never sought scholarship, but always "that thought-process which has as its sole object the transcending of the body and seeing the truth."

* * * * *

December 16.

No measure of success seemed possible today. Then all at once it commenced: Delightful quietness of body stole over me from head to foot, intensifying till I felt as if held in a vise. I found myself looking at a bright patch of light, which vanished as soon as I was conscious of its presence. I stayed this way about two hours, I think. When I got up to call Rex, where was my headache, my fatigue? Gone! And I have been well and rested all day. Fine inner vibrations come as I think intently about it. Glory to him who permits me to call him my Guru, without whom I could not possibly succeed in this work, with whom I cannot possibly fail.

* * * * *

December 23.

One thing that gives me joy is this: When I think intently and longingly of some future moment of realization, or if I begin to pray and invoke the Self, saying, "O Shining Self," etc., instantly and invariably fine vibrations come over me from head to foot. It is true I do not understand all this, and I remember what Swamiji said, that imagination does help, but that we should endeavor to pass beyond; otherwise we remain always in the field of imagination. So I realize that I may be deluded or led on by imagination; still, if vibration is the first projection of Spirit into matter, may I not believe that in those vibrations that pass through me as I write this, I contact my own spirit?

December 31.

My mind has been so outgoing and my body so tired during the Christmas season that meditation has not been successful except occasionally—a gleam through the darkness, a hint that it may be going on underneath. Swamiji so often says, "Strike a balance," and more and more I see that this is the true way of life. One's time should be properly proportioned between meditation and work.

* * * * *

January 2, 1927.

I love the "Recipes" in *East-West,** especially the spiritual ones, which call upon us to "put off the works of darkness and put upon us the armor of light, now in the time of this mortal life." I spoke of these recipes to one of the members of our meditation group last night, and she said she had not read them because she thought they were concerned with cooking and she lives in a boarding house.

A member of the group says to me often, "I wish Swamiji would come again." Of course, I too often feel the same wish, which is followed by the opposite one: I wish he would not come until I have been able to make better use of all he so graciously and generously gave me. I might feel ashamed to stand before him. O Shining Self, make me receptive to his holy vibrations!

* * * * *

February 22.

No entry in this book since January 2. Day after day of attempted meditation that did not seem even worthy of the name of practice. I have learned one thing, anyway—to

* Paramahansaji renamed the magazine *Self-Realization* in 1948.

appreciate the effect upon me of even a small measure of success. When failure is all the early morning hours bring me, I am so tired. Perhaps I should not call it failure because I always see light, and that is something. When discouraged, I think of Swamiji's coming.

Last night I woke at one o'clock with a headache, got up and sat in the kitchen reading till it subsided, then went into meditation....My mind became filled with peace, and a foretaste of Bliss stole over me. I was in this state over four hours. Just this little experience was so worthwhile. I have noted the peace and quietness that have filled my mind all day, and have thought of it as a chamber swept and garnished.

* * * * *

February 25.

Some words fall directly upon the heart: "With threads of sunbeams I will sew my tattered joy. With the moonbeams I will wash my sorrows. With the night I will obliterate my dark experiences. *With the dawn I will create my new world of eternal joy.*" It is 4:30 a.m. I go to meditate.

* * * * *

May 6.

Had some success this morning. For the first time I thought of the vibrations felt and heard as *one*. When I stopped my ears the vibrations seemed exactly the same in strength. I, the witness, listened and felt.

I have noticed how my attitude towards things changes in meditation. I had been feeling ashamed of writing to Swamiji, thinking it selfish to add the weight of a feather to his load, also that I would probably appear as actuated by a vain and foolish desire to talk about myself. But this morning I was glad I had written, and *sure* he would understand perfectly.

July 1.

When I have a moment of dark agony, it is because I am consciously shut into the narrow confines of my self. At other moments a stream, even though it may be a thin one, of Reality comes to me through intuition. It is that stream, wide and deep in some, shallow and narrow in others, that makes man willing to go on, for: "Who would have lived and breathed had not this sky of Bliss existed! When it finds in that invisible unembodied, unpredicated, abodeless Atman the basis of life, free from fear, then verily it transcends all fear." And, "He understood that Bliss is Brahman. From Bliss these creatures are born; having been born, by Bliss they live; and having departed, into Bliss again they enter. It is only by this *Ananda,* at once transcendent and universal, that man can be free in his soul and yet live in the world with the full active life of the Lord in this universe of movement." (Sri Aurobindo Ghosh)

As Swamiji says in the May-June issue of *East-West:* "The consciousness of man is made of God and is pain-proof." "Ye who have gained at length your palms in Bliss, victorious ones! Your song shall still be this, an endless Alleluia!"

* * * * *

August 6.

The doctor [an old friend of Sister's] has just spent seventeen days with me. I served him faithfully as is his due. We read books of Christian symbolism, they being the only ones he cares for. The main thesis in the books we read is that the same eternal energy works in everything; the doctor liked this concept very much. But I know where the same thing is said, and better: "One drop of water is in the sacred river Jumna," says Surdas's song, sung by the Nautch girl of Khetri. "Another is foul in the ditch by the roadside. One piece of iron is the image in the temple, and another is the knife in the hand of the butcher. Thy name, O Lord, is same-sightedness. Make of us both the same Brahman!"

I told him this time of the healing prayer vibrations sent me by Swamiji. I had not mentioned it before because I felt doubtful of his belief in them, and feared that my health was not firmly enough established to be convincing. But he noticed the improvement in me for himself, and said suddenly one evening: "You are better than I have ever known you to be." I replied: "Would you like to know why?" and told him all about it. He is a doctor, and so is more held by material laws than another man who had witnessed the same spiritual experiences might be. But he believed me, and the next morning asked if I had felt the vibrations that morning. He said, "There is no reason why they should not come."

I had felt them two or three times while he was with me. This morning it seemed as if Swamiji must be pouring forth power. It is useless to try to describe the effect upon me: rest, peace, general well-being while they last; afterwards, increased strength and endurance. It is wonderful.

* * * * *

Sunday, August 12.

Last Tuesday, the healing vibrations commenced in the afternoon, growing stronger toward the end of the day.... I awoke about 1:30 a.m., and felt really ill—my headache was severe. But the vibrations continued. I got up, but soon had to return to bed. I lay perfectly still and tried to meditate. The vibrations quieted me again, and after a time I fell asleep. When I awoke, and to my surprise and thankfulness, I still felt the vibrations and was cured! I had expected to be in bed all day and to take medicine.

I do not, of course, think that Swamiji was treating me all this time—though I am sure he could and would if necessary. My belief is that a few moments' attention from him may start vibrations in my body that I can feel for hours. I can also see that they might be the result of my own meditation, but I do not think I have sufficient power.

> Bless the Lord, O my soul:
> and all that is within me,
> Bless His holy name. [Psalm 103:1]

My body is being healed that I may seek more earnestly for Thee, and realize Thee more deeply in this very life. I turn to Thee in him, opening my heart to his holy vibrations, that I may find Thee in myself. "Praise the Lord, O my soul, and forget not all His benefits!"

* * * * *

August 20.

The wonders that others have in meditation are not for me. However, I do not ask for marvels—only the greatest marvel of all, the realization of Thy Presence, O Self.

If I count over my treasures, what have I? I have seen the third eye once, seen light of varying degrees of brilliancy, heard the flute once, heard something that sounds like the hum of bees several times.* Last of all, I see constantly now a beautiful little star. I am almost afraid to write it down lest it vanish.

The above sounds a little like a verse from the *Tao Te Ching:* "Knowledge of the Tao, how vast! I am like a sailor far beyond a place of anchorage, adrift on a boundless ocean. Common people are useful; I am awkward. I stand in contrast to them, but oh, the prize I seek is food from our Mother Tao!"

* Here Gyanamata is referring to experiences she had received in deep meditation—of the spiritual or "third" eye, and of some of the various manifestations of *Aum,* the all-pervading sound emanating from Invisible Cosmic Vibration, which may be heard through practice of Self-Realization Fellowship methods of meditation.

Changes come slowly in me. I was born with a bias against meat-eating, yet ate it because it was the custom. I could easily have been taught never to touch it. I could not endure the sight of rare meat—it was so suggestive of animal life. After long years, a feeling of disgust would come over me at such food and at myself for eating it. "Why do you persist?" I said inwardly. "It is not for you." Then I gave it up.

Other changes have come with like slowness. As I crawl along with my practice of meditation, still I believe, am sure, that changes are passing over my entire being—physical, mental, and spiritual. And as I write this, I vibrate inwardly, as though an Inner Presence gave me this confirmation.

* * * * *

September 8, 1928.

I often wish that I could see him [Paramahansaji], which is right and natural. But why should I, after all? If he had the power to touch Rex's little toy saltshaker and make it lie prone though it was its nature to stand upright, if he could touch me and start a force that I feel working in me, can he not do the same thing from a distance, even if he were to go back to India? *He could.* And while astral sight and hearing are slow in opening up in me, I am, I believe, very open to the action of vibration; and what he has commenced for me, he will accomplish.

* * * * *

October 9.

I received Swamiji's answer to my letter. His kindness, patience, and understanding never fail me. When I saw the Yogoda symbol* in the corner of the envelope, I commenced

* A lotus, ancient symbol of purity and soul expansion, in which is centered a depiction of the spiritual eye that Gyanamata had seen in deep

to tremble. How this increased when I read it, and found that the little star I see is really "the door"! Often I have said, when meditating, "Behold, I stand at the door and knock!" And now I know that is actually true, and more, I can see the door.

I see the little star constantly. At any moment of the day when I close my eyes it may flash upon me. This morning while doing the Energization Exercises* it came in exactly the right place. It had a white circle around it. Twice I have seen it with open eyes in the daylight, like a shadow that I could see through. Often as I go back upstairs after reading in the early morning, in the complete darkness, it comes before my open eyes. Once it had a blue circle around it, at another time a white one.

"And lo, the star, which they saw in the east, went before them, till it came and stood over where the young child was. When they saw the star, they rejoiced with exceeding great joy."†

* * * * *

October 15.

Swamiji says that the ego's process of cognition and any hurt-suggesting thought can only be linked by feeling. Yet indifference would not be liberation. Human relationships

---

meditation as a ring of golden light encircling a sphere of opalescent blue, and at the center, a pentagonal white star. By penetrating one's consciousness through the door of the white star, one experiences progressively deeper states of divine awareness, and ultimately, union with the omnipresence of God that is beyond as well as within vibratory manifestation.

* Originated by Paramahansa Yogananda and taught in the *Self-Realization Fellowship Lessons,* these exercises enable one to recharge the body with cosmic energy.

† Matthew 2:9–10.

have dealt blow upon blow upon my selfhood. I understand. Deep down in my heart I am saying, "Never, never again!" Why? Because I want to be selfishly free from pain? *No.* I do want to be free from pain, of course, but that is not all. I want to be free to really love—to love as God loves, as His sons love, without asking anything in return, without wishing to build up a separate earthly life. I know that sorrow springs from identification [with a mortal form].

* * * * *

October 19.

I have read to Miss Porter such a beautiful Hindu story by F. W. Bain—"An Incarnation of the Snow."

The Great God Maheshwara provoked his wife Parvati, the Daughter of the Snow, to quarrel. When she retired to the margin of Lake Manasa, He followed her, taking the form of a wild swan, and told her a story. As he talked, a bee came to her for warmth; and then a snake, which she allowed to coil around her neck; then a bear, who made of himself a footstool for the goddess. When the story was finished they all left her, and tears of self-commiseration were in her eyes, when Nandi the bull came. She leaned against him for comfort, but as she so leaned, she felt him changing, and looking up saw that Nandi was gone and that she was leaning against the Great God. And then, the great moment of the story, He said: "Know that I was with thee all the time. For I was the swan, and I was the bee, and the snake and the bear, and again I was Nandi against whom thou didst lean."

So it is. All the small loves are but expressions of the One Perfect Love and beguile us to Him. Should that against which we lean manifest its essence to us, we would find that it was Maheswara, the Great God. As with Parvati, so with *me*!

October 24.

Freedom is attained *in consciousness.* It is an unbroken mental attitude—perfect evenness, samesightedness, unchanging during moments of pain.

* * * * *

November 4.

All day, and at night when I go to bed, I look forward to the early morning when again I may practice meditation. "Tomorrow I will surely do much better," I say. Tomorrow, another day and another opportunity—and then still another day and opportunity. It is wonderful to think that days and opportunities will keep coming and coming and coming—until one day I will not need to seek for opportunities any more.

But even if I had no hope of succeeding, still I would rise early to read the lives and sayings of the masters and saints. This summer I have reviewed the teachings of Sri Ramakrishna and St. Thérèse, the Little Flower of Jesus, and read for the first time the life of Father Doyle, S.J., who fell in the Great War.

In the complete silence it is not hard to creep to the outskirts of some group on the other side of the world. I am not good at visualizing—I can *feel* better—but I get a dim picture. Sri Ramakrishna sits on his cot, or cross-legged on the floor. The devotees are before him in a half circle. I am at a distance, perhaps out in the hall. He says: "First reach the Lord, the Undivided Existence, Knowledge, Bliss, and then come down, back to the phenomenal world and perceive it as His manifestation. It is He who has become all this. The world is not a separate entity from Him."

Or, St. Thérèse of Lisieux says: "I would like to be a missionary, not only for some years, but from the creation of the

Sister on grounds of the Encinitas Hermitage

"If I were able to give you the gift that I would like best of all to offer you, it would be the right attitude toward God and Guru; toward life; toward your work; toward the others of your group. But the best gifts cannot be purchased and given. The gifts and graces of the soul must be acquired by patient, daily practice. All will surely be yours in time, for if you do not obtain them in the position to which God has called you, where, in all the world, are they to be found?"—Gyanamata

Gyanamata on the Encinitas Hermitage grounds, about 1938

Gyanamata in front of meditation caves below bluff-top site of Encinitas Hermitage, overlooking Pacific Ocean, 1937. The partially completed tower of the first Self-Realization temple in Encinitas, then under construction, is visible in the background.

world till the consummation of the ages!" Or, Father Doyle tells me that his aim was "never to feel even the smallest interior disturbance no matter what might happen." And, "I never have peace unless I am going against myself."

Or, Swamiji says: "Even through unfulfillment, if you still keep steadily, deeply believing that the Father is listening to you and will answer you, you will be rewarded with His presence. As the miser loves, dwells on, craves and works for money, so do thou love God. As the new lover loves the beloved, so do thou love God. As a drowning man pants for breath, so do thou pant for God. As the mother yearns for her child, so do thou yearn for God. As the drunken love wine, so do thou love God. As the diseased crave health, so do thou crave God. As the sleepy want sleep, so do thou dive into God."

When I remember what my beloved intuitions, speaking to me in the early morning, have liberated me from, I know that it is impossible for me to love them as I should, dear as they are. And when I think that I am permitted to approach a true guru, and pour out to him my longing for complete liberation, for perfect Light, I can only say, with Hans Christian Andersen, that "my life is a beautiful fairy story, told by God."

O blest communion, fellowship divine,
We feebly struggle, they in glory shine,
Yet all are one in Thee, for all are Thine.

* * * * *

December 31, 1928.

On the morning of Christmas eve, after meditating for some time without any apparent hope of success, peace came suddenly. Then fine vibrations commenced, and grew stronger and stronger, pressing upon me and holding me firmly, and I recognized the Power which I have not felt since last summer. Was it the Christmas blessing promised me on the card from Swamiji? That is my belief. It came again Christmas morning, and also yesterday morning, resting my body and quieting my mind; and, I hope, dealing a blow on the bars which hold me in, but which must someday break and let me go free. My devout thanks to him through whom I shall attain liberation.

* * * * *

April 12.

I have had a long period of what Catholic mystics call "dryness." It is a good word. It helps to watch the mind. I mean, it helps to suppress weary, downward-tending thoughts; to say, "It is the mind." Another help is the affirmation that Truth is not changed by a mood, and that I have only to hold steady, and success is sure. "The effect must follow the cause." For long years I wanted to know the technique of meditation.

A true guru from India came to my house and blessed me. This seed, lying apparently dormant in my consciousness, must, *will* germinate, grow, bear flower and fruit in the fullness of time.

O world invisible, we view thee,
O world intangible, we touch thee,
O world unknowable, we know thee,
Inapprehensible, we clutch thee!*

* * * * *

[No date given.]

The Self gives forth an effulgent light; it is light, peace, joy, bliss. The self is dense and dark; it casts a shadow over our lives, causes bitterness and disappointment. Clouds do

* From "The Kingdom of God" by Francis Thompson.

not come from the Self. When your spiritual sky is obscured, know that it is the work of the self. We meditate and pray and work, that we may bring about our freedom by the death of the self.

* * * * *

August 28.

One of the things I know is that all earthly love can be carried up into the love of the Self. When I listen to love songs like, "Ah, Sweet Mystery of Life," I thrill with love of the Self. I really have no trouble at all, except to hold my mind serene and quiet, while I await the hour, already on its way, that brings me another and deeper realization.

* * * * *

Questions to Paramahansaji, and his answers:

Q: "What does the word 'salvation,' as you use it, mean?"
A: "*Mukti,* liberation."

Q: "Will I be God-conscious and free from entanglements in my next life?"
A: "There will be no more entanglements. Of this much I am certain. This is the last life. There should be the desire to return for the sake of others."

Q: "When you say, 'Try to see the star,' do you simply mean concentrate as steadily as possible?"
A: "Yes."

Q: "I think you said that if the light, the star, comes and goes, it is because our consciousness has not become steady; and to this end we should hold the mind steady and calm during all the hours of the day. Is this correct?"
A: "Yes."

Q: "Can a yogi lose all body consciousness without going into a trance-state of ecstasy?"
A: "Yes."

Q: "What is God?"
A: "Universal Intelligence. Absolute Existence. Eternal Consciousness. Ever New Joy. Cosmic Vibration. Ever conscious, ever new Bliss. All things come from Vibration. In the beginning was the Word or Cosmic Vibration, and the word was God. Vibration is the cause of all things, therefore vibration is God. God is manifested as Cosmic Vibration."

* * * * *

Other quotations of Paramahansaji:

"If the fires and mosquitoes of heat, cold, anxiety, care, fear, sickness, etc., singe and sting you, seek the remedy with a quiet mind. Always keep the mind steady and indifferent."

"When the sensibilities become sensitive, then the pain becomes intense."

"Always keep yourself on the spiritual plane. Sleep is the enemy of meditation. Anything that takes the consciousness from God is sleep."

"Rejecting all allurements of things seen, entering into the One, the Real, the sphere of blessedness, intent and alert without and within, let us endure until the bonds of former works pass away."

"God is contacted in meditation as Light, Sound, and Joy."

"Do not mind His silence. *Remember, He is listening.*"

CHAPTER 19

Meditations

Gyanamata wrote the following inspirational thoughts, essays, prayers and "meditations"—one for each day of the month—for publication in early issues of *Self-Realization* magazine.

It was the custom of a certain saint, who was a public accountant, to write at the head of each page of his ledger a spiritual poem or thought. One was: "I am keeping track of dollars and cents. Teach me to keep track of Thee."

* * * * *

I am a musician. Through my mind and heart pass countless harmonies and melodies. They come, I listen, they fade away, to be succeeded by others. These beads of music are strung upon the golden thread of the divine harmony that Thy voice hums ceaselessly in my ear, O Heavenly Musician of the Universe.

* * * * *

I follow the plow, running a straight furrow through the earth. May my eyes, O Lord, be quick to discern the print of Thy feet upon the moist earth and the dewy grass.

* * * * *

I am keeping track of an office. My mind is full of the petty details of business. Yet let me not forget, at the noon hour, at sunset, at midnight, in the early morning, to listen for Thy voice, O Lord!

I am keeping track of many things—of children, of food, of the telephone, of the doorbell. Voices call my name all day long. Let my ears not be too dull to catch Thy whisper before I sleep at night.

* * * * *

Through countless earthly mazes our feet seem doomed to find their way. O Thou who makest the crooked path straight, and can illumine the darkest midnight of the soul, teach us to keep track of Thee.

* * * * *

A great saint sat down upon the banks of the Ganges to meditate. But while his spiritual posture was secure and immovable, his earthly seat was not, and a big wave came and swept him away into the river. Do you pity him? Do you chide him for carelessness? If you do, consider upon what your own security rests. Is it upon your ability to select a safe place, or upon your inability to lose yourself in meditation? O glorious fate! There are many bodies, but only one God. May I forever lose myself in Him!

* * * * *

Only the fearful, the cowardly, never take a chance. Launch your boat upon the vast waters of adventure and sail to a port of heavenly peace and bliss.

* * * * *

Make me an instrument of Thy peace, that war may cease. If not world war, at least the war of hot words and arguments, unworthy efforts to prove oneself to be always in the right. May quarrels and unkindnesses be stilled in my presence.

Consider the *Kumbha Mela.** For days a seemingly endless procession of saints and devotees pass, to gather at the appointed place. They may come riding or walking, wearing flowing robes, half-clad, or naked. What are they seeking? To commune with their equals, to worship at the feet of their superiors, to impart the blessing they have received to others. Let us pray the holy ones to come to us in the hour of meditation, and hold a *Kumbha Mela* at the confluence of the sacred rivers of our soul.

* * * * *

In the cool evening, Adam heard the voice of God calling to him from the garden. But he knew that he was naked, so he did not answer the call. Satan had stripped him of his robe—his robe woven of threads of loyalty, fidelity, honor, gratitude, devotion, and love. He knew that he was naked, and he hid himself. Think of the misery of such stark nakedness!

* * * * *

A student said: "I cover my naked soul with God." Naked is the soul without this heavenly robe. Invincible, impregnable is the soul that has woven a garment of God-consciousness.

* * * * *

The slang phrases, such as "standing the gaff," "taking it on the chin," and "can you take it?" have a deep underlying meaning. Can you take it? You protested your changeless devotion, a devotion that nothing could undermine. God smiled, and said, "Let us see." Now He has taken away your tools when you thought you had done your best, saying,

* A religious fair held periodically in India.

"That is not like the pattern I gave you. Try again." The honor, the reward you expected is given to another. Your seat at the feast is the humblest. Your portion is neglect. At best you are ignored. Can you take it? Is this Thy way, O Lord? Yes, it is His way of stretching out His hand to you and raising you to a higher level of consciousness.

* * * * *

"Make life a little easier, O Lord. Then I will have strength to find Thee." The Eternal Goodness answers by adding weight to the burden. What does His smile mean?

* * * * *

Many speak of sickness and suffering as a stigma on their characters. They have not yet "demonstrated over them," they reluctantly admit. What is the way to rise above them into the clear, spiritual air, where they cannot touch us? It is by accepting them, and humbly admitting that they are the agents of redemption. The Divine Potter has us upon His wheel. Without them we would develop into a sort of spiritual cream-puff—good, perhaps, but not good for very much. Difficulties develop steel in the muscles of our soul.

Lord, we desire to escape from these Thy messengers, but the only way we can is by running to Thee. This is the interpretation of the Biblical saying, that without the shedding of blood there is no remission of sin—which is to say, without suffering we do not attain.

You weep—but why? Could you attain without these experiences? No. *Then glorify them.* "For this cause came I to this hour." There is no escape. It is a necessary part of my development.

* * * * *

On this Mother's Day, let us also remember to offer our flowers of devotion at the feet of the Divine Mother whose infinite heart has showered causeless and unconditional love upon each of us since the beginning of time.

* * * * *

When one considers the world's saints as a group, the fact of their great sufferings obscures for the moment the glory to which they have attained. The Blessed Virgin had to watch her son die upon a cross of agony. Jesus had to endure that cross, after a life in which he was misunderstood and deserted. Buddha, possessing the very cream of earthly happiness, nevertheless chose years of privation and torture that he might know the truth. St. Francis stripped off his rich clothing and laid it at the feet of his father, standing up naked before him. The list of the names of those of whom the world is not worthy is long, and they live in endless glory.

How different are modern methods. We, the latter-day saints, point out that the laborer is worthy of his hire. The modern saint-in-the-making takes the best possible care of himself and carefully avoids those things that he believes will interfere with what he calls his "development." The ancient, on the contrary, accepted all that came to him as from the Giver of every good and perfect gift. His goal was reached when he could so die to self that he lived in God.

* * * * *

When self comes into consciousness, God goes out. Watch!

* * * * *

All pain, grief, sense of frustration and failure lies in the lower self. Where would you be if you never thought of yourself? Experiment with this thought and you will notice that the "self" has vanished. What is this self that you should hold it dear, when you are worthy only by its loss?

* * * * *

What suffers? The self. It suffers that it may die; for if one does not die to self, he cannot live in God.

* * * * *

"When the I, the me, and the mine are gone, then the work of the Lord is done." When these words are meditated upon properly, the soul will feel itself ascending into pure spiritual regions of thought and aspiration.

* * * * *

Only the mentally strong, only those of dominant wills, can carry on the work of the world. Why then are we told by all great spiritual teachers to surrender the will? The will spoken of is the little personal will. If that is given into the hands of God and Guru, the disciple is freed from chains that make him an earthly prisoner, and his own higher will becomes operative. The devotee makes this surrender at first, perhaps reluctantly, only to find himself in possession of a divine will of which he was entirely unconscious. Also, he feels an influx of power from those to whom he has made the surrender. It is said that no one, while in the body, can make this surrender so perfectly that it covers everything. When this is at last accomplished, one is a fit messenger of God.

* * * * *

If you would be to the Eternal Goodness, to your earthly Master, all that a man's right hand is to him, then learn to bring your self into subjection, and watch what the power of God will do for you, and what it will work through you for your chosen cause.

It is through the power and grace of the guru that God draws ever nearer and nearer.

* * * * *

Deeds of service appear in the spiritual life, in the fullness of time, as naturally as do oranges on an orange tree. Special treatment does not have to be applied in order that an orange tree may bear oranges. Give the tree what it needs for its personal life and health, and leave the rest to the Divine Gardener. A life that is rich in meditation cannot be poor in service.

"I want to serve" is the cry upon many lips. "I want to do something for the world. I want to give." Then seek God with no thought but that of finding Him, with no other object in view than the Beatific Vision. The day will surely dawn when golden fruit will hang upon the tree of your life. Service is the natural result of the holy life.

But do not forget that at the last, when our soul is withdrawing from its earthly abode, not one good deed will appear at your side to sustain you. All will appear worthless, if they even come to mind. What will matter is whether you have seen the King in His beauty. It is the rare but unforgettable moments when you have touched the hem of His robe that will be with you then.

* * * * *

"Blow the little bubble of joy." These words are from *Whispers from Eternity*. The intention is to create in the mind a picture of a child blowing soap bubbles. Not content with a small bubble, he continues to blow until it has fully expanded. So blow your little bubble of joy, child of God. Do not despise your tiny bubble of meditation. Do not neglect it. Keep blowing until your effort and its beauty attract God to you as Bliss.

Carefully, persistently, blow the little bubble of joy, until in its iridescent beauty you behold the face of God.

* * * * *

The heavens declare the glory of God. Nightly they spread their majestic canopy over heads that never turn upward to observe them, over hearts burdened with trifles.

The angels of the Lord, the powers of the Lord, the seas and floods, the sun and moon—all, all fittingly praise their Creator.

The showers and dew, the winds of God—their chant never ceases.

The night and day, the light and darkness, the heat and cold, the growing things upon the earth—their *Aum* is plainly heard by the initiated ear.

Only man, having become twisted and distorted by the misuse of his God-given powers, creates a discord. His voice—most wonderful of all—he has allowed to sink to a whine of fear and complaint.

Students of Self-Realization Fellowship! Awake! Sleep no more! The clue has been put into your hands, which, if grasped firmly, will lead you from the pit where petty jealousies rend families and organizations, and stupendous and horrible wars drench the world with blood and tears, to a high place in peace, joy, and bliss.

* * * * *

We thank Thee, Heavenly Father, for the glorious example of the saints. These holy ones climbed the steep ascent of heaven, taking every test, enduring to the point where endurance is no longer necessary, and now pass on from glory unto glory. We pray Thee to hasten the day when we shall be one with them, as they are one in Thee. O blest communion, fellowship divine!

Watch for His golden smile. Any moment it may shine through the darkness.

* * * * *

Listen for His voice. Shut out the noise of the world, or you will miss it.

* * * * *

Would you like to feel His hand take yours and hold it? Then drop your earthly treasures.

* * * * *

Hark to that sound which seems to come ever nearer. He will join you at the appointed meeting place.

* * * * *

The King's children are glorious within. Tear off the covering that obscures the light of your own soul.

* * * * *

Let it not be said that he who might walk with God prefers some earthly companionship, some earthly occupation.

* * * * *

He is the Self of your self.

* * * * *

The Infinite may be enjoyed, but never fully found.

* * * * *

Surrender thoughts and feelings to God. Know Him to the exclusion of all else, and swim in that perennial Bliss.

* * * * *

But if pain be your portion, then suffer, and die to self that you may live in Him.

* * * * *

"I am Spirit. What is this trifle to me?" This thought gives both peace and power.

* * * * *

The love of God is the beginning of wisdom. Its end is Bliss.

* * * * *

I pick and eat the fruit of karma, bitter and sweet, from the tree of my life.

* * * * *

All are eager to accompany the Master to the Mount of Transfiguration, but few have devotion enough to stand beside him in the judgment hall—or forgo an hour's sleep for his sake.

* * * * *

Have one idea: God.

* * * * *

Overcome restlessness by meditation.

* * * * *

Observe some rule of silence. Outer silence is not to talk with the mouth. Inner silence is not to talk with the mind. It is in the silence of body, mind, and senses that you will hear God speak.

* * * * *

He comes, and joy floods your being. He goes, and your mantle is woven of sadness. But this is only in appearance. In reality, He is ever at your side.

* * * * *

There is no such hour on the timepiece of fate as "too late."

* * * * *

When you become luminous there is no pain. There is only Bliss.

* * * * *

Listen to a voice from the fourth century [St. Augustine]: "For Thou hath made us for Thyself, and our hearts are restless until they rest in Thee."

* * * * *

Watch your thoughts.

* * * * *

How much do the offerings that you lay at the feet of the Master cost you? "Neither will I offer burnt offerings to the Lord my God of that which doth cost me nothing."

* * * * *

Touch my lips with the flame from Thy altar, O God, that they may speak Thy truth, may sing Thy praise!

* * * * *

I am safe in the everlasting arms.

* * * * *

Where to us God shows least, said a great Christian saint, He is often most. Since, therefore, it is possible that what seems very small and unimportant to us may loom large in the sight of God, it behooves us to accept everything as coming from His hand.

* * * * *

The value of all situations in life proceeds from man's attitude toward them.

* * * * *

It is not the work given you to do, nor the physical weariness caused by it, that separates you from God. It is the attitude of your mind.

* * * * *

The aspiring attitude of man builds schools for the ignorant, stores the wisdom of the ages in libraries, erects laboratories for scientific research, hospitals for the sick, structures of use and beauty all over the world, and—best of all—ladders by which his soul mounts to God.

* * * * *

When anything painful enters the shell of your ego, consider the origin of the pearl. By the right attitude of patience and humility, exude a transforming secretion, and behold a miracle—a beautiful spiritual pearl!

* * * * *

There is no pain, nor sense of disappointment, frustration, or failure that has not its roots in desire. Put this to the test, and you will see for yourself.

* * * * *

Drive out the two princes of darkness—desire and resentment—that the King of Glory may come in.

* * * * *

Oh, speak to me out of the darkness, touch me with Thy finger, expand my limited consciousness into Thy limitless ocean of Bliss!

* * * * *

Out of the wound in Jesus' side flowed blood, mingled with water. Out of the wound in our heart may flow deep understanding, divine love, renunciation, liberation, and that Perfect Joy which follows the death of the self.

* * * * *

Asked by his disciples in what lies Perfect Joy, St. Francis stated in the strongest possible terms that it lies in victory over self. So near! So far!

* * * * *

Every tree must grow upon its own piece of ground.

* * * * *

Describing the perfectly liberated, the Buddha used these words: "He whose conquest cannot be conquered again, into whose conquest no one in this world enters." He has become a Leviathan of the deeps of God-consciousness. The most ingeniously woven net cannot recapture him.

* * * * *

Francis Thompson says He is "so near it mocks our pain." Paramahansa Yogananda says He, who is so great, has made Himself small, and concealed Himself in our hearts. But though He is so near, we, made blind and insensate by the human will and desire, cannot perceive Him.

A Persian saint, meditating on "the nearness of God," fell into a trance, and walked deep into the forest before he regained consciousness.

* * * * *

The greatest joy of all is to discover Him in our own consciousness. Concentration and meditation open the door. But unless the will is purified and united to the Divine Will, unless surrender and devotion are so complete that all rebellion is driven out, you cannot pass through the door. You may experience phenomena, but you will not "see God."

* * * * *

Said the disciple to his master, "How may I see God, and hear Him speak?" The master answered: "When thou standest still from the thinking and willing of self, then the eternal hearing, seeing, and speaking will be revealed in thee. Thine own hearing, willing, and seeing hindereth thee, that thou dost not see or hear God."

* * * * *

Is there, after twenty centuries, still no room in the inn for his holy nativity? Be born in my heart, Christ Consciousness; let there be room in my heart for thee.

* * * * *

O divine magnet of my soul! Joyfully I yield to Thine irresistible power.

* * * * *

There are inner experiences that are spoiled by speaking of them. Feel them and rejoice.

* * * * *

Let your will dissolve in the Divine Will, as a lump of sugar dissolves in a glass of water. Then you may say with Juliana of Norwich, "My Me is God." She also says to avoid the fog that envelops the soul when it concentrates upon the wrongdoings of others.

* * * * *

I thank Thee, Lord, for Thy inexorable demands upon me. No struggle to escape has availed me aught. Now I turn upon Thee, and wrestle all night with Thee, even as Jacob wrestled with the angel, saying: "Behold! I will not let Thee go, except Thou bless me." As day broke, he prevailed and obtained the blessing. And in the Morning it shall be with me even as it was with Jacob.

* * * * *

Essays written by Sri Gyanamata for early issues of Self-Realization:

Christmas in Your Heart

Soon there will be worldwide preparation for the greatest festival of the year. Trees will be set up and decorated with many-colored lights. Gifts will be wrapped in gay paper and appropriately tied. Special food will be cooked, and special attempts made to give the poor a share in the good things.

At our Mt. Washington headquarters the whole of Christmas Eve will be spent in meditation; visions of the Holy Ones will be seen; and the bliss that God can bestow will be tasted. Why?

Because over twenty centuries ago a great Master, a great Yogi, a great Savior, made the descent into matter; was born a little baby whose only shelter—so the story goes—was a stable; his only bed a manger, put there for the use of the cattle.

He came to awaken the world, to break the bonds of matter that hold the sons of men, to announce their true lineage, to persuade them to accept the power he can give them to take possession of their rightful inheritance as sons of God.

Do you know the name of any great conqueror or statesman whose fame is equal to his? Though he taught for only three years, never wrote a word, simply walked around the hills of Galilee teaching twelve disciples, time has not dimmed his glory, and of his kingdom there shall be no end.

Meister Eckhart, a saint of the fourteenth century, in a Christmas sermon stresses the lack of importance of the details of the birth of Christ—of the time or country where it took place. He puts the question: "But if it happens not to me, what does it profit me? What matters is that it shall happen in me."

If we dwell only on the externals, we are like spectators at a pageant. After it is over we go on our way and nothing further happens. Not for this was the holy child born. Not for this was our Master born in India, nor did he labor tirelessly, unceasingly. It was, it is, that Christ may be born again in our consciousness. This is the second coming of Christ.

Eckhart concludes his sermon with the prayer: "May the God who has been born again as a man assist us in this birth, continually helping us, weak men, to be born again in him as God. Amen."

* * * * *

The Eternal Birth

In a house that I shall never see again, save in poignant memories, I used to stand by a window and look out at a cherry tree. I did this in the early morning, and only upon days when discouraged by spiritual failure, or, if not complete failure, at least failure to attain the success I especially desired. It must have been in the winter time that this happened, because, as I now stand at this ghostly window and look through it at the cherry tree, its branches outlined against the sky are beautiful, but bare. This is the first scene that presents itself, and as I look at it, my soul passes again into the darkness of despair because this eternal birth, the birth of the Christ-Child Consciousness, has not taken place in me.

Wordlessly my soul cries unto God: "O Lord! Is then my birth to be without fruit? Shall nothing be born in me?" Without sound comes the answer: "Whatever takes place in time must have time to mature. What would it avail if you went out under the tree and wept, demanding cherries on the instant?" Then, in pictures presented to me I followed the tree through the season. The clouds came and it was washed with rain. I saw it drenched with sunshine. The blossoms appeared. It was a pink glory. The leaves, the hard green fruit. Then the last transformation of all: baskets stood under it, piled with red fruit.

As with the tree, so with the eternal birth. In darkness, in the rain of sorrow, in the sunshine of joy, the new consciousness is taking shape in you. On a day that may be distant, but is sure, it will be born, and you shall enter into the golden consummation which you have sought through many lives. Believe, stand firm, and you shall see the Glory of the Lord.

* * * * *

I Will Seek Thee

I will seek Thee in the golden glow of the sunrise of my life. In the freshness of this hour, I will lay the opening buds of my devotion at Thy feet.

I will seek Thee when the sun is at the zenith. I will make a garland, glistening with the dewdrops of my tears, of my daily toil, cares, hopes and aspirations, and lay it before Thee, upon the altar of my heart.

I will seek Thee every hour of every day and night, until my restless heart finds rest in Thee.

I will seek Thee when the sun is sinking in the West. Wayworn, I will kneel for Thy touch of blessing, and rising will go forth with more than the courage of youth, against the foes of ignorance, idleness, and forgetfulness of Thee.

I will seek Thee in the evening, when the last golden glow of the sun has died away. I will fix my eyes on the Pole-star of my life, and will listen intently for Thy pipes of peace to pipe me Home.

I am Thine, O Lord! I will make myself worthy of Thine acceptance.

I will not make a burnt offering unto the Lord my God of that which doth cost me nothing. I will lay myself, with all my prejudices and pettiness, with all the flesh holds dear, upon the burning pyre.

I will lift my heart daily to Babaji, Lahiri Mahasaya, Swami Sri Yukteswarji, and my Guru Paramahansa Yoganandaji, asking for their many-jewelled gifts of Self-realization.

In the stillness of night, out of the depth of my heart, I will cry, "Speak, Lord, for Thy servant heareth."

When the call to disagreeable duty is sounded, I will answer, "Here am I, Lord; send me."

AIMS AND IDEALS
of
Self-Realization Fellowship

As set forth by Paramahansa Yogananda, Founder
Sri Daya Mata, President

To disseminate among the nations a knowledge of definite scientific techniques for attaining direct personal experience of God.

To teach that the purpose of life is the evolution, through self-effort, of man's limited mortal consciousness into God Consciousness; and to this end to establish Self-Realization Fellowship temples for God-communion throughout the world, and to encourage the establishment of individual temples of God in the homes and in the hearts of men.

To reveal the complete harmony and basic oneness of original Christianity as taught by Jesus Christ and original Yoga as taught by Bhagavan Krishna; and to show that these principles of truth are the common scientific foundation of all true religions.

To point out the one divine highway to which all paths of true religious beliefs eventually lead: the highway of daily, scientific, devotional meditation on God.

To liberate man from his threefold suffering: physical disease, mental inharmonies, and spiritual ignorance.

To encourage "plain living and high thinking"; and to spread a spirit of brotherhood among all peoples by teaching the eternal basis of their unity: kinship with God.

To demonstrate the superiority of mind over body, of soul over mind.

To overcome evil by good, sorrow by joy, cruelty by kindness, ignorance by wisdom.

To unite science and religion through realization of the unity of their underlying principles.

To advocate cultural and spiritual understanding between East and West, and the exchange of their finest distinctive features.

To serve mankind as one's larger Self.

BOOKS BY PARAMAHANSA YOGANANDA

Available at bookstores or directly from the publisher (www.yogananda-srf.org)

Autobiography of a Yogi
Autobiography of a Yogi *(Audiobook, read by Ben Kingsley)*
God Talks With Arjuna: The Bhagavad Gita—A New Translation and Commentary
The Second Coming of Christ: The Resurrection of the Christ Within You—A Revelatory Commentary on the Original Teachings of Jesus
The Collected Talks and Essays
Volume I: Man's Eternal Quest
Volume II: The Divine Romance
Volume III: Journey to Self-realization
Wine of the Mystic: The Rubaiyat of Omar Khayyam —A Spiritual Interpretation
The Science of Religion
Whispers from Eternity
The Yoga of Jesus
The Yoga of the Bhagavad Gita
Songs of the Soul
Sayings of Paramahansa Yogananda
Scientific Healing Affirmations
Where There Is Light: Insight and Inspiration for Meeting Life's Challenges
In the Sanctuary of the Soul: A Guide to Effective Prayer
Inner Peace: How to Be Calmly Active and Actively Calm
How You Can Talk With God
Metaphysical Meditations
The Law of Success
To Be Victorious in Life
Why God Permits Evil and How to Rise Above It
Living Fearlessly: Bringing Out Your Inner Soul Strength
Cosmic Chants

A complete catalog of books and audio/video recordings—including rare archival recordings of Paramahansa Yogananda—is available on request.

Self-Realization Fellowship Lessons

The scientific techniques of meditation taught by Paramahansa Yogananda, including *Kriya Yoga*—as well as his guidance on all aspects of balanced spiritual living—are presented in the *Self-Realization Fellowship Lessons*. For further information, you are welcome to write for the free booklet *Undreamed-of Possibilities*.

Self-Realization Fellowship
3880 San Rafael Avenue • Los Angeles, CA 90065-3219
TEL (323) 225-2471 • FAX (323) 225-5088
www.yogananda-srf.org